In 2003, whe ⟨⟩ *as*
unearthed ben ⟨⟩ *·gi*
Mountains, it b ⟨⟩ *for*
Romania and their new partner, the United States, whose
advanced technology enabled the discovery to take place.
The primary custodial agency of this remarkable chamber
full of holographic technology is Department Zero, a secret
service unit that answers only to the Romanian president.
Ever since, there has been a continuous and persistent
effort by certain Romanian and American factions to
undermine the authority of Department Zero in order to
gain access to and control this technology.

The Secret Parchment — Five Tibetan Initiation Techniques
tells the story of the detailed political intrigues behind this
remarkable find and also how these matters have been
subject to intervention by superior spiritual forces, one of
which concerns the arranged discovery of an ancient Tibetan
manuscript which is revealed and explained in this book.

After the ancient manuscript is translated, a mysteri-
ous antenna-like structure reveals itself as a result of
melting ice near a secret American base in Antarctica.
Acting as some sort of cosmic buoy, it has an energy
signature connecting both to Jupiter's moon, Europa, and
an area of Transylvania where the remains of an ancient
civilization were uncovered in 1990 amidst vast tunnels
of solid gold. Long ago classified as the top state secret
of Romania, this location becomes the center of intrigue
in and around Department Zero. Although not actually
penetrating the underground area itself, Peter Moon
visits the general area and determines that this ancient
civilization is still very much alive and active.

✸

THE SECRET PARCHMENT
FIVE TIBETAN INITIATION TECHNIQUES

By Radu Cinamar

INTRODUCTION, EDITING & PART TWO
By Peter Moon

SkyBooks
NEW YORK

The Secret Parchment — Five Tibetan Initiation Techniques
Copyright © 2009 by Radu Cinamar
Part Two Copyright © 2013 by Peter Moon
First English language printing, February 2013
International copyright laws apply

Cover art by Sky Barbarick
Typography by Creative Circle Inc.
Published by: Sky Books
Box 769
Westbury, New York 11590
email: *skybooks@yahoo.com*
website: www.skybooksusa.com
www.digitalmontauk.com

Library of Congress Cataloging-in-Publication Data

Cinamar, Radu / Moon, Peter
The Secret Parchment — Five Tibetan Initiation Techniques
224 pages
ISBN 978-1-937859-13-8 (hard copy format)
ISBN 978-1-937859-14-5 (for ebook format only)
1. Body, Mind, Spirit: Occultism 2. Body, Mind, Spirit: General
Library of Congress Control Number 2012956179

This book is dedicated to the Inner Seeker in you

OTHER TITLES FROM
SKY BOOKS

CONTENTS

LEFT PROFILE OF THE ROMANIAN SPHINX

This is the sphinx beneath which, according to Radu Cinamar, there is a chamber built some 50,000 years ago which contains technology that is far more advanced that our current human technology.

RIGHT PROFILE OF THE ROMANIAN SPHINX

This is the same rock as the above sphinx but the photograph is from the other side. Behind the "cat's whiskers" is the shape of a woman with long hair which is more pronounced in color. It is not graffiti but seems to be crafted by nature. There are many rock formations in this part of the world that appear to have been designed by superior beings who utilized the elements of nature to create mysterious art work.

INTRODUCTION

The publication of this book is a major milestone for the progenitors of the remarkable series of volumes by Radu Cinamar which we can now call the Transylvania Series. I use the word progenitors in conjunction with the name of the author because the events, circumstances, and agendas that he describes in his written work reach far beyond the personal or microcosmic view of Radu Cinamar. In the larger macrocosmic aspects of existence, Radu was a chosen vehicle to set in motion certain agendas for forces that extend into the realms of infinity.

So, where do you fit in?

I cannot answer that last question save for the fact that you have opened this book and have read it thus far. I can tell you, however, that you have accessed a report of information that is not only astonishing in its very nature but is also unprecedented in human history. And this last statement applies whether the information is true or not. It is completely unique, and it will send your mind into unexpected directions and into recesses of mental consciousness that have been dormant or inaccessible until now.

While I cannot tell you exactly how you fit into any of this, you have come across this information for some reason under the sun. I can, however, tell you something of how I came to be responsible for assisting and fulfilling the will of the progenitors of this remarkable series of books; but first, I will give you a description of those who have made these stories possible and how their agendas dovetail with mine. This will include a concise summary of the three previous books in this series.

During the Cold War, there was a natural alliance between the two communist nations of Romania and the People's Republic of China. Trying to keep up with the West in regards to the most advanced and esoteric methods of reconnaissance and espionage, the Romanians sought out the help of the Chinese as they did not really trust the Russians. As part of a cultural exchange program whereby Chinese students were able to participate in educational programs in Romania, the Chinese government sent the Romanians an expert in parapsychology who would set up a secret department that would deal with all abnormal occurrences. There were referred to as "K events," but in pop culture terms of today, these might now be termed as "X-File" events. Known as Department Zero, this special unit was only known to the head of state and the head of security. Besides housing and caring for paranormal subjects, Department Zero also trained them. The expert in parapsychology who set up this unique department is known to us as Dr. Xien, and he was introduced to us in the first book of this series, *Transylvanian Sunrise*. Although Dr. Xien is an intriguing character, we do not learn too much about him in that book. We do know that he was called in after the birth of another very interesting character who also turns out to be one of the progenitors of the *Transylvania Series*. His name is Cezar Brad, and he is born with an umbilical cord that is so thick, the doctors have to use an ordinary saw to sever it. As this is an anomaly, Cezar comes under the scrutiny and eventual tutelage of Department Zero and forms a close personal relationship with Dr. Xien from a very young age. Cezar is trained in a host of spiritual and psychic disciplines that would rival the best your imagination might offer.

As fate would clearly demonstrate, Dr. Xien was grooming Cezar to serve as a steward and guardian for what is arguably considered the greatest archeological discovery in the history of Mankind: a secret and previously inaccessible chamber beneath the Romanian Sphinx containing futuristic holographic technology that was put together some 50,000 years ago.

In what could be termed a virtual Noah's Ark that far exceeds the thinking and experiential capacity of those who lived in biblical times (or even in our own times for that matter), this chamber includes technology whereby one can place their hand on a table and see their own DNA rendered in three-dimensional holograms. Other devices on the table enable one to see the DNA of alien species from other planets with accompanying star renderings so that one can see where they actually originate from. By placing two hands on different parts of the table, one can also "mix" the DNA of two species so as to see how they might look if hybridized. As the tables themselves are six feet high, the creatures who built them were gigantic compared to humans of today.

This remarkable chamber also includes a "projection hall" whereby one can see a holographic rendition of the history of Earth that is particularly tailored to the individuality of whomever might be viewing it. This history, however, abruptly cuts off in about the Fifth Century A.D., perhaps because it requires some sort of software update. One of the more intriguing aspects of the Projection Hall is that it also contains three mysterious tunnels that lead into the bowels of the Earth and similar facilities in Iraq, Mongolia, Tibet and also beneath the Giza Plateau in Egypt. One of the tunnels leads into the Inner Earth itself.

Although Cezar was set up by fate through the tutelage of Dr. Xien to be the overseer of this remarkable archeological discovery, it was not his role to write the story of what was found and its implications. As these events were unfolding, Cezar handpicked Radu Cinamar to write these volumes. Serving as a mentor to Radu, Cezar gave him a rapid fire education in all of the political machinations going on behind this discovery while also introducing him to the world of psychic phenomena and esoteric studies. We learn about this in the first volume, *Transylvanian Sunrise*, but we are not told exactly why Cezar picked Radu. What I can tell you from what I have learned thus far is that Cezar is a remarkably adept individual, and he knew precisely what he was doing. His psychic sensibilities are quite formidable and proved to be accurate in this case. Radu got the job done, and with the release of this book, the entire series of all four volumes are now in English as well.

You might think that this discovery was a wonderful opportunity to enlighten Mankind and take advantage of all that this newly discovered technology has to offer for the benefit of humanity at large. Many, if not most, of the Romanians in the government who were privy to the discovery viewed it that way. Circumstances, however, dictated otherwise.

Cezar informed Radu that the actual discovery of this secret and previously unknown chamber took place when the Pentagon discovered it via the use of ground penetrating radar that operated through satellites. It is understandable that the Americans would use all technology at their disposal for reconnaissance purposes as well as to scrutinize all geographical anomalies and resources on the planet. Right or wrong, this is the purpose of the Department of Defense. What was most challenging about this intelligence, however, was that Masonic interests in the Pentagon funneled this information to a leader in Italian Freemasonry, a Signore Massini, who represents a hidden global elite that wanted access to and control of this chamber for themselves. Accordingly, Massini approached Cezar who was then the head of Department Zero and sought his cooperation. Cezar, who did not trust Massini, was forced to cooperate to a certain extent due to political circumstances. Thus, the evil interests of an Italian Freemason forged an unprecedented alliance between Romania and America with the former suddenly being admitted to NATO. The specifics of these political intrigues are detailed in the book *Transylvanian Sunrise* which is primarily the story of Cezar's life and his involvement with the uncovering of these amazing artifacts.

While the enigmatic and mysterious Dr. Xien set the stage for Cezar to uncover this secret chamber through rigorous training and education, he is a distant memory when the discovery is made and seemingly completely uninvolved in any tangible way with the political machinations and evil intrigues which allowed it to even take place. He is, however, an interested party and a definite progenitor of the information revealed in these books, and this comes into clear view in the second book of the series, *Transylvanian Moonrise — A Secret Initiation in the Mysterious Land of the Gods*.

Transylvanian Moonrise begins with an editor's note from the Romanian editor, Sorin Hurmuz, who includes numerous excerpts from the Romanian press that not only corroborate Cezar's story as told by Radu but give insights into why it is credible. Above and beyond these facts, it might interest you to know that a key area near the Romanian Sphinx is blacked out on Google

Earth. Besides that, Americans were seen en masse during the time of the excavations that were taking place near the Romanian Sphinx in 2003. I have also spoken to several well-placed people in Romania who believe the general story to have merit. Exactly what has taken place and all of the details are still largely a mystery, but Radu's books offer us the only clues. In addition to that, they are remarkable stories and teaching devices which integrate the mundane aspects of politics with some of the most esoteric concepts of occultism as well as the cutting edge of technology.

Radu's narrative in *Transylvanian Moonrise* begins with a mysterious man named Elinor trying to contact the enigmatic author through his publisher, Sorin Hurmuz, who has generally been instructed to stonewall any people wishing to meet with Radu. In fact, Sorin has never met with Radu and only communicates with him by special courier or with a prearranged phone card. When it is eventually discovered that Elinor is speaking on behalf of a Tibetan lama, both Sorin and Radu change their tune and a meeting is eventually arranged. This meeting is filled with a panoply of metaphysical revelations which present an entirely new paradigm by which to view the events described in *Transylvanian Sunrise*. After an amazing indoctrination into the ancient art of alchemy and the prospects of immortality, Radu meets the lama who reveals himself to be none other than Dr. Xien and explains that he once served in the royal court at Lhasa under the name of Repa Sundhi at the time of the Chinese invasion of Tibet. Escaping that purge, he somehow ended up in the employ of the Chinese government and adopted a different identity as Dr. Xien.

Repa Sundhi has a very specific agenda for this meeting with Radu and it has to do with what is the focal point of the book you are now reading: an ancient parchment that reveals five Tibetan initiation techniques. In *Transylvanian Moonrise*, Radu learns that the lama wants to take him to the Apuseni Mountains of Transylvania. Once there, a mysterious but well-described space-translation takes place that literally transports them (as well as Elinor who remains in their company) to certain rarefied high peaks of Tibet which are inaccessible to humans by normal transportation means. Radu is escorted into a cave where he meets another progenitor of the *Transylvania Series*. Her name is Machandi and she is a blue goddess and tantric dakini who not only educates and initiates Radu but gives him an ancient manuscript which is to be translated from ancient Tibetan and published, first in the Romanian language. Having finally been translated into English, it is now the centerpiece of the volume you are now reading.

While *Transylvanian Moonrise* refers to the characters in *Transylvanian Sunrise* and the lama is included in the dramatic events that take place, the two books are astonishingly different and offer complimentary views of the overall scenario from completely different perspectives. The third book in the series, *Mystery of Egypt — The First Tunnel*, is no exception. Radu is recruited to join Department Zero on a journey with Cezar into the mysterious "first tunnel" in the Projection Hall of the Bucegi complex. This leads to a hidden chamber beneath the Giza Plateau in Egypt. What they find there is no less astonishing than what has already been offered in the first two books. The purpose of the mission is to recover neatly organized slate-like tablets that are in fact a type of ancient "DVD" that project holographic "memories" of the history of the world. The tablets do not require a projector and are so numerous that they can only hope to return a portion of them to their home base, after which they will be sent to America for detailed study. Even though they cannot recover everything in one mission, what they do retrieve would take a team of viewers a considerable amount of time to view.

There is also an occult chamber containing a device consisting primarily of huge crystals that facilitates the projection of one's consciousness back into time. It is not a physical time travel device. It should be noted that it requires a certain amount of psychic and esoteric development to be able to withstand the rigors of projecting oneself into time, even if the physical body is not being utilized. We also learn that this device is bioresonant in that it is tuned to the physiological, mental and emotional conditions of the subject as well as their own past experiences. In other words, you would have different experiences than would I and so on.

Another intriguing aspect of the time device is that there is a certain amount of censorship present. When Cezar attempts to project his consciousness into time in order to see who created the device, he encounters blockages. While it is informative and useful in certain respects, it contains mysteries which it does not want penetrated, at least at this particular time. All of this gives rise to interesting speculation.

These censorship issues further fuel the controversy Cezar ignites by relaying his initial experience in the time device whereupon he returns to the time of Jesus in the First Century. Radu also recounts what he saw in his original experiences in the Projection Hall (beneath the Romanian Sphinx) when he witnessed events surrounding the crucifixion of Christ. This account contains UFOs wreaking havoc amidst a virtually insurmountable thunder storm while a fearing populace scrambles to save their own lives. It leaves us with a hornets nest of information, the result of which has been more than a few questioning the veracity of the authors. I should add, however, that most of the reading audience thus far has not blinked at the accounts given. They have enjoyed the book and are not judgmental about the authors. While this surprised me, I am happy that the book is being well received. More importantly, these controversial issues about Christ explain, at least to some extent, how I fit into this rather ornate tapestry that has been woven by my mysterious Romanian friend, Radu Cinamar.

While I do not have any personal passion nor indoctrination towards the Christian religion, there are some bizarre experiences in synchronicity which have given me cause to take note of interesting phenomena that is worthy of further consideration. I have written several books about all of this so will only summarize these right now but from a new perspective.

In 1982, after reaching the most exalted spiritual state of my life, I was summoned to a council of jinn, angels, or whatever you want to call them. As I had successfully cast off my karmic baggage, I had either earned the right or was being allowed to change and/or redirect the entire course that my life would now take. I did not actually see jinn or angels in the conventional sense as if this were a cinematic drama, but they were most definitely present. I could definitely feel them. What was most important to me was that I had reached a certain point in my evolution where I was reaching out to a new and higher calling. In the schematic of the Tarot, this is representative of the card entitled the World. Although I did not know it at the time, I was following the path of this Tarot card to the letter. I do remember thinking of the card in deference to my situation but not so specifically.

All that I knew at the time was that I had put myself in a position to choose my destiny and that I could manifest whatever I wanted. There were no limitations. If the odds were stacked against me due to a particular challenging choice, I would have been able to overcome them. Without even weighing too many different options, I chose to dismantle or rearrange all hurtful conditions of physical existence. Although I did not realize it at the time, I had taken on the challenge of a Bodhisattva, or at least one definition of that multi-used term. I am referring to one who has achieved relief from suffering and chooses the path of relieving others from their torment. There was nothing romantic or theatrical in my decision. It was very matter of fact and with no thought of aggrandizement. I was, however, a Bodhisattva on my own terms that was fashioned after my own design. There was no pandering to the approval of a higher authority. The angels or jinn, however, saw to other elemental issues that would give my path a significant degree of actualization.

In terms of the Tarot or Cabalistic Tree of Life, it is said that any occult operations begin in the realm of Chesod, the sepiroth ruled by Jupiter and the number 4. One of its main attributes is infinite mercy or compassion which I had unreservedly embraced. Even so, my life was not exemplary or a show-case in terms of reaching out to quell troubled souls, etc. I was primarily concerned with my own survival in a rather crazy world. The jinn would take care of or feed my higher aspirations in due course. Assisting others can usually only best be done once one has secured a strong position for themselves. This is why mothers are alerted on airplanes to secure their own oxygen mask first. Then they can tend to their little ones.

14

In any event, I was embracing the World. With decades of hindsight, I can see such rich symbolism in that card that I am inclined to share it as it also explains my collaboration with Radu and his friends on a very deep level. Part of the interpretation of this card reads as follows.

"The World represents an ending to a cycle of life, a pause in life before the next big cycle beginning with the Fool. It is completeness. It is also said to represent cosmic consciousness; the potential of perfect union with the One Power of the universe. It tells us full happiness is also to give back to the world, sharing what we have learned or gained."

The card itself contains a naked woman surrounded by a green wreath rendered like an ouroboros (a snake eating its tail). She is holding a staff in each hand while being watched by four creatures in each corner which are a human face or head, a lion, an ox and an eagle. In astrology, these represent the four fixed signs of Leo, Scorpio, Aquarius, and Taurus which also signify the four elements of Tetragrammaton, represented as the name of God in Hebrew: *Yod He Vau He*. This card not only represents the fourfold elemental nature of the physical world, but the Goddess is in the center as Sophia, the spiritual or sacred center that is the goal of all mystical seekers. She represents the secret and sacred letter *Shin*, the Fifth Element which becomes Pentagrammaton evolving out of Tetragrammaton which, in Christian Cabala, is represented by Christ as *Yod He Shin Vau He* which is *Yeshua*.

In between the time of my great awakening and my involvement with Preston Nichols and the writing of *The Montauk Project: Experiments in Time*, I invoked positive beings that would help in my mission. I was non-specific as to whom they might be. My work with Preston would take me to the cutting edge of quantum physics, and publishing his theories and stories literally changed the way scientists have looked at the subject of time. Trying to verify his stories resulted in me having unprecedented experiences with the principle of synchronicity.

Carl Jung, who coined the word synchronicity, worked closely with Albert Einstein and Wolfgang Pauli, the pioneers of relativity and quantum physics. He believed there were serious and significant parallels between synchronicity and aspects of relativity theory and quantum mechanics. Both Jung and Pauli postulated that life was not a series of random events but rather an expression of a deeper order which they referred to as Unus mundus. This deeper order refers to a cohesive connection of "super strings" of consciousness that follow an orderly pattern that the person himself is embedded in. The realization of such a pattern results in a spiritual awakening. In ordinary religious terms, Jung stated that synchronicity shares similar characteristics of an "intervention of Grace." Jung also believed that synchronicity in a person's life serves a role similar to that of dreams but with the purpose of shifting a person's egocentric conscious thinking to a greater wholeness.

15

Essentially, my own awakening led to my own discovery and exploration of these various "super strings." As these are the subject of many previous books, I will not elaborate on them. Most of you are already familiar.

What I will add at this point is the subject of markers in time. Across the various streams of time, there are certain events which stand out for one reason or another. This is the perspective from which I believe Repa Sundhi, the Tibetan lama who is also known as Dr. Xien, operates. Although not involved in the day-to-day operations which made the discovery in the Bucegi Mountains possible, he came in at certain points on the time line to efficiently expedite certain matters which made this possible. He also was very much involved with key events that took place in the other books and personally saw to it that Radu would receive the manuscript that is translated and presented in this book. We also learn in this book that the lama is keenly mindful about exactly when the secret parchment should be released to the world. There is no question that he views it as a marker in time. If we once again consider the Tarot card known as the World, we see that the card itself also represents a very important marker in time.

With the advent of the Age of Pisces, the wisdom of the Tarot was converted into Christian terms by Gypsies where the four fixed signs were transmuted into the four beasts of Revelation. This was seen in Medieval decks where the four fixed signs were also converted into the four evangelists who wrote the Gospels with Christ who, as the ultimate expression of Divine Mercy, was placed in the center. What is more important than whether the Christians or Magi were correct is that this card points to an outpouring of compassion. In the Orient, this is recognized as Quan Yin. The manuscript you are about to read relies on compassion as the impetus for all it represents.

The publishing of this book, which is coincidentally being released as the traditional Mayan calendar comes to an end, would therefore represent a marker in time where a shift is taking place from a universe that appears ruthless and predatory to one that is compassionate. By a shift, I am not referring to something that is quaint, cute or trite. I am talking about a fire hydrant that has been opened up in comparison to a tiny leak.

Thus it is that I have become involved in the English language publishing of this unique manuscript as well as the entirety of the *Transylvania Series*. How this interrelates with all of the other fascinating information presented in these books is interesting and invites much intriguing speculation. While I will not indulge in this for the moment, I can tell you that time travel scientist Dr. David Anderson was dead-set on getting me to Romania from the day I met him. There is no doubt that he viewed my presence there as an important marker in time and he went out of his way to get me there. I have now visited Romania each summer for the last five years and have built considerable friendships and relationships in that mysterious and beautiful country. As an ancient crossroads between East and West, it is viewed as a strategic point with regard to future politics and economics on the world stage. As you will read in this book, it is also the ancient homeland of all of our ancestors. It does not matter what color you are.

That is all I have to say for now. I will make further comments in Part Two of this book.

You are now about to read the adventures of Radu Cinamar that took place immediately after he returned from his journey to the Occult Chamber beneath the Giza Plateau as was described in *Mystery of Egypt — The First Tunnel*. As is the case with his previous books, it takes us in a completely different and unique direction. Personally, I find this one of the most delightful aspects of his books. They are always full of unexpected surprises that reveal new twists and turns to already fascinating subjects.

I would also like to add one word of warning. When you read the manuscript and Radu's accompanying comments, do not underestimate what has been offered. It is very easy to dismiss words you read on paper just as you might do with any other text, sacred or not. These principles are potent, but they have no meaning or impact unless they are absorbed, contemplated, and applied by the reader. There is no limit to what you can accomplish with them. I hope that you can awaken to the point where you can see all the "super strings" that make up your existence.

Enjoy the book.

Peter Moon
Long Island
July 8, 2012

PART ONE

by Radu Cinamar

CHAPTER ONE

REMOTE VIEWING — EVOLUTION IN THE USA

After a considerable break from writing *Mystery of Egypt*, the third volume in this series, I have returned to present some new aspects that involve both the spectacular modification of my professional status and also some unexpected features of man's knowledge and existence. While they seem to be two different things, they are both integrated into the natural flow of events that took place after the return from the expedition through the tunnel to Egypt. I can even say that the experiences I had then, as well as the precious knowledge I gained through Cezar Brad's kindness, have contributed to both my spiritual evolution and to the surprising integration into an area which had been relatively unfamiliar to me up to that point.

I know that I have kept silent for almost two years, but I am asking the reader to understand that things took a completely different turn regarding myself and that unforeseen elements intervened whose development I hope will compensate, at least up to a point, for all the waiting. I will only narrate the chain of events as I lived them during this period of time. This is the easy part. The difficult part, however, will be to manage to explain as well and correctly as possible the elements included in the parchment I received from the goddess Machandi as was mentioned in the book *Transylvanian Moonrise*. It is true that I shall be guiding myself by the important indications and observations that I received from Repa Sundhi, meaning Doctor Xien, when he translated the secret text, revealing to me some of its occult aspects. Still, given my responsibility to present the above-mentioned translation and comments, I think this is the most difficult part of the book. Depending upon everyone's power of understanding and affinities, the concepts revealed in the text of the parchment can open for attentive readers a completely different way of perceiving life and life's goals.

"You should neither tell everything nor leave things unclear," Cezar advised me. "Anyway, to understand the specific elements of the text, the person who reads these explanations must show good intentions, reason and an ability not to be proud. Do you think you will find this in many people?"

"I'm thinking that, this way, the young people will be especially receptive and will perceive the profound meaning of the teachings in the parchment given by the goddess," I replied.

"And I'm telling you that you might have great surprises in store for you from this perspective. Most of these people are narrow-minded and are even half-learned. They look only towards ideas that lack spiritual support, and they mistake everything with science and its 'evidence.'"

"How do you know this?" I asked.

In his own special way, Cezar smiled slightly.

"We have certain programs for research and selection from this particular age group. There are special tests that show their true capacities, but you can also search the internet, especially the forums. That's enough to get the main idea. Each one of them wants to look smarter than the others, each one wants to astound with his knowledge, but when it comes to reason or spiritual and occult aspects, the majority of them show their helplessness, pride or arrogance."

"Aren't you being a little harsh?" I asked, shyly.

"Would you like me to say something else? Sure, they're not all the same, but there are statistics on this matter which cannot be ignored. The social system is simply embarrassing and it baffles them. I feel that you want to ask me what should be done about this now, but we will not discuss that for the time being. Let's hope, however, that the text of the parchment will have an effect upon them and show them that, in a way, not all that glitters is gold."

After I received the text from the goddess Machandi and after it was translated, I wanted it to be published as soon as possible; but Repa Sundhi said that it was not the right time yet and that I had to wait a little longer. Suddenly, by an astonishing chain of events, the urge came to make this secret text known to everyone interested. This was preceded and facilitated by a major change that took place in my life which changed the very orientation of my existence. While this change opened great opportunities, it also created special responsibilities.

It all started a few days after I returned from the expedition to the underground Occult Chamber in the Egyptian underground beneath the Giza Plateau and very near the Great Pyramid. I was still pretty shaken by the time travelling experiences that had been accomplished with the help of an ancient device, and I could still feel the energetic effects. Unexpectedly, Cezar insisted that I remain a few more days at Alpha Base and stay in the chamber that was assigned to me in order to rest and relax. I gladly accepted his proposal, particularly because this meant that I was going to be spending more time around him. The second day after we returned to the base, General Obadea arrived to receive the report directly from Cezar. It soon turned out that this was not the only reason for his arrival.

The next day went normally. Cezar and the General remained in the office most of the time while I relaxed on the sport grounds of the base, breathing the clean mountain air and thinking about what I had just seen and felt throughout the expedition. I was so caught up in these thoughts that I lost track of time and did not notice that it had gotten dark until the cold numbed my body. I was just preparing to return to my chamber when I saw a courier on duty approaching me. He respectfully halted at about two meters and let me know that I was requested in the protocol chamber.

"Cezar relayed this through you?" I asked.

"Colonel Brad and General Obadea," he answered without a blink.

I nodded my head affirmatively. I had forgotten that I was in a secret facility with a special status which had its special action and speech rules.

"The General?" I asked, surprised. "Do you know by any chance what the reason is?"

"I have no idea, Sir."

Accompanied by the courier, I left towards the building in which the protocol chamber was situated. As I was getting nearer to that place, I felt more and more that I was being taken over by an inexplicable feeling of excitement. It was almost as if my thoughts were no longer taking a definite shape in my mind anymore.

When I entered into the elegant hall, I was greeted by Cezar who, smiling, asked if I was feeling well. Mumbling an affirmative answer, I headed for the table in the center of the room where General Obadea was going through a file. Feeling like a small, timid and fearful child who was in front of people older than him and did not know what was going on, I shook hands with the General who invited me to sit. Massive, forceful, serious and rough, General Obadea had a great impact on people. If it were not for Cezar's calming influence, I would have fled that place in a hurry. Although I knew that the General was a righteous person and devoted to the good of this country and full of dedication, I still felt sort of timid in his presence.

He spoke to me directly and without further ado.

"Radu, I gather that the expedition was of good use to you and that you successfully passed its physical and psychological rigors well. Cezar has informed me in detail, and I want you to know that what you saw in your time travel is of great interest to us. It is not a novelty to us, but any extra information is welcomed. We will be discussing this further."

General Obadea stopped for a few moments, letting his eyes down as if he were searching for the right words. I looked respectfully at his shortly cut grey hair, bushy eyebrows, strongly lined face, and pronounced chin which showed a great strength of character. In all his being, one could feel the experience of many years of hard trials, battles and sustained efforts, part of which I already knew. All of this did not knock him down but made him even stronger. His relations and connections were now stronger than ever and were directly linked to the political sphere as well.

I was startled at the sound of his powerful voice.

"In the current situation, Cezar has made a proposition that, frankly, I accepted with some reserves. But the fact that you have been with us all these years and respected our conditions in the books that you published, as well as the existence of certain abilities which Cezar seems to have noticed within you, have convinced me to agree. Anyhow, this is a unique case, an exception concerning which I take full responsibility."

I still had no idea about what this was about, although an idea started to take shape in my mind.

"The proposal that we are making is for you to enter into the ranks of Department Zero. It stands from this point on, if you agree. Exceptionally, your incorporation will be as a civilian, but your position will come first."

I had been on the right track. My intuition, corroborated with an old and unspoken desire, came true. The moment seemed unreal and yet full of content. Hardly managing to hide my joy so that it would not get out of the somewhat solemn frame that the presence of General Obadea imposed, I immediately accepted and also asked about my future activity.

Cezar gave me a few details.

"There are some areas that our department wishes to initiate and develop. We are thus taking advantage of the cooperation with the Americans, and your task will be, in principle, to coordinate the section whose area of activity will be concerning 'borderline' or that which is on the line between the real and the unreal. Our people need this because we have recently been orienting ourselves more towards tactical and administrative events. The pace was imposed by the discoveries we made."

I suddenly became worried because I thought I might not be ready for such an activity. I understood the importance of this role in the department, but it was more difficult to get used to the idea that I was the one that was going to coordinate it. Seeing my inner agitation, General Obadea spoke to me with kindness.

"I told you I was also skeptical with regard to Cezar's proposal in the beginning. In such a position, however, we cannot afford an outside person, regardless if that person is competent in the field. The situation is too delicate and we have to be cautious. The agency personnel are one thing, but the coordination of a 'twilight' section involves access to a great deal of secret elements. Given his current position, Cezar can no longer take care of this particular activity."

The General took a short pause, looking at me inquisitively.

"I gather that you have found out a lot about this domain and have a special interest in it. Then, there are the special connections that you have with Doctor Xien and the Goddess Machandi. In a way that is not too clear, even for me, you have been constantly pushed towards us. Cezar has an important contribution here, too."

I was already feeling more relaxed and more confident in the future that was revealing itself in front of me. After all, there must be a beginning for everything.

"Don't worry. You will take certain specialized courses," the General continued. "I have analyzed the situation together with Cezar and he will train you in connection to the tasks that you will have to fulfill here. Still, you have to understand that from now on you have certain obligations that are specific to the secret services and, even more, to our special department. Think well for there is still time to refuse."

I nodded my head, determined to accept the position. I had seen too many things of an exceptional significance to feel restrained by some inherent rules of such an activity. Apart from this, as I later learned from Cezar, the fact that my social situation did not bind me had weighed a lot in the General's decision. As I wasn't married and had no other family obligations, I started with an important admittance asset from the very beginning.

A few specific procedures then followed. I signed a maximum confidentiality contract and was initiated into the less known to me directorates of Department Zero. Usually, candidates take a series of very difficult physical and psychological tests. The selected ones then undergo three months of special training after which the final evaluation takes place in the field.

"There have been situations when, in the end, none of the candidates were eligible," Cezar confessed to me. "There are generally a few hundred who subscribe. After the tests, only about forty remain; and at the evaluation, only two or three pass at the most. Many times, there is only one left; and at some selections, like I said, not one was left."

The technical department agents must be very well trained. After the discovery made in the Bucegi Mountains, Cezar made the admission conditions a lot harsher. This was not necessarily in order to be at the same level of training as the American soldiers, who were detached here from the special forces, but mostly to cope with the problems and unpredictable conditions of the expeditions that could take place in the three tunnels. This intense professional training was also for other types of operations on Romania's soil. The candidates who were finally admitted, however, learned only after their admission that they would be part of Department Zero, later fulfilling separate formalities.

For a few weeks, I got use to the rhythm of the base and it was pretty intense. It goes without saying that I am not granted permission to describe the main activities that happened there or within the internal structure of the location. I will only say that I was shown the study hall in which I was going to form different specialized groups. In fact, there were two such halls. One of them, however, had a different compartment arrangement. At first, I did not understand what it was all about, but Cezar explained it to me quite quickly.

"I have agreed with General Obadea to set up a group specialized in remote-viewing which is the ability 'to see' at a distance. We have to create our own team of experts in this field, and you will start and lead the specific activity. It is important to achieve this objective."

It looked like my hiring in Department Zero was starting to take shape. I had only read a few references about remote-viewing thus far and without going more deeply into the matter.

"I don't know. I need knowledge. I need time," I said. "From what I gather, I am the only one that will be in charge of this in the department."

"Yes," Cezar answered with determination. "You will, however, go to an intensive specialization course in the United States. There is a proposition from the Americans that was sent to a few secret services of certain countries, ours among them, to ensure an elaborate training in the field of remote viewing. We are not so sure what their kindness is hiding, but we can use the opportunity. If it had not been for the Projection Chamber, I don't think they would have called us at all."

Things went ahead at a rapid rate and, after approximately a month and a half from signing the contract, Cezar announced to me that I was going to depart in a matter of days for an intensive preparation course. In the meantime, I seriously sought out documentation for myself on the matter at hand. Sadly, what I found on the internet on remote-viewing only touched the surface of the domain. I soon realized the fact that, to go deeper into the mysteries of this extrasensory ability, the elements presented in different courses or dedicated papers are not enough as there is need of highly competent practical guidance. Maybe this was the exact purpose of the intensive training proposed by the Americans. Simple logic stated that, if this initiative was to involve the secret and national security services of eight countries, it can be safely assumed that this training would be far more than the generally circulated notions on remote-viewing to which anyone has access.

Secondly, this course was to enrich my connections and my knowledge in a world of special agencies where I still had many gaps that needed to be filled. I found myself to be a completely unusual case in this field because my situation made Cezar break out with amusement.

"I do not think that there is any other secret service agent with so little experience who can still take part in this course! There you will meet with several famous military figures; and most probably, you will have some discussions, but the subject related to the discovery in the Bucegi Mountains must remain a closed one."

Initially, the department wanted to send Lieutenant Nicoară, but he was in charge of tactical operations on the country's territory, and his presence at the base was indispensable from this point of view. Although I was somewhat nervous and was thinking that, in a way, I was entering the lion's den, I still felt self-assured and that I was master of myself enough so as to withstand the probable contextual "pressures" I could expect. The advantage of this opportunity opened by the Americans was that the secret services could send the agents that they wanted. Despite this, Cezar told me that there were some question marks and raised eyebrows arising from the Americans with regard to me being sent because they did not understand this choice and suspected an infiltration of a different nature. General Obadea intervened here because he was a good friend with the American program director, General Roddey. In 2004, after the first months following the discovery in the Bucegi Mountains, he had been one of the American collaborators with the Romanian side and proved to be a righteous and reasonable man. In the panic that marked that period, any hasty decision could have unleashed actions with irreversible effects which could have thrown the situation of both countries into chaos. After questions arose with regard to myself, General Obadea had a short telephone conversation with his counterpart, and the result was that I received the clearance to take part in this special training.

Before leaving, in parallel with my training in the activity at the department, I also received special training from Cezar and General Obadea. This concerned some state secrets and aspects related to the interaction of counterintelligence agencies as well as some communication directives which, for obvious reasons, I cannot reveal here. The reader should not feel frustrated because of this. As time has gone by, I have been informed about accusations lodged against me with regard to the fact that I cannot disclose the exact location of the discovery in the Bucegi Mountains. After everything stated in the first volume, I think such accusations seem even childish. In such a case, the reader might think that our society no longer needs secret services, that there is no need for barriers in the collaboration with the great powers, that people can receive members of other civilizations from the cosmos with open arms, and that such discoveries should become sort of a museum which is opened to anyone at any time.

I have explained that, besides the resistance shown on the fulminating developments for Mankind – and I am not referring here only to the Projection Chamber but also to the three underground tunnels – there is also a strong faction that sustains the opposite current, that of the good and of informing the population; but this information must be made in a just manner which is suitable for the situation of the respective moment. To judge such complicated situations with simplicity brings no benefit for intelligence and deprives the impatient and arrogant of a more profound knowledge. Still, I am sure that the careful reader will correctly understand the reasons that do not allow me to reveal extremely important information and that they will not fall into the net of cheap observations and extraordinary conclusions on this subject. Some things can be told and others cannot, at least not for now; but even those that can be revealed are only partially mentioned due to government interests and because of the unforeseen impact on society.

Based upon decision making factors, I understand that these are very delicate aspects which cannot and must not be treated lightly.

My growing up in the secret services was quite quick because I was already familiar with the said problems from what Cezar told me and from the incursions that I was a part of. My "take-over" in the relatively small framework of this secret activity was done without any problem and, after a short period of time, I already felt perfectly integrated into the work chart of Department Zero. Thus, being enthusiastic with the importance and novelty of my mission, I wasted no time in making an intense documentation of remote-viewing extrasensory capacity in order to be as well prepared as possible for that start of my training in the USA.

Until I was integrated into the Department Zero structure, I only generally knew that remote-viewing meant the process of "seeing at a distance," meaning in places that our regular senses cannot comprehend. After I started to study the matter, I realized that, even from the beginning, this paranormal capacity does not refer only to "seeing in space" but also to "seeing in time." Being somewhat initiated and familiarized with many esoteric notions, it was relatively easy to understand what this phenomenon was based on and how it is possible to overcome the limits of our normal senses. At the same time, I quickly understood that this field is vital in military operations and also within the secret services. It is useful to know where a top-secret base of the enemy is located, and it is comforting to know ahead of time the secret weaponry of the opponent. These techniques are also necessary to find out the location of certain people who possess secret plans. The range of operations can, of course, be greatly extended.

"The Americans have intensively developed this field and, from what I know from General Obadea, they have achieved extraordinary results," Cezar explained to me. "Initially, the Russians had reached a high level in this research in the seventies. It was during those times that the USA was completely taken by surprise in the case of a particular incident where they thought that their security network had been breached by Russian espionage. In fact, things were totally different. Counterintelligence provided proof that what the Russians had found out was not a direct result of active espionage, but had a paranormal nature; thus, they realized that the studies by the Russian 'comrades' were already quite advanced in this field. They became very scared because they were not only unable to control the process by which the Russians could learn of their greatest secrets but also by reason of the fact they had no idea of where to begin fighting back."

Still, the Americans mobilized quickly. Cezar told me that a training facility was set up and the first protocols or stages in connection to what they referred to as "remote-viewing" were conceived. I found it most interesting that the people from the team that started the research made hundreds and even thousands of experiments with human subjects in order to gradually understand the basis of the process of perception that occurs in remote-viewing. They realized that rigorous training is needed in order to enter a modified state of consciousness in which relevant intelligence can be detected on a proposed target which is at a great distance in space and even time.

This perception actually refers to the correct interpretation of a type of energetic information that has no connection to our three-dimensional space. It is transmitted by what we can assess as types of energetic information "waves" that exist in a space or level that is superior to the physical one we live in, a level with more spatial dimensions than the three we are accustomed to. When the Americans reached this conclusion, it was relatively simple for them to understand the process through which information gathered in such a manner can be used. The difficulty stands only in the correct decoding of any state or form of information coming from a level superior to the physical one but to which we are nevertheless connected every second, even if we are not aware of this. I confess that I did not understand very well how this was possible, but I hoped Cezar would clarify this. The opportunity came very quickly because, during that period, we met daily at the base.

"You already know that man is more than the physical material body," he said, "but what man is besides that is hard to say for the common man. If we were only flesh and blood, we would not have very great expectations in life nor a well defined goal, but our being is much more complex and exists simultaneously on several levels of its universe or, better said, in Creation."

"I did some research and learned about the three main levels of existence in the order of their increasing vibrational frequency: the physical level, the astral level, and the causal level," I mentioned, "but you've also told me about this."

Nodding his head approvingly, Cezar continued.

"Yes, the three fundamental dimensions of Creation each have a general vibrational frequency which is typical for them. Better said, an array of vibrational frequency like a kind of radio scale. Together, the physical, astral and causal dimensions form what occultists call the Macrocosm, meaning Creation itself."

"An interesting comparison with the radio scale," I noticed. "It gives me a clearer image on the Macrocosmic structure."

"If he develops the respective frequencies in himself, one can access any of these vibrational frequencies. It's like trying to listen to a certain radio station from the many that you have at your disposal on the frequency band of your radio. So, there is a precise correspondence between what man has inside and what is outside him."

Thanks to the books in Elinor's library, I was in relatively familiar territory because I had knowledge in this field.

"I know," I said. "The correspondence is synthesized in the famous Emerald Tablet assigned to Hermes Trismegistus. What is above, on a Macrocosmic level, must also be found below, at a microcosmic level, which is the level of the human being."

"When I speak of the microcosm, I am not referring only to the physical body but also to the other structures of a subtle nature that exist simultaneously with this one, and this means I am also taking the astral and the causal body into consideration. I think you understand this well."

I nodded my head in approval.

"Just the same, when I speak about the Macrocosm, I am referring both to the physical universe or cosmos as scientists define it but also to the astral and causal universe. I see you are already familiar with the relations between the Macrocosm and the microcosm. This is very good. Some think that it is a metaphor when it is stated that the whole of Creation is found in man as a microcosm, but this metaphor expresses a great truth because you now know that the microcosm of the human being that includes its three bodies, the physical, astral and causal, is the Macrocosm in miniature. This is about a very precise correspondence in the sense that all that is in the Macrocosm is also in the microcosm of the human being."

"I understand; but, is this correspondence also valid regarding the spiritual essence of man that you spoke to me about in the past? If man has a self and if there is such a correspondence, does it mean that there are two kinds of self, a smaller one and a larger one for the Macrocosm?

Cezar laughed loudly.

"No, of course not. But you must know that the essence of the Macrocosmos is, in fact, God's self. Occultists call it the omniscient, omnipotent and eternal spirit which is, in fact, God's ultimate essence. This essence also exists like a 'divine spark' in every human being. And, even if man cannot tell and does not believe that this is possible, he still has a divine nature which is eternal."

Although I now had that matter sorted out, there were others left to be cleared. I thought a little before speaking.

"I cannot quite understand how the three dimensions are differentiated in the Macrocosm. Is there a border between them? My idea, as a representation, is that they are like overlapping layers of different thickness. First, there is the physical one at the base; then, the astral one in the middle; and then there is the causal one which is the most refined one. I can tell, however, that this is not just a mere representation of the mind. How are things really in this respect?"

"First of all, you have to accept for a fact that the three universes that together form the Macrocosm (the physical, astral and causal) exist simultaneously and are intimately related to their correspondence in the microcosm that is the human being. We cannot speak of a manifestation at the human being's level that does not correspond at a certain level in the Macrocosm, too. For example, emotions connect the man to the astral universe whether he knows this or not. His physical aspect connects him to the physical universe that we can notice around us or by looking through a telescope. Likewise, the causal universe is in close relation with the world of ideas. Even if this universe is more difficult to understand and to perceive around us because of the fact that it is very subtle, it is present in every man through the 'causal body' which is an esoteric term."

"Most people, however, have no idea about the existence of the astral and the causal body," I said. "Almost all of us concentrate on our physical bodies which we see and feel."

"It is true because man's action with the other two invisible bodies, the astral and the causal, is closely related to the extent to which he has awakened his consciousness in these fundamental worlds. Usually, the human being is satisfied to live almost on instinct, only at the level of the physical body. If man, however, becomes conscious enough of the astral world, he can then manifest more in that dimension and will act in full awareness, just as he does in the physical world."

I was still a bit puzzled.

"If we have everything in us, if we have these energetic structures or fundamental bodies in our being, then why are we not aware of them just as we are aware of our physical body?" I asked.

"Be assured that, when your consciousness is in one of those two subtle bodies, in the astral or the causal one, you are fully aware of the existence of that body."

Cezar took a small pause, staring right at me.

"Tell me, when you sleep or dream, are you aware that you have a physical body?"

"No," I replied, imagining what was going to come next.

The explanation came immediately.

"In those moments when you are asleep, you can say that you are living and acting with your astral body while your physical body is resting in bed. You are not then aware of it although it is clear that it exists. It is the same when you wake up. You become aware of your physical body but you are no longer conscious of your astral body. This shows that, next, adequate purification training of the consciousness is needed in order for it to engulf a larger area of knowledge that is, in a way, somewhat like expanding. If there are no difficulties in being aware of your body and of the manner in which you can act in the physical world in which you live, things are different in the astral and causal world. In order to manage to perceive and understand them, you must make efforts so that you can afterwards act in full awareness of them.

Their vehicles, which are invisible to normal perception, must be elevated and purified as much as possible."

"What 'vehicles' are you talking about?" I asked, puzzled.

"It is a specific terminology in esoteric and spiritual literature. Your physical body is the 'vehicle' that your consciousness has at its disposal in order to act in the physical world that you are in. In the same manner, your astral body is the 'vehicle' which helps you act in the astral world. Of course, the causal body is the very special 'vehicle' that helps you to know the causal world and to act in it. I have already told you about this."

I continued to ponder a little. Things seemed pretty clear to me, yet I still wondered where and how man's evolution appeared since he is born with the three above-mentioned bodies in his every existence. I asked Cezar about this, and he replied, smiling slightly as he was happy about where this discussion was going.

"Structurally speaking, the physical body remains the same from one existence to the other, meaning it cannot modify itself fundamentally. What I mean is, if you now have the well-known look of a human being, you will not be born in the next life with a totally different shape. That is to say, you will not be an oddity in relationship to the form of the human body. Personal karma and genetic information will guide you towards the same structure of the human form in the physical level. What is modified, however, are the being's subtle structures, meaning the astral vehicle and the causal one. They are, in fact, the ones that evolve more or less from one life to the other, and it is within them, in essence, that the main vectors that will define the features of your following existences are encrypted. As you know, of course, these vectors rely on how you acted in the respective previous existence."

The discussion clarified a fundamental element: nothing that resides in the Macrocosm, which is all that visibly or invisibly surrounds us, is not lacking from the microcosm that is our being. But, although the Macrocosm is always active, we are confronted with a "dormant" state of these elements. That is why it is very important to awaken what is in a latent state in our microcosm, for it is in this manner that we can fully understand the Macrocosm. As every man contains a proportion of what exists in the Macrocosm and in God, this allows us to achieve, to a certain extent, what God achieves in His Creation. Cezar clarified this aspect for me in an admirable way.

"The fact that man can achieve proportionally what God achieves in His Creation, which is the Macrocosm, is correlated to what is written in the *Bible*: namely, that the human being is made in God's own image and likeness. The profound significance of this aspect is tied to the fact that all that resides in the Macrocosm is also in the microcosm of the human being. I'm telling you all of this because you must be aware that in your being there is everything, but this everything has not been awakened yet. Be sure, however, that your consistent efforts will gradually lead to this enabling of what is latent in your being and then you will understand that the differences that exist between men are in fact determined by the extent to which they have awakened what exists in each man's microcosm."

I listened carefully to what Cezar said and, in the end, I synthesized a few main ideas. First of all, we are a complex whole, a real miniature cosmos which is what the word microcosm signifies. I also understood that the microcosm that we all are is, at the same time, a miniature replica of the Macrocosm, that is, of Creation, the Great Whole of which we are an integrated part. It is out of the question to be outside this whole; or better said, to separate us from the Macrocosm. It is an incomprehensible mystery that we are embraced and comprised in the whole, the Macrocosm, and that this is simultaneously reflected in the microcosm of every being that exists in the physical level or in any other of the subtle levels of Creation. It would be strange to imagine, for instance, that angels or any other deities do not have Everything in them. What separates one being from the other is, as Cezar specified, the preponderance of one type of energy or another which makes that being possess a certain "affinity" or inclination towards something in the Creation that is specifically for himself.

Meditating thus on what my good friend revealed to me, I understood even more profoundly the fact that the Macrocosm is reflected proportionally in the microcosm of our being. Almost all the esoteric texts leave this to be understood but do not precisely state it. The main idea is that, through spiritual evolution, man can access the energetic sources that reside in a latent state within the microcosm of his being by using certain initiating methods or techniques. This determines, in time, the possibility of gaining colossal powers through affinity with the great Macrocosmic energies. This fact itself is thus a direct result of awakening the force and energy sources that are correspondent in the microcosmos of our being. And still, if this process is not fully understood, it can lead to utterly erroneous ideas. With his remarkable tact, Cezar exemplarily revealed this aspect:

"Some might imagine that by evolving and awakening the corresponding force sources from the Macrocosm, they could even become masters of it, meaning God. The truth is that, no matter how much we evolve and amplify these energies, even if we reach the maximum, we can never say that we are equal to God. This is a dementia that only Lucifer, in his immense stupidity, could think of. It is therefore very important to keep in mind that this analogy between the Macrocosm and the microcosm of the human being, or any other being in the Macrocosm, indicates not equality but proportion. Sure, to quote the metaphor known in spiritual texts, the drop may unite with the ocean; but it would be insane for the drop to imagine that it is the ocean and that it can do what it wishes. In reality, there are forces that make the ocean manifest the way it does and cannot be controlled by it because it is just a drop. I hope you understand the analogy. Any part in the microcosm of a being is like a cell in an immense organism and surely, through the actions that it does, it can contribute by its specificity to the harmony of some plans of Creation."

"So, that is how I can explain the actions of saints or some of Mankind's great spiritual teachers," I said, captured by the explanations I was getting.

"Exactly! A being that aspires for its divine manifestation will be in full agreement and in harmony with that divine reality. It will be a part of that unity. The Whole of that reality will then be reflected in it, and it will be in solidarity with the Whole. In this manner, you can understand how miracles work. You can understand the holiness, purity and sacredness of some extraordinary beings and you can understand how states of mystical ecstasy and some people's paranormal powers appear. In such a being, evil will never appear, and that is exactly why I told you some time ago that the absence of evil means good. The same can be said in the case of a being that brings evil in his deeds. That being will then represent evil and show it in the surrounding world accordingly. Through personal choice, every being can contribute either to the building of good or evil. Of course, however, the consequences of those actions will differ radically as well."

"Yes, that is clear," I said. "Still, it is quite difficult to grasp how something virtually infinite, like the Macrocosm, can fit into something finite like the microcosm."

With patience, Cezar explained this misunderstanding, too.

"You can now better picture why it is said that the human being is, in fact, a microcosm made in the image and likeness of the Macrocosm but in a metaphorical way. This is the key. Without understanding this aspect deeply, it is virtually impossible to know how it is possible to discover God and His Creation within yourself or how it is possible that inferno and demonic lights but also paradise exist in man. If you do not understand this fundamental truth fully: namely, that all that exists in God's Creation is also proportionally and similarly within yourself, you'll not be able to find the answer to some paradoxes. You'll not understand, for example, how it is possible for some people to say that God does not exist while others say that He exists. Some say that love does not exist while others say that it is endless. Just like God has created the Macrocosm, man is also a miniature universe like a microcosm, similar to the Macrocosm but by analogy. Because God exists and He is omnipresent, He is also in man; and this divine presence in our being is like a spark from God, eternal and indestructible. The saints and the enlightened men of past times strongly state this because they got to experience this divine presence in themselves in a profound way."

These clarifications that Cezar provided to me have been a revelation for my understanding because he has mentioned certain nuanced aspects.

I am a microcosm after the metaphorical pattern of the Macrocosm, and everything exists inside of me in a latent and proportional form. In order to get all that I want, I only have to bring these latent features up to date.

The process that involves remote-viewing is also a latent capacity which waits to be awakened in me. I now understood why decoding information through remote-viewing, which comes from a level superior to the physical plane by means of energetic waves, is so difficult. Even if all of the dimensions and realities of Creation in the microcosm of my being reside there, I am still not aware of many of them. This is also true for most people, and this aspect itself is the very basis of our current civilization's ignorance. In remote-viewing, pieces of information which already exist in the structure of my microcosm, or that of any other human being, are waiting to be brought up to date. No matter what the target of my research already is through this procedure, I already have the right answer in me. Finally, it all consists of giving enough stimulation to the access path to this piece of information which can be found on a more complex subtle level than the physical one. In fact, the informational range of the remote-viewing process is actually the collective subconscious.

As in any other field, anyone can learn to successfully practice remote-viewing. Every person who decides to do this will have accomplishments and successes depending upon how much effort they make and based upon their experience. If you listen to the ones that will tell you that you cannot do this because you must have certain capabilities you were born with in order to perform remote-viewing, I can assure you that you will only be allowing that person to limit your possibilities and potential. You will thus allow someone to say what is and what is not possible for you and that means human conditioning. Fortunately, I was not only proposed and encouraged to develop my remote-viewing abilities, but I also received precious esoteric knowledge from Cezar which permitted me to understand the phenomena more profoundly. I offer all this information to my readers with openness in the hope that it will represent a turning point in the conception of life and the world to many of them.

Remote-viewing means a step further beyond the common and the routine, even a dive into the ocean of collective knowledge. The people that have the necessary faith, will and urge to convince themselves that something else exists beyond our physical universe all have what they need to perform remote-viewing. It is necessary, however, to mention that the final stages of the accomplishment protocol are subject to special military and secret service intelligence and research; but even without these superior phases, there are enough ways and means to transcend the human condition and sensory limitations successfully.

I wish to mention again that every man who has a normal state of physical, psychical and mental health can achieve the ability to remote-view. Through such perception, we develop our ability to travel in time and space in a practical manner in order to see different people, places or things and to gather information about them. Many readers may imagine that this is similar to watching a movie on the television or at the cinema, but they are seriously mistaken. Except for the superior secret phases mentioned earlier, remote-viewing precisely refers to only two actions that every man manifests almost all the time: to detect and to decode. We will thus detect information and data from a level of vibration which is superior to the physical level; then we will decode this into coherent three-dimensional thought-forms; and in the end, we will objectify these three-dimensional thoughts into bi-dimensional information. The latter we will record using dimensional contours, meaning sketches. It is also possible to write words that describe color, texture, temperature, taste, smell, and sound. In conclusion, remote-viewing is the detection of some data and information from another dimension of manifestation in which Mankind's collective subconscious ocean is integrated. After that comes the decoding of this data into coherent tri-dimensional thought-forms. In the end, we objectify and capture this data in bi-dimensional information in the form of sketches and sensory verbal data.

If we think about it a little deeper, this is a process that repeats itself every day in our life. Let's say we are listening to something on the headphones. What we say that we are hearing is, in fact, energetic information waves that are in motion, heading towards us. Our ears hear this, and our brain electrochemically decodes the data which is in the form of waves. Thus, we get tri-dimensional coherent thought-forms that have a meaning or significance. We call these new thought-forms sounds. Afterwards, we can reproduce the impressions caused by the sounds we hear in words or even images.

It is the same thing when someone speaks to us in a language that we do not understand. We cannot decode the information and we will thus have to rely on something else to understand what the other person is telling us. We will have to use another capacity that each of us has, like significant gestures. Initially, my idea was that images received through remote-viewing have a direct nature, like when we look at a painting or a screen where a film is projected. In reality, when a person justly applies the steps in remote-viewing to learn information about a distant place or time, the visual images are in fact perceptive images. It is like that person is dreaming. Although the visual images in a dream can seem to be completely real at the respective moment for the dreamer, they still do not imply visual processes inside the eye. What is then happening is that the product of the eye is connecting to the universal capability of the "eye" within the mind to visualize, meaning to imagine. Anyone can and has the capacity to imagine. When we dream, we are, in fact, visualizing by using our own imagination. In a way, the same thing happens when we read a book or imagine a landscape.

I feel indebted, however, to mention once again that the visualization that I am referring to is an inherent quality of thought and not a biological process that implies the sense of sight at eye level. Everyone does that constantly during the day when, for example, they are day-dreaming in the car or when they imagine things. In the case of the remote-viewing process, all that is asked is to modify the quality of visualization. This implies the modification of perception (from the external stimuli which are decoded by our brain into tri-dimensional thought-forms being interpreted as our outer reality) by concentrating towards inner mental stimuli which are always present in our thinking processes but to which we usually do not give conscious attention. The main focus of our attention is usually towards the so called outer world, but the perception that lies at the basis of remote-viewing is connected with the deeper levels of our mind and especially the subconscious.

As we achieve more and more remote-viewing experiences, there is a tendency to change the focus of our attention from the symbolic tasks and activities which we perform in the exterior world and to concentrate more and more on the messages that we receive through the subconscious mind. This originates in the Universal Mind that operates outside the limits of space and time. Certain esoteric societies have the purpose a obtaining a single-directional focus towards the most profound levels of the subconscious mind which has direct and immediate access to infinite knowledge which can be accessed from the Universal Mind.

It seems difficult; but in reality, it is not. When we perform the remote-viewing process, all we need to do is to ask correctly and observe the answers appearing in a form which is compatible with our cultural and religious programming. In the web of life's infinite connections, knowledge is the key and it comes to us in a more and more exact form as we amplify our capacity to focus ourselves towards the profound levels of the mind. It is all in there in the mind.

One of the officers who trained us at the Maryland base used to tell us: "The whole of life is like a safari through the mind. You are exposed to dangers, but you can also defend yourself from them efficiently if you get to the depths of the causes."

When you go deeper into the remote-viewing process technique, you realize more and more how complex and vast the mind is. In the meantime, you realize that the dangers of this jungle are as real as we want to perceive that they are. It is our choice to consider ourselves threatened or surrounded by all sorts of dangers or to impose a calm, relaxed and profound attitude of the mind which automatically changes the universe in which we live and act.

Of course, the intensive remote-viewing training which I followed at the American base involved certain mental abilities that had to already have been stimulated in the subject. There were numerous tests and scores; and in the end, there were only five of us left.

I do not know exactly what contributed to my promotion to the upper phases of the training. Perhaps it was the long talks with Cezar or the explanations that I had gotten from him, Elinor and Repa Sundhi over the years. Perhaps it had to do with my individual studies of the occult and spirituality or perhaps my timid attempts of meditation practice under Cezar's guidance. Or maybe it was all of that together. The fact is that out of fourteen agents, only five remained: two Americans, a Canadian, a Brazilian, and me.

Western secret services used and still use many protocols to achieve remote-viewing. The preferred protocol in the USA involves distracting the mind. If we keep our conscious mind completely distracted from some tasks that modify rapidly or are irregular, we can concentrate on the messages of the subconscious mind since this is the source of the "instrument" tied to the information flux which is remote viewing.

Some countries use techniques for a quick transformation of the state of consciousness of the mind in order to have access to the level or state of mind known as theta. Here, the remote-viewing ability becomes a natural state for anyone who operates on these very profound levels of the subconscious. The results obtained are truly impressive. Theta is the ideal state of mind to achieve remote-viewing because, when the specific theta waves are predominant in the brain, anyone can easily achieve remote-viewing. Experience has shown me that to be successful in remote-viewing, it is not strictly necessary to have an intense visualizing training but rather an adequate training to obtain the theta state of the brain where visualization becomes a natural ability.

Even from the beginning, we were told that in order to achieve serious progress in this respect, faith is the basic key to success. On the contrary, skepticism is the key to failure and restriction. We were also warned that although all of us who were present there had faith in this process, which was somewhat at the edge of scientific knowledge, our individual faith was still structured on different levels for each and every one of us. That became visible as we went along as more difficult tests started to show the blockages that some agents had on some levels of their subconscious. Not managing to get over those steps, they did not have access to the superior levels of the training, and they left the base immediately.

The problems regarding faith and skepticism act as a universal law. Just as faith can move the mountains of doubt, skepticism or excessive reason block transformation and restrict the person in a cage of doubts. This, in time, generates fear, paranoia and a false state of comfort.

The essence of success in remote-viewing is somewhat the same as in any other field. It does not refer to efforts but rather to faith and enthusiasm. I had a strong dose of both. On one hand, I was experiencing the spiritual formation that Cezar had provided me; and on the other hand, the joy of being part of Department Zero and having access to great secrets of state. Even without these particular "ingredients," any person who has enough faith in his or her capacity to reach his goal and wishes it strongly has automatically opened the door to success.

I feel, however, that I must specify that the remote-viewing process is not easy. The protocol to accomplish this involves many stages, and lacking one of them or a blocking on one of the intermediate levels results in missing the proposed space-time target. The training gradually opens the way towards the Universal Mind which represents a "warehouse" of pure information that can be accessed instantaneously at will. Only through transcending the other levels of the mind and by direct connection to the more profound levels of the subconscious, which operates as an interface with the Universal Mind, can we transcend the physical reality of our perception. This is how we can explain the fact that, by entering into communion with the Universal Mind, we virtually have access to any kind of information. At this level, all is simultaneous. We have the feeling of omnipresence, and the past and future are reunited in the present. The Universal Mind is like a common background for all life forms; and it can give any kind of information about space and time which is exactly what the one performing the remote-viewing process is searching for. Here, imaginative visualization and sensory perception are more intensified. Senses are then particularly perceptive and less biological. You feel like you are in an ocean, having everything at your disposal, instantaneously.

It was clear to me from the first days that the Americans wanted to train us in order to see which ones of us would reach the very high level that goes beyond even the brain's theta waves. As in Cezar's stance, it was not clear to me why they were doing this. I am sure there was a reason but that remained hidden. Naturally, the most apparent reason at hand was that they were planning to use the abilities of such a person for their own personal purposes.

The ones that achieve remote-viewing — and here I am referring particularly to the military domain — train intensely to obtain this state of hyper-concentrated and consciously receptive creativity that is available to them at their will and even when they have their eyes open. The secret to operating in this manner at the profound theta level with your eyes remaining open is to stay very centered and focused towards the interior of our being and especially on the flow of thoughts while simultaneously achieving exterior perception by applying the process of remote-viewing. Presently, I only know one person capable of such a thing. He is the Canadian who was finally selected from the group of five that I was a part of as well. He had a phenomenal ability to interiorize and a great sensibility. To my knowledge, he only made one mistake on the targets proposed during the tests.

I had prepared myself theoretically as well as I could before I left for the USA. The protocol imposed a certain level of security and a well designed contact system. Still, even as things went into the home stretch, there were certain interferences from Bucharest which seemed political to me. I have no pleasure in speaking about these things, but I do so now by virtue of the fact that I was directly involved. As I later found out, it was, in fact, an intervention from above due to the other faction in the Romanian Intelligence Service which cannot stand the independence of Department Zero or its leadership. Unfortunately, I have to admit that there are a lot of treacheries and complications at this level. Things do not always run smoothly by reason of the fact that, many times, responsible parties interact with the missions that they have to fulfill with regard to their own personal interests. State secrets of the highest level that exist in the archives of Department Zero considerably incite the imagination of some people who would like to obtain certain advantages from it. As they cannot to this directly and in such a way that there will be no traces left, they resort to pulling strings. Bit by bit, a chain of dependencies is created which sometimes reaches very high political levels. This was exactly the case with regard to my situation.

A member of an important Senate committee started exuding pressure in order to visit the Alpha Base. We already had signals about this, and we tried to invoke legal aspects which forbid such a request save for force majeure cases such as treason or important leadership changes that might occur. In fact, the real purpose of this pressure was to create tension in the relations between the committee and Department Zero, especially with General Obadea, so that our refusal, even if justified, would be interpreted as unnatural. An investigation would then follow that would permit the committee to access the subtleties of the department. With regard to me, their pretext was that a fresh employee could not be sent on a mission like this and that someone with more experience in the field was required in order to cope with the proposed theme. In reality, they wanted to break the monopoly that we held over a certain segment of state secrets and to affect the centralization of intelligence into a new command structure.

Both General Obadea and Cezar knew very well how much trouble would come from such a modification if it were to take place. First of all, the horizontal expansion of the chain of command meant that more people would know the sensitive points of national importance concerning certain locations or highly important areas regarding our country. This would have created confusion and become a source of security leakage. Regarding the underground complex in the Bucegi Mountains, the sharing of this information would have blown up all the cooperation with the American faction. We believe that this was actually the direct target for the action coming from "above," and I did not doubt for a second that there were a few "honorable" persons behind it who were willing to do everything in their power to get there as quickly as they could.

General Obadea and Cezar had to cope with a situation that, without being too complicated at the time, was nevertheless annoying. If it was not treated seriously, it risked unleashing something on a greater scale that would endanger the well-defined and very secret status of Department Zero. Cezar told me that there were three rounds of discussions between the respective members of the committee and General Obadea. At two of them, he was present as well. Almost directly, this politician threatened to alert the committee and initiate the analysis procedure if his requested security modifications were not done. By this, he was referring to my trip to the USA, but that was only a pretext. He did not even hide the fact that he was speaking on behalf of a group of hidden interests. Such aspects are common at a certain level of government. Things were even more complicated due to the fact that one of the reasons on which the attack was based was that I was writing about certain secret subjects and even published them. This was a delicate aspect which had already appeared a few months earlier but had been put to rest at a secret meeting of the RIS (Romanian Intelligence Service) directors. I was never informed too much about that issue, but both Cezar and General Obadea assured me that I could continue to write within certain boundaries which I have followed completely.

Now, however, this problem was being raised again and was a sign that the "trouble" was not only not forgotten, it was being amplified. Besides being an effort to obstruct my books and future writing , the parallel intention was to create a small breach in the current RIS system by using this little "scandal" in order to take control over Department Zero. In these conditions, it is obvious that I could not have added fuel to the fire by publishing the fourth volume of the series immediately after these events transpired. I therefore had to wait, hoping at certain moments that all would cool down and I could keep on making known the main aspects that I was having to deal with at Department Zero. My waiting was prolonged long enough; and only now, two years after publishing the third volume, have I gotten the clearance from Cezar to continue writing.

I am asking the reader to understand this complicated situation in which I, metaphorically speaking, had my arms and legs tied. If it were not for a certain group of strong people with financial and political power who favored me, there would have been no chance at all for this book to be published. Of course, I cannot expose here all of the backstage aspects that exist and of which I am aware. Besides these, there are elements which Cezar said it was best I did not know as they are part of the incredible web of interests and goals which have taken over a large part of the powerful men in this country. I was only permitted to underline certain issues in order to keep a relative balance in a situation where waters "boil" virtually all of the time.

When General Obadea considered that the group behind this Senate committee was applying too much pressure by touching on some very sensitive and dangerous points, he acted in a special manner. By means of some highly placed connections that he had, he nipped the destructive initiative of some of the committee members in the bud. As I would later learn, the General had been very surprised when certain aspects regarding terrible secrets of state were presented to him that only his department and a section of the army could have known. Hilariously, those problems were used to blackmail him. This is why he had to call upon the high connections he had.

At least for that moment, his decision to counterattack the committee's very virulent and subversive attack was salutary. The aspects put on the table by the committee were extremely serious with regard to national safety. In consequence, and in order for things not to become even more twisted and to have more time to gather information that might help, General Obadea sought out political aid. Even so, the pressure still continued and went overboard more than a few times.

At that level, the tone of those discussions were unofficial. The committee was represented by one of its members who was also a high dignitary. His intentions were obviously hostile to Department Zero. For instance, one of the critical points of the discussion referred to an incredible discovery that took place in the Orăştie Mountains in the '90s which was very quickly and finally blocked but involved important state interests. The approach of the committee was unorthodox, and although Department Zero was not involved with this discovery from the beginning, their purpose was to give credibility to the idea that this was just a cover-up and that, in reality, many things were hidden from the entitled state bodies which was a very serious crime. Being curious about this subject, I asked Cezar about it. He mentioned only one aspect related to those events, adding that we would discuss it further after my return from the United States. I have to indeed admit that what I found out afterwards not only dazzled me but also made me very eager to learn what happened at that time. I thought this would come in somewhat handy to me given the abilities I had acquired through the remote-viewing process. It turned out, however, that these abilities were of no use to me in this case. Still, I do not want to anticipate with regard to these matters because I will address the subject widely in the last chapter of this book. If I am to express my personal opinion, I would say that the discovery in the Orăştie Mountains represents the quintessence of the nature and origin of the Romanian people and the undoubtable and inalterable proof of what it truly was and is. In their ignorance, maybe some will hurry to accuse me of exaltation and exaggerated patriotism. In their place, I would first suggest they be patient to get to the presentation of those events and afterwards make a general opinion. On the other hand, it is known that we can never please everyone. I hope, however, that the respective information will raise many questions in skeptics; and for those who feel the thrill of ancestral times, it will bring to their hearts the certainty of the true origins of our people.

These matters were not settled as fast as I had hoped. The intervention of the politicians calmed the spirits to some extent and helped me to leave for the military base in Maryland, USA. There remained, however, certain obscure aspects that the General and Cezar had to take care of. As a result of this, we decided together that it would be inappropriate for me to write and publish the circumstances surrounding these events after I returned to Romania. Once again, I had to postpone the publishing of this book during that period with regard to the background of those discussions and tensions.

Two years following those events, however, things seem to have fallen into place and the political situation tended to take another turn so I got the green light for publishing. I have told all of this so that the reader may form, even approximately, a general idea of the context and reasons that existed in relation to my previous silence which many do not understand.

Let me now return to the period before my departure for the USA. Even after the political intervention requested by General Obadea, harassment from the Senate committee continued under different forms and this disturbed our daily activity to some degree. The idea that we followed was to avoid a decisional or legislative act from superior structures of the government, at least until I left. The apparent reason for starting this mess would therefore have been overcome and the situation could have been settled more easily. The events, however, did not happen as we wanted. Five days before my departure, General Obadea announced to Cezar that they were invited to a new discussion on the matter. As you all know, such meetings always assume equally beneficial negotiations and settlements. In our case, however, there could be no advantage as the matter at hand was itself fraudulent. Still, the meeting was not to be avoided even if it had a semi-official nature. Once they arrived, Cezar knew that the pressure would be great. Therefore, in order to undermine these backstage maneuvers, he proposed to the General for me to be present at the meeting as well, especially because I was involved in the problem. He immediately saw the advantage and agreed on the spot. Not only would this be an uncomfortable surprise for the representative of the committee, it would also stop the representative from acting with danger- ous freedom with respect to certain threats or decisions. There was also the possibility that, faced with this fait accompli, he would back down and ask for a new meeting with more precise discussion terms. I knew the person in question since I worked in the Ministry and knew that, when he hung on to a problem, he badly wanted to obtain an immediate result. He lacked diplomatic reason and patience in action. Choleric and selfish in nature, he persistently tried to solve all problems of personal interest in a harsh and authoritarian way. I could thus sketch a viable psychological profile for the scheduled meeting and agreed on a certain strategy with Cezar and General Obadea.

The meeting took place in one of Bucharest's fancy restaurants that is considered to be a main hub for political affairs. We arrived there first, and after a quarter of an hour, the representative of the Senate committee also arrived. Shaking the hands of Cezar and the General with nonchalance and sitting down, he spoke to them without looking at me, cold and distant.

"Who's this?"

The General introduced me and specified that I was going to depart in a few days.

"He already has all the credentials for Maryland," he added.

"I don't like this business, gentlemen," the character said, indisposed. "We have things to talk about and you knew very well that I can't do it in front of someone else."

General Obadea suddenly became harsh.

"Mr. Domotei, things have been settled clearly and there is no need to apply any more pressures. If it is necessary, we will go to the President."

The discussion got fired up between the two. Cezar and I kept quiet because it was all part of our anticipated plan. The man would get nervous and his blood sugar level would drop. Because we already knew he had problems with his stomach, he would have to eat at once, and that is why we arranged for the plates to be already prepared. Domotei had to be convinced to delay any decision until after my departure. What he did not know is that once I entered this American training program, there were certain external cooperation protocols which individualized Department Zero whereby it could not be absorbed into larger structures without notable repercussions with regard to the relations between the two countries at the level of the secret services. That would have meant solving our problems.

That evening was long and tiresome. Domotei had that type of street intelligence that is fast, slick-like, and highly adaptable. Even if he did not see the nuances and did not have a general view of the matter, he still could not be fooled easily. It took several hours to slow down his vigilance and to persuade him that there were chances of solving this problem in the future in the way he and the group which he represented wanted. We knew that, later on, when they would learn of the Romanian-American normative act, there would be nothing left for them to do and a great scandal would emerge; but in this manner, Department Zero remained on its own feet and would not depend upon political or any other kind of interests.

I left for the USA at the beginning of December 2005 with a special RIS (Romanian Intelligence Service) flight. The plane was also carrying a few American officers which included three colonels. They were the special envoys in regard to the Bucegi ensemble. After a short stop in Spain, we safely arrived in Maryland and started the training the very next day. The Americans were very serious and punctual. After all, they were spending their own money. The equipment was interesting but not spectacular. There were several Marines and USAF officers moving around, peeking and trying to figure out which one of us was the most promising. Surely, they wanted to claim the respective agent for the service that they were working in and which they led, after an agreement with the secret service that he was a part of.

Knowing that the stakes were high, I concentrated as much as I could, remaining almost all the time in a relaxed and receptive state that would be good for any remote-viewing (RV) investigation at any time. Still, from the array of colonels and generals that came and went, one seemed not to like me and that was Colonel Foreeth. Every time he passed near me, he would never lose the opportunity to mock me or even to scold me, more or less seriously, which did not look good for the general picture nor for the final report that was going to be made on me. I admit he was getting on my nerves because it was obvious that it was mere dislike and nothing more, but it could cost me. I had been sent by Department Zero as a kind of "insurance" with regard to the value of the RIS so I could not afford to make a bad image there. I do not know the thinking of the secret services of other countries that sent their representatives, but already there were only five of us left, the others being sent home. The matter was ruthlessly and directly clear: you go or you stay. The ones who stayed had to take some more tests.

I had a special respect for the Canadian, a very sensitive guy with certain extra sensory abilities. He was by far in the lead, but at least I recognized his value for what it was. If Foreeth had not stressed me with his idiot jokes, perhaps I could have improved my abilities even more. Fate, however, solved this problem admirably.

I had already spent two months in Maryland practicing hard. I have also said that the Americans took things very seriously, the military base being an important one that was almost always being visited by different important military personalities. Among these was the Chief of the Pentagon, who at that time was General Inossanto, and he came a couple of times. Although severe and cunning in everything, the General kept a joyful tone that he did not fear to share with his subordinates whenever he felt it was right. I even had the impression that, to a certain extent, he liked me and was somewhat interested in my situation. I could not say if this was a direct consequence of the American Counterintelligence Service in relation with the Bucegi discovery, but the first impression that he made on me was a favorable one. Besides, he had an exceptional stateliness which had the effect that, when he entered a room, not only did everyone rise — a natural element of rank — but they also stayed silent a long time after that until he brought up or said something.

On that day, Foreeth's misfortune was not to see the General who was bent and discussing something with one of his aides at a table in the back of the room. We were in the middle of a small break preparing for a secret and important test which had to be taken in the Chief of the Pentagon's presence. As usual, Foreeth entered carelessly and started to pick on me with no reason whatsoever. With the corner of my eye, I noticed how General Inossanto turned his attention to me and Foreeth, the latter continuing to remain unaware of the presence of the Chief of the Pentagon in the room. A few of the other officers responsible for the test tried to warn Foreeth, but the General signaled them to stop. The situation became somewhat embarrassing until, with a subconscious intuitive reflex, I told the Colonel rapidly what he did between 9:00 o'clock and 10 o'clock in the morning, underlining that his wife would perhaps not be so pleased to find out.

A grave-like silence settled. I was as red as a crab and had already started to collect my things, considering I had no longer any reason to be there. Then, the sound of the vigorous laugh of General Inossanto was heard, filling the silence in cascades. Still, no one dared to take any position as Foreeth's vengeful nature was known as was the importance of his rank. He remained with his eyes gouged out, red with furry and incapable of saying a single word.

"Ha-ha-ha, Foreeth," said General Inossanto, who did not stop laughing. "You've been keeping that hidden away from us!"

Only then did the Colonel see the General. He saluted, and taking the Chief of the Pentagons's reaction as favorable to him, he was preparing to give the order to send me back to my country.

Then, an amazing thing happened. From the laughter and joyful tone he had, General Inossanto suddenly changed his attitude, speaking in a cold loud voice.

"Do you want to do something I do not know, Foreeth?"

His tone also took a vaguely threatening tone.

The colonel stumbled, stuttered and excused himself.

"Sir, no, Sir…I…just…Sir…an offence…"

The general looked at him with cold eyes.

"Tomorrow you are transferred from Airborne to Marines."

"But…Sir…I…"

"That is an order, Foreeth!" the General raised his voice. "You will find it signed on your desk first thing tomorrow. You have no reason to be here."

Saying this, General Inossanto came next to me and was very friendly as he made several slightly ironic remarks about Foreeth whom he now ignored completely. He went out with his tail between his legs; and from that moment on, I never saw him there again.

It is easy to understand what a boost this intervention of the Chief of the Pentagon was to me. In a certain way, things in America are as they are in our own home. Immediately afterwards, I recorded a significant "stock" increase and was given more attention and shown more respect. I am sure that all of this did not come from a real appreciation or judgment but more because of conjuncture aspects like the ones listed above. Anyway, I finished in fourth place which was considered a real victory. It was not clear to me what use this would be for me, but the fact that I finished among the first gave me a certain self confidence.

We were just getting ready to move to a new and more advanced round of RV studying when I got a telephone call on a secured line from Cezar. He was calling me home in haste without telling me the reason why. I did not ask another question either. I reported directly to the chief, General Roddey, who expressed his regret that I had to leave unexpectedly but told me I could continue my training in a year but only with the selected ones. He left me to believe without any ambiguity that I was one of them. Happily, I rushed to catch the jeep which was waiting for me in the yard. American efficiency was worthy of envy.

When I got to the airfield, I properly saluted two officers whom I knew from Romania as being attaches to the Bucegi mission. I was glad to see that they also responded with responsibility, as if they knew too well who I was and what I was doing there. Without losing any more time, I embarked on a B-52 and followed the same line as before: a short stop in Spain and then finally to Bucharest on a secluded runway. The snow mixed with mud and rain gave me a small feeling of discomfort. It was something totally different than Maryland. From the runway, I directly embarked on a helicopter belonging to Department Zero which rose immediately, heading for the Alpha Base. I could not suspect the grand surprise that awaited me there.

CHAPTER TWO

IMPORTANT MISSION

At the base, Cezar was smiling as he met me. Having heard about the Maryland "incident," he had reported it to General Obadea who laughed in satisfaction. "Did you see? Did you see how the General 'fixed' Foreeth?" he repeated to Cezar. "Even if we haven't met for a while, I always got along well with Inossanto."

Then, turning towards me, Cezar spoke.

"You did a fine job there, Radu! But now things are going on a different path."

I raised my eyes, expecting that there would once again be problems with the Senate committee.

"Aaa, it is not about Domotei," the General rushed to comfort me. "For now, we have managed to keep that situation under control; but the man is always watching and we have to be on guard all the time. Please step into my office."

I followed the General, curious about what my next assignment was going to be. I, however, remained still in the doorway. Doctor Xien was sitting at the elegant chrome and nickel table.

"Repa Sundhi!" I almost involuntarily shouted with great surprise and joy in my voice.

Doctor Xien looked exactly as I knew him: small with a spot of baldness and dressed in one of those well known Chinese uniforms except that it was now dark blue with white sleeves. He slowly bowed in front of me and smiled. I rushed, taking and shaking his feeble hands strongly. I had not seen him for some time, and I knew this was a matter of great importance if the government of Romania was seeking his advice. I did not have the time to express these thoughts, however, because he intervened directly.

"That matter has been settled. All is well now; but here, meet Shin Li."

Out of emotion, I did not get to analyze the situation in the chamber very well. Doctor Xien was sitting at the table next to a very young and superb woman while Cezar and General Obadea sat on either side of her. She was the assistant who had accompanied Repa Sundhi in the '80s when Department Zero was founded. I could not help but thinking: "Don't these people ever grow old?" According to Cezar's description, it seemed that they remained untouched by the rigors of old age.

"I've told you before that time doesn't pass for us as it does for you," Doctor Xien continued my thought verbally. "But, let us leave that aside. There is something important that you must do, but it is all up to your decision. Shin Li will help you to understand this better."

I was still pretty confused. What was I suppose to do, who exactly was this woman, and how did these two manage not to age? There were many questions that were colliding in my head and agitating my mind. Slowly, however, and thanks to the training gained in Maryland, certain mind functions started to put themselves in order and offered competent answers. I realized that the arrival of Doctor Xien was something important and without a doubt was not related to just me. I understood that this extraordinarily beautiful woman with Malayan features was going to guide me through the thicket that I had to pass; and I also thought that I could use RV to understand more about Doctor Xien and his companion.

"Do not even think that the Americans' method will give any results in our case," he immediately comforted me, reading my mind as usual. "I advise you not to waste any time and begin studying as soon as possible together with Shin Li."

Intuitively, I realized that before this meeting there was another important one between Doctor Xien, General Obadea and Cezar which referred to the secret parchment received not so long ago from the Goddess Machandi. It seemed, therefore, that the time had come for the information it contained to be made public. Doctor Xien had already assisted me in translating this text from the old Tibetan dialect, but he specified that it was not to be published yet. Now, the situation had changed radically. I was told that I had to act without any further delay in order to publish it. Still, Repa Sundhi told me that it would be useful to add some short comments to the five stanzas of the parchment in order to enhance the enlightenment and understanding of interested readers. The nature of these comments was to be revealed by Shin Li, and that is exactly what her decisive role in my mission was to be.

"But, Cezar cannot explain this?" I asked.

Doctor Xien stopped, slightly smiling.

"No, this time someone else must provide the necessary explanations," he said.

I looked upon Shin Li. She was truly perfect in her body's features, and her smile fascinated me. I found myself opposing her smile with some small resistance because I felt defenseless. I gave one last effort towards this end.

"How long will I need to learn of the mysteries of the parchment? I have many other duties to perform here."

"Exactly as long as it will take," Repa Sundhi comforted me as he patted me on the shoulder. "Not a moment more."

Cezar told me that Doctor Xien was going to remain at the base for a while longer due to some supplementary national security aspects that the government had raised. They were asking for his help once again. During this period, Shin Li was going to be around me almost all of the time. I confess that I did not understand the "tactical maneuver" coming from Doctor Xien and Cezar; but at the same time, I felt a shiver that engulfed my heart when I looked at Shin Li, being glad of her presence. That woman far exceeded any beauty standards that I was accustomed to. The features specific to the Malayan land gave her that inexplicable Asian sweetness of the face without straying too much from Western features. At the team's meetings, she barely spoke; but when she did, her voice was strong and expressed precisely all that she wanted, sometimes with a slight accent which made her even more charming. My speculation regarding her space-time "consistency" and her youthful mystery found no solution for I did not have enough data. With regard to Elinor, the matter was clear: his organism's functions were influenced by that metallic object which gave him phenomenal longevity. In Shin Li's case, I could not find a single support to explain her time "suspension." Later, I tried to find out something from Cezar, but it seems that the subject was taboo.

"You don't need this knowledge for now. It will only get you lost in a jungle which you will not know how to get out of."

"But how can I speak to someone about such important subjects without having any information about her person?"

"Sometimes it is best to leave things like this," Cezar concluded.

Obviously, Repa Sundhi and Shin Li were two highly spiritually evolved beings who had to accomplish certain specific duties and missions and thus gave their help voluntarily. Compared to what I did in Maryland, the current job seemed tens of times more difficult. Lately, I noticed a sort of rational and spiritual "laziness" regarding myself that was especially prompted by the ordered and precise schedule from the American base where I had trained. Somewhat drunk by some successes gained through RV, I started to lose sight of the true teaching which was the spiritual one. I realized that remote-viewing was not the main piece of my "education" but rather the correct understanding of the mysteries of spirituality, especially with regard to the fact that Doctor Xien had called on Shin Li for this.

Despite these appearances, the "lessons" did not begin immediately. For two months afterwards, I continued my daily routine, selecting staff and taking part in several tactical actions together with Lieutenant Nicoară. I had so much to do and my attention was so clenched that, rightfully, I do not think that I would have been able to assimilate any of Shin Li's explanations. Besides, during this period, she was gone most of the time with Doctor Xien in the capital regarding the same delicate problems of national security that I did not have access to.

In May 2006, our department received a visit from General Roddey. As I said before, he was a pleasant and wonderful presence; a very intelligent, serious and righteous man. To my surprise, Cezar gave me the task of receiving him until the discussions that were soon to take place. He was probably counting on a certain mutual sympathy and respect that he had felt between me and the General which had been indicated by the excellent references which he sent after my departure from Maryland.

I felt honored to take the role of the host and to be able to engage into discussions with the General which were actually quite dangerous for me as I had not fully mastered the subject. The old officer was a man of vast military experience; and without a doubt, he thought of me as "easy game" as if this was a pause or a break in his busy affairs. He was a very good friend of Cezar, but in this very fine field of national security and counterintelligence, things are always like quicksand. Later on, even Cezar asked himself if the General's attack was not, amongst others, also an arrow sent over Department Zero which had sent me to the protocol offices to receive him. No matter how great was the sympathy and friendship between him and Cezar, it seemed that there were certain limits which made the General think that being received by a new employee was somehow beneath his dignity.

Later, however, while analyzing the matter with Cezar, we realized that things weren't that simple. General Roddey had made a reference to the Orăştie Mountains in the western part of our country, asking me if I knew anything about this undoubtedly exceptional case. As I said before, I was surprised because Cezar never did clarify this subject with me which had been approached by an American official.

"In this regard, things are more complicated," Cezar explained to me. "Believe me, even for us it represents a great mystery. We will talk about it but not right now."

If everything had stopped here, the matter would not have been significant, but what got the attention of and worried General Obadea and Cezar was that the American officer left it to be understood that there was data which proved a connection between those mountains and one of the Americans' most secret bases.

"If Roddey let this escape him, it means that it is indeed something serious," Cezar commented. "I know the General and he has always been sure of the intelligence he has. This shows that there are important things going on which we do not know about yet."

"But it seems that he is feeling the ground, too," I noticed. "Otherwise, he would have approached you with this piece of information directly."

Cezar stood silent for a moment.

"He did come," he said, "but this is what worries me. It was not the Roddey whom I know. The impression he left me with was that fear was taking him over and that he is no longer sure of the intelligence flow."

"There hasn't been any official discussion?"

"Official discussions begin when both sides know that they can rely on something. This was not the case for either of us."

I stood in perplexity. I looked at General Obadea as he was holding his head on his hands. Cezar was also quite gloomy.

"Okay, but this means that we don't know what is going on in our own backyard," I mumbled in astonishment.

The two remained silent. At last, Cezar spoke.

"That would not be the problem, but the fact is that General Roddey thinks we know but that we don't want to tell him when, in fact, it is not true at all. This creates tension in our relations."

"General," he spoke to Obadea, "not even the last round of discussion were efficient?"

The General raised his head slowly. His eyes were tired and an expression close to helplessness was installed on his face. He spoke, heavily, with long pauses between words.

"You know to what a standstill we came in this case. He didn't believe me, and I'm really sorry because I feel that here something is being ruined for nothing. It is as if all is piling up just now."

I then asked the General if Doctor Xien could assist us in solving this crisis. Americans knew about him, but the subject was always diplomatically avoided.

"Doctor Xien told me that there is a certain limit to his interventions and that some things must be solved by us alone. Cezar knows this better. He spoke to him in person."

"In this case, the solution must come from the involvement of both sides," Cezar explained to me. "It is necessary for it to be so for now. The officers on the American staff are very good men, but they still have a certain degree of understanding. To begin to explain the subtle nuances of this matter and why it has to be like this and not any other way seems, however, a bit too much for them."

General Roddey left and nothing had been settled. The spiky problem was that the relations between the Romanian secret services and the Pentagon were beginning to deteriorate due to a lack of confidence. When I am speaking about the Romanian secret services, I am referring to Department Zero, which was the link to the Great Discovery in the Bucegi Mountains. The background of these events became even more complicated after a very short visit of the American Secretary of Defense which followed only a few days after General Roddey's departure and had a very well stated purpose.

A government meeting behind closed doors was held and attended only by the Prime Minister, the Ministers of State, General Obadea and the American dignitary. I have never seen Obadea as troubled as after that meeting. Even Cezar was worried. It seems that, right then and there, disclosures were made revealing that the Pentagon and the CIA had been financing for many years, with funds amounting to tens of million of dollars, vast research programs in the field of parapsychology and that contracts for such were with both state universities and with private institutions. The American side stated that they were doing this "because, in this field, it is better to keep our eyes open than to pretend that we don't know." In the center of these preoccupations were clairvoyance and telepathy; but in practice, there is no area of these phenomena that was not studied by the military or secret services of the USA. In the minutes of the meeting, which were sent to our Department two hours after the meeting, it was stated that the Americans underlined the fact that several experiments were being conducted in order to establish how extrasensory groups can decipher documents closed in safes or can precisely see objects or people with the focus being on atomic submarines. As the most complex and expensive machines built on Earth, they are of key interest, especially because of the multiple warhead torpedoes and their secret double-encrypted launching codes.

I felt like laughing at the content of the minutes.

"What is here is mere rain water," I said, detached. "We have done all of this a long time ago with remote-viewing, and as the minutes state, it is clear that it is just more money drained from the American state budget for clandestine operations."

Indeed, I knew what it was all about with these secret programs because I had just taken part in one of them, and I understood too well that what the Americans were saying was mere sand in the eyes of officials in order to better hide the progress that had been achieved. But, as always in these cases, the best defense was offense.

In the room with me were also Cezar, General Obadea and Shin Li who had returned with him from Bucharest after the secret meeting held with the government. I did not understand why they all remained silent although the situation was clear for all.

"It's complicated because the Secretary of Defense made a numb threat," Shin Li spoke unexpectedly.

General Obadea suddenly became attentive because Shin Li had not been present at the meeting. I quickly went over the sheets of the minutes but noticed no threat.

"And still it exists," Shin Lin continued. "The Americans did not say: 'We are asking you for the complete protocols regarding the Orăştie Mountains,' but coldly mentioned, 'We will take the complete protocols.' This means that there was a prior agreement at governmental level."

I looked at the General, wanting him to save the situation and to deny this diplomatic deal because I did not like the way the Americans had raised the issue. The old man looked overwhelmed by the concerns and pressures which he had been always subjected to, but this lasted only for a few moments. He then stood straight in his chair and passed his hands through his grizzled hair and over his harsh face. Then, looking with admiration at Shin Li, who had silently remained standing and looking down, he spoke.

"Shin Li is right. There have been backstage fires. All this has been happening since '94 — Cezar knows. They will not believe us that we don't have any intelligence and that the dossier is very thin. They put me to the wall; they said that this was incompetence. The Prime Minister drew my attention to the fact that if I did not have this matter sorted out in three months, he cannot help me and would intervene to the President to remove me from the department. It seems that there was an agreement with the American secretary. But, if this happened, it would be hard for me to impose Cezar as leader since they will zero in like vultures."

We all stood, perplexed. I at least did not fully understand what this was all about. The General then continued.

"Still, I managed to obtain from the Prime Minister the promise that this piece of information will not be revealed outside. This may give us some time to arrange things around here."

He then turned towards Cezar.

"Tomorrow I am leaving for the Pentagon to speak to Inossanto. I might still have a chance to achieve something. Call for Nicoară and tell him to prepare the departure. While I am gone, I will give you the codes."

I saw the old man rising from his own ashes. As ideas came to him, he became more exact and more precise in his actions, hoping to be able to save something. Nevertheless, the situation seemed quite serious because an order of the Prime Minister or the President could not be ignored, and if this order were actually enforced, then no one would have a precise answer about what would happen with regard to management and security of the Projection Chamber. Most probably, USAP agents would infiltrate it immediately, and military competence would combine with the civilian, or better said, political faction. Everyone knew what this meant: the certain penetration of Masonry's representatives into the command and control levers of the Bucegi Mountains complex with unprecedented consequences.

Amidst all the fuss that had been created, only Shin Li remained idle. When the General said good bye, wanting to leave the base, she spoke to him naturally.

"General, the chief of the Pentagon will not see you. You are making this journey without a precise end. I just want you to save time and energy."

The General said nothing but could not hide a displeased gesture. I do not think that anyone present there, except Cezar, did not think that this was possible. Obadea left for the capital to take the plane bound for the United States, but the second day following, at noon, Cezar told me that the Oval Office knew about the General's visit to the Pentagon. After the secret discussion with the Government, this might look even worse as it could be interpreted as defiance. In the elegant halls of Washington D.C., old friendships or connections were not taken into consideration but only the pragmatic and immediate aspects of a certain matter.

"Our service received a confirmation from the White House that the Secretary of State has ordered that General Inossanto should not meet with General Obadea," Cezar told me after a few hours. "This will be a hard blow for the old man," he silently added, clearly preoccupied by the dangerous turn that things were taking.

After a couple of days, Obadea returned to the country without having met his friend, General Inossanto. I could make out the traces of a beginning of resignation on his face. Without a doubt, he knew very well the dangerous implications of his removal from the leadership of the department, but perhaps fatigue and the repeated "attacks" on his person were starting to take their toll. From my point of view, Department Zero was now very well equipped, both tactically and theoretically. The last months had meant an almost continuous work schedule for the remaking of protocols, secret codes, tactical schemes and, most of all, personnel. A new leadership, however, would have destabilized the entire activity because of political interference. This was, in fact, the great difference. For over 20 years, General Obadea had managed to keep a certain balance in this sense, not letting others enter into the department's "backyard." But, the latest repeated pressures and threats had managed to heat up the atmosphere surrounding this problem, and it seemed that this was bringing matters to the very edge of an inevitable outcome.

It was then for the first time that I heard the General saying that he wanted to retire. I felt a thorn in my heart. The whole of Department Zero was virtually equal to his work of a lifetime. It was a long career that was threatened with being blown away. But, as I said, beyond General Obadea's career, name, and prestige, there was the country's interest to consider as well as not permitting certain hostile forces to take control over the complex in the Bucegi Mountains.

Although I had learned a great deal up to that point and knew enough subtleties in the field of spirituality, I confess that I felt a panic, anger and helplessness engulfing me as I faced an injustice which I, at the very least, considered totally inappropriate in this context.

I then felt Shin Li's light hand on my arm.

"Let us go. Time has finally arrived," she said. "We have nothing to do here anymore."

We were in the protocol chamber after a short briefing with Cezar, Lieutenant Nicoară, two other officers of the department, and General Obadea who had remained silent and absorbed by thoughts. I saw how Cezar exchanged a look full of implications with Shin Li. I do not know why, but this made me feel a bit more relaxed. The woman slightly bowed her head and followed me into my office. She maintained that same unaffected air, that impeccable posture and that same naturalness in her gestures. I, however, was pretty confused about what was going on in the department. Up to the last moment, I had hoped that things would change and that all would be repaired, just as it had happened countless times before. It is fair to say that no major decision had been taken yet, but I had a feeling about it. Feeling down, I was upset and searched for an explanation.

"A short while ago, I received an intelligence note. The Duchess of Halberg is coming on a visit to Bucharest. Right now, in these tense moments, it is like something is up."

And, wanting to make sure I was not talking to the walls, I asked Shin Li a direct question.

"I think you know she is a standing member of the Black Nobility?"

She bowed her head affirmatively.

"Sure, and that she is also part of the Club of Rome, but these organizations are not of too great importance as their names tend to show it. Others are more dangerous. It is, however, strange that they mobilized so quickly. This means that they have been waiting for this signal for a long time."

I sat powerless in the armchair, looking downwards and frowning. If things kept going this way, my contract would probably be canceled in a short while, leaving me only with the provisions related to security. Sadly, I made the observation that it seemed we had been overwhelmed by political pressure and that I did not understand how it was possible for God to allow this.

Shin Li suddenly became cold.

"If I hadn't known about you from Doctor Xien and if Cezar hadn't made a resume of some features of your character, I would have said that you are as dumb as the dark night after hearing you speak like this. In this case, however, there are still some hopes of recovery."

I stood as if stricken. I could not believe my ears and, in the end, I told myself that the woman was full of surprises. Even so, I would not have imagined that the beautiful Shin Li would ever be capable of such daring. In my inner forum, however, I admitted that I fully deserved the name I had been called.

As if nothing had happened, she continued to speak in the same natural manner.

"You should be more careful and meditate more deeply on these aspects."

"And what do you think, I pray, should I meditate upon?" I asked, still baffled by her responses.

I didn't expect any answer however. In the end, who was this woman to judge me so sharply? I was being consumed on the inside, being highly concerned about the faith in Department Zero and the General, and here she was whipping my character out of itself.

"Now is not the time for you to play the victim because you will not solve anything. This will lead you to panic and discouragement and you will never fix things with these. In fact, it is not about you fixing anything. Forget about the concern regarding the department. There is someone to take care of it. What you cannot yet understand is that what seems to be very bad now is, in fact, a way towards the good."

"Phooey! What are you talking about? Is it better that General Obadea will no longer be in command of Department Zero? What bad thing is, in fact, good?" I insidiously asked, hoping to catch her stumbling in her own statements.

Shin Li looked at me with her superb eyes and with a radiant smile.

"I am looking at you; and I realize how, in your great lack of reason, you really manage to be as sincere and pure as a child. Somewhat not knowing but pure and innocent. And, it is very well that it is so because, if you tried to use this gift and to obtain purity and innocence 'on demand,' then you would become pragmatic and everything would go to waste. Purity and innocence are your very freedom. They are even that which exceeds you as an individual being, as a person, except that, as I have said, being somewhat stupid, you yet fail to see this."

"Please stop using words of this sort!" I strongly said.

"Forget that. Concentrate on what surpasses you. Don't become petty. I once knew a human being who, when he was a child, used to play with some spirits of nature. Everyone, including his parents, thought he was retarded; but he actually played with those wonderful beings of nature whom only he was able to see. If you allow this childlike frankness, purity and innocence to surround you more and more, but in an unprogrammed manner as you did now, you should know that you still have a chance not to be stupid. But, if you abandon yourself to petty and pragmatic calculations in order to obtain something only for yourself, then that will be your doom."

I was beginning to be immune to her appeals because I realized more and more that the force and energy involved in those expressions did not put the accent on the bothersome words but had a totally different meaning that for now escaped me.

"But, let's return to bad and good because this is where the discussion started," Shin Li said, undisturbed.

"Aaa, you haven't forgotten," I noticed, half-mouthed.

"How can such 'wit' like you expressed earlier be forgotten? Of course, in many cases, what is bad is actually good. But it is also true that this analysis can shock some people who have made a unilateral idea about God because people associate God only with what is good and beautiful without being capable of understanding the hidden significance of the fact that great divinities also love obscurity.

56

"And what is the hidden significance?" I asked.

"Have patience. The statement is paradoxical; and it implies the fact some divinities are highly above the domain of good and evil and that is why they are detached from these dual aspects."

"You go and convince someone who suffers great losses or hardships in life of this fact," I said, upset although in essence I knew the subject of the discussion.

"The problem is rather delicate here. Of course, we cannot state under any circumstances that God is evil, but for us it is wise to understand that we can discover God even in the existence of evil. This truth represents a great conceptual barrier for most people and this is why they fail in life so many times."

"And how would this be better understood?" I asked, becoming more conciliatory.

"It is very important not to forget for a single moment that God always, in every second, is everything. This will help you quickly get rid of the dualist idea that both good and evil are absolute."

Yes, I had read about the aspects of absolute dualism and that brought into my mind, for example, the eternal problem of Christian Puritanism: original sin, presented in the Eastern Liturgy as Felix Culpa (a happy blame). I knew that, to solve this dilemma, Christianity had to justify the "original sin" by the fact that it represented the very way in which man could reach his spiritual salvation. I only wondered if the acceptance of this obvious thesis can overcome the narrow prejudices of Puritan Christianity which have lasted for almost 2000 years. But, since my purpose was not to see how many parishioners could understand this, I listened further to the explanation provided by Shin Li who seemed not just very elegant but also full of wisdom.

"The statement that God, in reality, can be discovered and felt like supreme goodness, even in what is evil, expresses in its essence the idea that the evil which appears is not absolute evil and that, as a consequence, it does not oppose good absolutely."

"If things are like this, then why do we confront ourselves with evil and good?" I asked for good reason.

"Because the experience of evil confronts us, in fact, with our own weakness, with our own sin. That is why — because what you do badly now most times has a justified trace in your past actions. Of course, we cannot say that the evil is not real; but even so, we know that if we sincerely admit something bad we did, it then becomes, in a certain way, a sort of bad thing that is a bit more 'good.'"

Here she was right. In fact, not only here but all of the time. I was thinking that the experience of daily life many times gives us occasion to notice that the ones who have never known anything bad are, generally speaking, lacking love or are behaving inhumanely towards others. There are a number of cosmogonies in which evil is regarded as the original sin, a sin that also determines the actual condition of the Creation or the Macrocosmos. One can talk about such a mystery as evil because it cannot be understood by regular means of the mind, logic or reason respectively and an explanation cannot too often be found by the common man. This is why, for an ignorant human being, evil appears to be almost impossible to understand. If man was truly able to explain it properly, evil would look more like a bomb whose detonator has been removed; and once its mystery would be fully discovered, evil will cease to exist.

My Oriental and esoteric oriented readings came to good use at that point. I remembered a significant quote from the great Hindi epic, *The Mahabharata*, which made me deduce the wise way to act in this matter. I searched for that quote for a long time until I found it again and I'll include it here completely. A great wise man, who had realized the Supreme Truth, gives the following advice: "Renounce good and evil now, renounce truth and lie; and after that, renouncing all of these completely, finally renounce the act of renouncing itself."

This idea is expressed in the Kata-Upanishad when the hero, Nashiketas, asks Yama, who is the deity of the realm of the dead, "O Yama, tell me, I beg of you, what is in reality beyond good and evil?"

Still, I do not want to prolong these philosophical considerations which had Shin Li's subtle explanations as a basis. It is enough to observe from the careful reading of these quotes that we cannot be above good if we cannot be, at the same time, above evil. In connection to this, however, I allow myself to observe the need for a metaphysical analysis without which we cannot even hope to understand the matter of good and evil in a superior manner.

Shin Li made the observation that evil is still an unquestionable fact, a reality that we can neither deny nor avoid, at least while we are still confronted with a state of ignorance. She has also shown me that there was a sort of mystery of evil, the reality of which cannot be the focus of reason or logic. Thus, this metaphysical dimension appears which causes us to notice that evil is almost incomprehensible to human intelligence, but this statement is not valid with regard to divine omniscience.

"Think a little," Shin Li urged me. "If God would do harm, then He would not be that God. So for God, evil simply does not exist. Torture, hatred, injustice, and sadism are only man's 'short-sightedness' towards some aspects of life, and they are interpreted as being evil. However, if God allows their existence, this surely happens for reasons that He knows for certain; but for the time being, man cannot know them because of the state of ignorance which he is in. All that he can do is to hope that sometime later, even in a future life by spiritually evolving, he would learn the answer to this enigma."

I remained pondering. The arguments were valid but human nature is too strong to let these principles manifest freely. Our tendency to search for an immediate solution when we are harmed, even vengeance, is too strong in most of us to make us lucid and wise. Even if rational thinking shows us very clearly every time that it cannot even explain evil and cannot succeed in eliminating it, this habit repeats because the mysterious action of evil can only be transformed and "alchemized" in the heart; that is, through the formidable power of love and innocence which always spring from a pure heart.

"Other problems might arise here, however," I said, "because, for example, if a person goes even deeper into evil deeds, the accrued suffering and pain can become unbearable for him or her and push that person to even more reckless deeds that are also evil. It seems like there is no exit."

"Only at first glance," Shin Li underlined. "Most of the time, man is at first confronted with suffering and what is evil so that afterwards, having these two experiences, he or she can spiritually evolve to a state of spiritual maturity. When he or she willingly breaks rules and principles that he or she considers compulsory, suffering is generated in his or her own being by the strange and dangerous world that he or she entered into and becomes so great that forgiveness or desperation seem the only alternative to the mistakes made because for him or her there is no turning back. Due to this necessity to overcome this terrible fear and to go beyond the evil that was done, the human being can then find, as a ray of light, the divine transcendental experience. This is how we can explain the fact that when faced with great suffering or soul trials, man almost always seeks his escape in God. Of course, this passing over must come after a fully conscious and responsible deed because, if this aspect is treated as petty, one can then no longer speak about a severe mistake but rather a simple wrong step. The severe breaking of certain principles or rules then confronts us with our own liberty and, through this, with the responsibility that we hold."

Shin Li touched a sensitive subject here, the one of fully conscious freedom and acting. This matter was considered very dangerous by the Church who regarded with great concern the possibility of man manifesting his individual freedom fully and breaking the laws and regulations which the Church had pre-established. This is why the Church rushed to forgive ignorance in regard to a certain deed or action which is wrong, stating that ignorance is enough to release us fully from the respective sin. In other words, you were forgiven at the holy confession if you said that you did not know that what you did was in fact bad. Let us not forget the biblical texts which show the meeting between Jesus and the man who was working on the holy day of the Sabbath and to whom the Savior said: "Man, you are happy if you truly know what you are doing now by breaking the strict rule of the Sabbath which is the day when nobody works. But remember this, for if you do not truly know this, then you are doomed for you are breaking sacred law!"

Jesus' statement therefore takes into consideration man in relation to the Sabbath and not the Sabbath in relation to man as the Church does. For this reason, the text has been considered very dangerous and destabilizing, especially for the conception and interests of the clergy because it subtly underlines the necessity of freedom of choice and makes us deduce the power which freedom – when it is assumed consciously, responsibly and wisely – gives to a man. In the opinion of the Christian Church, however, it is dangerous to offer man freedom. This doesn't mean that the necessity of being free is an apology for sin and anarchy which, over time, is a reason that has been invoked by most representatives of the Church in order to justify the rules which they imposed.

Assuming the prototype of a perfect human being who has never sinned up to now, has never "fallen" and has never done any harm, we will notice immediately that the respective person lacks that experience of weakness, mistake, sin or pain that is often felt both in body and soul. In my opinion, which is shared also by Shin Li, without the experience of these weaknesses and mistakes, it is difficult if not impossible to achieve a just understanding of some fundamental realities that exist in Creation. If it were not so, it would be difficult to accept the human condition, human society, meeting another human being, and relations of all sorts that intervene. Most of the time, these kinds of experiences give birth to the purest and most uplifting love which is full of compassion at the same time. It cannot be claimed that we can fully love only from heights because we also have to be below, among the ones we love, thus getting to know their sufferings, sins and troubles through a profound, intense and alive experience. Therefore, if we think about it deeply, we can immediately realize that the matter of evil has crushed in advance once and for all many of the schemes that some men make for themselves regarding God, making us become more humble and more realistic about the different complex aspects of God's creation.

That was a memorable day when Shin Li demonstrated her extraordinary psychological finesse and dexterity of argumentation. I would say even more that she was the one who caused me to go a bit beyond and to see over the barriers of my own ego. It was a journey inside of me which prepared the explanation of the text of the parchment that I had received from the Goddess Machandi. Still, four more months were to pass before the situation arranged itself in such a manner that would permit its complete drafting.

In the meantime, my hopes for the continuity of General Obadea's activity proved to be in vain. It seemed that the old man had indeed reached the end of his patience, but surprises did not stop even then. With countless relations and connections in the obscure field of the secret services as well as in the political arena, the General was still a very powerful man. Although he filed his resignation from command, he remained on active duty and did not choose to become a reserve officer. This was an act of resistance that opposed the prime-minister's political decision, also under diplomatic pressure, that shook Department Zero like a lightning bolt. If anyone thought up to that point that the General's removal from command of this unit was highly improbable, it did happen and amazingly fast, too.

Still, things worked out better than we had hoped which encouraged all of us who were left at Alpha Base to clap our hands under the table in a frenzy. As I said before, General Obadea was not a man to give up that easily, but in this case, he just did not have enough control levers anymore and, as the intention of removing him from the head of the department came from the highest political spheres, he had to give up the command of the department which he had taken care of for over twenty-five years. He did, however, have enough high level connections and relations to pull some strings that would leave us at least partially covered. Personally, I am absolutely certain that the Duchess of Halberg's visit had speeded up the outcome in the General's case. As there are unwritten laws in diplomacy and politics, we were left alone without much of a fuss after Obadea's departure from command. I did not doubt that this was only the calm before the storm, but at least we had a little time to recover from the "quake."

It is very interesting, however, how things fell into place in regard to the spirit of Shin Li's explanations, even when you think that it could not get any worse. I always suspected that the General could not get over the refusal of his visit to the Pentagon. This was either because of the personal relationship he had enjoyed with General Inossanto or simply because he did not have access to all the intelligence elements in this case; or maybe he did not want to find out about them. Several times, we tried to clarify the situation and present it to the General as it really was with the order from the White House; but every time, he refused to receive any details without providing any explanations.

The interim transfer of power lasted quite some time. As it was natural, Cezar took over the lead of the department while Lieutenant Nicoară took over Cezar's tasks, especially the tactical ones. I kept my office with a small improvement in the sense that I became responsible for administering the main protocol for the Bucegi complex. That meant, of course, a higher position but also more bureaucracy in the relationship with the Americans. Nevertheless, because I had developed excellent relations with the Pentagon officials, things were going smoothly and everyone was happy.

As we had the habit of evening discussions around the table in the Alpha Base's protocol chamber, we all agreed that this was, most likely, a temporary situation created by the apparent "void of power" left by General

Obadea's departure. Cezar was known as a close confidant to the General and was respected in the occult area of the RIS; but in the end, the command of the department was going to be political. His interim stewardship of the department could last only a few months, let's say a year at best, but after that, the state of things would change. Nobody in the occult management of the government had an interest in keeping Cezar as head of Department Zero when it was known too well that he followed the same agenda and the same vision as the old General who had freshly resigned. Then, that element of surprise I was talking about came, and it was like a bubble of oxygen that made us feel not so completely isolated anymore.

In my opinion, General Obadea never did manage to get over what happened a few months before at the Pentagon. I do not know if this assumption is true, but things suddenly took another turn. By November 2006, shortly after the General signed his resignation, the tempestuous visit of the Chief of the Pentagon was announced, but not in Bucharest but at the Alpha Base. This was an event that got us going even if we were told that the visit did not have an official character but rather a niche-like one. General Inossanto's specification was to meet General Obadea on the base grounds for half an hour. As the visit was going to be a detour from a scheduled flight towards Pakistan, it looked more like a courtesy being extended towards an old friend, a "sweetening" of the situation created a few months before.

Although he had just relieved himself of the command of Department Zero, the General was in neither the posture nor the position to refuse such a visit. Beyond the personal aspects involved, which did not suit him, there was still the matter of good relations at the level of the secret and military services between Romania and the USA, and these were not worth ruining.

I was present when the helicopter landed inside the base, and I only could catch a quick exchange of sentences between the two generals.

"I'm glad to see you, Bill, even after you didn't receive me at the Pentagon," Obadea said, meeting the General with a sharp remark.

"Do you have a secluded place? We have to talk," General Inossanto replied seriously.

They went inside the building, but instead of meeting in the Protocol Chamber, they went into the office that had belonged to Obadea. They stayed there about twenty-five minutes, the General's order being that they were not to be disturbed by anyone and that nobody was to have access to that section of the building. During that entire time, the helicopter did not even stop its engines. After almost a half an hour, the two got out and I could notice that the discussion was not only fruitful but surprisingly good for our General. He was now much more relaxed; even serene and in a good mood. He said his goodbye to the Chief of the Pentagon who hastily boarded the helicopter accompanied by his personal guard.

The General entered the Protocol Chamber where I, accompanied by Cezar and Lieutenant Nicoară, was waiting impatiently for him.

"Even as the helicopter is heading towards Bucharest, the necessary papers are being drafted," he said without any introduction. Then, after making a short pause which had its own definite effect, Obadea spoke.

"Hmm … The 'Wolf' hasn't disappointed me. I am leaving the office I had here, but I will remain close! Bill told me that he regretted the diplomatic element from back then, but he couldn't help it. The order came on a direct line from the Secretary of State. But now that the waters have settled a little, he needs a permanent 'connecting bridge' with the Bucegi complex. He knew about my resignation so he stopped here to propose me for the position. I will be working directly in the Pentagon with my office in the same aisle as his."

That was some news indeed! Besides, this stronger backing would prevent a divide and conquer strategy being used against us.

"It will be difficult with the cooperation protocol," Cezar mentioned, also happy with the outcome of the meeting but keeping an objective view. "The American part will want bureaucracy."

"We have already discussed this aspect in general. It will be an adaptation, within certain limits, of tactical operations. For the rest, I hope that there will not be a great deal of changes."

"It will make waves," I said, also quite excited. "It will be a certain blow to some 'customers'!"

"Yes, it's true, but they will not be able to help it. I asked Bill twice if he is willing to risk this, but he told me that, in the general picture, no one has anything to say about it because he is covered."

At last, after almost a year of sustained tension and hard labor, we began to see a calmer horizon. In the end, the change of the situation in Department Zero did not seem so bad. Maybe this modification of the levels of influence was even necessary inside the department.

Doctor Xien and Shin Li had been absent for almost two months, but it was obviously not my business where they were and what they were doing. I only felt that the final deadline of editing the parchment was approaching and that this was a special mission which was entrusted to me. I had a few general discussions with Shin Li on the matter in which we had generally revised the text of the translation and drew a few guidelines upon which I had insisted along with some comments.

"It is not important how much you write," Shin Li told me. "On the contrary, the text must be as concise as possible, but very explicit. Here, quality comes first. Some will understand while others will lose themselves quickly in their mental thicket and will no longer know how to get out of it.

My role is to guide you so that you are able to present as clearly and adequately as possible the ideas of the five stanzas of the parchment."

When it came time to refer to this secret text, all faded in importance in comparison to it.

"Then what is my role?"

Shin Li gazed at me intensely for a few moments and then answered with a voice that seemed to come from another world.

"Your mission is to make it known everywhere. Nobody with bad intentions can stop this anymore. There have been countless obstacles, but now all is arranged. Your time has come."

CHAPTER THREE

THE SECRET PARCHMENT –
FIVE SECRET TIBETAN INITIATION TECHNIQUES

At the beginning of 2006, I was already in the middle of the process of drafting the text of the parchment under the strict supervision of Shin Li. A series of factors had almost miraculously led to a "breach" in what had been our regular activity and enabled this work to take place. Things were calmer after General Obadea left for the Pentagon. Cezar had easily taken over the management of the activity of Department Zero, and I had performed my tasks very well and often had constructive initiatives, especially with regard to the Romanian-American collaboration concerning the Bucegi base. Shin Li and Doctor Xien had returned to Alpha Base and the "octopus" of backstage settlements had withdrawn a bit, everyone being amazed by the sudden change of the top-level situation concerning General Obadea, High Representative of the Romanian-American Commission concerning the Bucegi base. Since it was considered a highly important strategic point and also an invaluable source of technological information, the origins of which were unknown, the base in Bucegi represented a top concern at the Pentagon, and this led to General Obadea's office being very close to General Inossanto's.

To all of this, I have to add the mysterious and troubling presence of Shin Li, who always spoke with carefully chosen words and a lot of consideration. I had been silly enough to consider her expressions from the previous months as a personal problem, believing that she had something against me. In reality, as she later explained, her tough behavior was necessary in order to eliminate a great part of the "residues" of my identity which was absolutely necessary with regard to the important context of me drafting the comments to the text of the parchment. With some help, yet still on my own, I had to come to the fully conscious realization that the often unpleasant aspects I was confronted with in my daily life, especially given my job, were practically meaningless in comparison with the light fullness of charming love given by the deep knowledge revealed in the text and the understanding of its subtleties.

This endeavor was supposed to bring the peace and quietness which cannot be troubled to both my heart and the hearts of careful readers, no matter how big and important we think our daily activities are. As I was right in the middle of this reality through Shin Li's "corrections" and explanations, I fully enjoyed this "fine tuning" of my personality and knowledge. Shin Li explained to me that it was absolutely necessary to maintain that refined level of consciousness in order to be able to present and better understand the hidden meaning of the text. With this training, I realized that I had almost no states of mind where there was a lack of attention nor the evil thinking which is unfortunately common to so many people who have states of mental disorder or inner violence.

"You have achieved a state of relative inner balance, harmony and coherence which now stops you from reacting with pride," said Shin Li, "but don't think that you'll remain like this for a long time. You have to conquer this state forever in order to really move on. Most people fail this test. This is where groups, societies, great wishes and ideas fail. It's a very difficult test."

"I'm thinking of our department. Do you think this also applies here? As you can see here, we also have a fight of wishes and ideas against a certain segment of those who don't want the good of this country."

"This is a totally different situation," Shin Li answered. "Consider that there are many variables which are based upon physical conditions and these include hierarchies, order, and interests. But, we can still say that what goes on in this department is a reflection of certain hidden intentions manifested by a certain category of people. This can ultimately be repaired from bottom to top as well, meaning that Department Zero can act so as to obtain effects in the groups that want to control Department Zero, but this needs a lot of energy and is also very complicated."

"I understand," I said, "but the 'rule of the group' is still universally valid, isn't it? I am referring to the way it works. Does it not matter, for example, that the main members are at a great distance apart from each other?"

I was, of course, referring especially to General Obadea. No matter how present the General was in our thoughts and intentions, the huge distance was still an impediment. Even so, I wanted to convince myself of the contrary. I wanted to believe that almost nothing had changed. In the current situation, the General had limited power of action, especially at executive level, but his strong influence was still felt through his relationships and the "strings" he pulled, both in Bucharest and at the top of American military diplomacy. With his resources, the General tried his best to help us so that we would not abandon the fight.

"This does matter," answered Shin Li. "It matters a lot. First of all, it's the group coherence and then the way it can be torn apart. When I say coherence, I mean the state of harmony which is fundamental in any strong group that wants to accomplish an important goal. This state is like an indestructible monolith in the face of evil forces that want to destroy it, and this is the very reason why the standard of evil actions is reduced to "divide and conquer." When evil imposes itself, alliances are born and die before opening their eyes. They were torn apart without being able to manifest the force of their union and harmonious cooperation. Usually, the evil forces act through persons or organizations against the good. They first of all try to destroy this coherence and harmony. Let us say that, until then, the group was coherent in ideas and actions. By destroying its harmony, the state of coherence disappears and thus the efficiency of the group is dramatically decreased."

I understood these aspects very well because I had discussed them with Cezar many times, and they were an essential way of understanding what the fight should be based upon, especially the fight against Masonic interests.

"I know," I said, "and a classic way of manifestation of such disharmony is the exaggeration of pride which appears and sometimes increases like a monster in some of the group members. Then, the tendency to act separately and without harmony occurs. Yes, I think I've understood this mechanism correctly."

"It's okay; we'll discuss it again," Shin Li said without backing off. "What you said is correct. This is why such members, when they exist, must be eliminated from the group because they are like a 'microbe' which tends to severely sicken the group. But, what happens if, for example, harmony is created between the members of the group?"

I was amused.

"Well now!" I said. "As if we were in kindergarten! Of course, the power of the group, be it spiritual, esoteric, political or of another nature, can greatly increase."

"Don't rush," she tempered me, "because there is a very good reason why I wanted to talk about this. Remember that, in such cases, when a group displays harmony and coherence, its power greatly increases; but this is not about transmitting the state of harmony to each group member but rather about an exponential increase of their capacity. This is a very important aspect if you understand it correctly. You'll thus be able to see that, even though some persons know many fundamental spiritual and esoteric concepts, what leads to the decrease of efficiency or even its total destruction is the increase and exaggeration of ego which leads to disharmony and lack of coherence of the group members."

Inspired, I immediately made an extrapolation to the microcosmos of our being, to the universe we create through our personality and identity. As far as I could tell, the troubling factor is the individual ego which manifests a whole series of disharmonious features such as pride, selfishness, and wishes of grandeur. All of this separates us from a unitary and holistic view of reality and make us see only fragments of reality which are often meaningless. If we manage to "conquer" our pride and manage to show humbleness and true love, then we understand that the state of harmony and energetic coherence is produced at the core of our being. We are then able to vibrate in harmony with other coherent harmonious fields of the Macrocosmos which will make us stronger, inspired and efficient because subtle connections are established between us and those harmonious force spheres which also favor the occurrence in our being of amplified states of harmony, force and coherence.

Shin Li especially appreciated my comment and sincerely congratulated me.

"However," she specified, "you should never forget that, in order to achieve this state and to exceed man's mediocre condition, man must first of all show will. And understand that, without will, almost nothing can be done. I am not referring to the common automatic will but to an effort of conscious significant will which causes changes in man's existence."

"Of course, one can't exceed oneself without the manifestation of will," I said.

Shin Li immediately corrected me.

"You speak, but you don't yet understand. Try to grasp the deeper meaning of will. You express your will to move but also to write about this secret text. In both cases, we are talking about will and yet it does not manifest itself identically. What makes it differ? What is will after all?"

I looked at her with amazement.

"I thought you are the one who explains to me," I said, a bit discouraged.

"Don't worry. I was not expecting an answer. I only wanted to bring you closer to the subject. There is a great difference between unconsciously exercised will and fully responsible conscious will. This is due to the fact that will is a fundamental energy which makes possible all manifestations as well as the maintaining of these manifestations as we see them every moment. For example, cosmic laws are an expression of God's will. It's a subtle and even hidden energy. Of course, the ideal situation is when our will is in harmony with God's will because then we know that we are not wrong and that our will is benefic and harmonious. But, if our will is opposed to the divine laws, then it is an evil will and can be generally defined as stubbornness. It's true that man also has an inferior and subconscious animal will which is integrated into the unity of the being and also has its role. What is more important, however, is that men have a fully aware will which involves refining its specific energy."

"Am I to understand that, in every person, the energy of will is nuanced: there is an automatic or subconscious will and a conscious will — in other words, a low or inferior manifestation and a high or superior manifestation of will?"

"Yes, with the mention that I still see that you don't understand. You imagine that this inferior subconscious will is just an accessory to accomplish certain body functions, especially movement and automatic actions. But, I am telling you not to ignore the force and importance of inferior will because, in some cases, this aspect can be dramatic in a man's life. Low instinctual aspects often tend to grasp the whole being in their manifestation and even to subdue it. In the case of vices or passions, these inferior aspirations of will are strongly manifested and can lead man to regression and even dramatic decadence. Here is the problem. Precisely stated, this automatic subconscious will tends to put the human being in chains, makes man give in to inferior impulses, and pushes man gradually on a descending path. It's also the energy of will, but it is an inferior energy. But, if you awaken the superior will energy enough, this can efficiently oppose such impulses and inferior tendencies and can dominate and annihilate them. In such situations, the role of superior will is essential."

"Okay, but I believe you know that there will always be fluctuations," I said.

"They will only exist as long as the inferior will is not overcome by man's superior will. But, as inferior tendencies are controlled, we witness a process of "training" the being and refining it. Therefore, it is essential for the superior energy of will to be awakened and amplified in the human being. For example, with its help other beings can be exorcized and given an impulse when they request our help. Sometimes there is a true battle between the two types of will."

I still had to clarify one aspect.

"What if someone thinks they possess that superior will and imagines that they heal, exorcize or help others? What kind of will is that?"

"In such cases, it's the manifestation of a certain lack of common sense and spiritual maturity without which one can't evolve. Indeed, I have personally known many poor fellows who imagined having certain capacities or powers and, talking about some occult concepts, they managed to twist the minds of weaker persons. The interesting part is that these human beings were actually convinced of their mission; but of course, this conviction was based on the common man's naiveness and ignorance.

No matter what we say, we can't delude ourselves or others forever if we don't have a real basis for what we claim, if we don't demonstrate a force and a high energy which truly proves — if only through common sense — that our respective speech and actions have true value. Words or pathetic gestures will not be enough for long because, after all, everything is measured by the effects produced. In order to have a true effect, this higher energy of will is necessary. In its turn, in order to be amplified, the superior energy of will needs an adequate and fully conscious effort. That which ends in failure by a person without this superior energy, even if he or she desires success, will surely be accomplished by one who has awakened and amplified this superior energy inside of themselves."

Here Shin Li had touched on an essential aspect.

"You must understand a fundamental aspect. It is not enough to want. It is also very important to sustain this wish with the energy of conscious will. Once again, it's not enough to want. It is very important that when you want something, you also have the energy that later facilitates what you want.

This will allow you to test how much energy of will you have, by measuring the time that passes between your wish and its realization. The shorter the time, the greater is the energy of conscious will in you — because, from an outside perspective, man can't know if he or she has this subtle energy of conscious will; however, these "signs" I told you about can show his or her force of conscious will. Let's say that you are hungry, but you don't have anything to eat. If you have this energy of will, you'll see that, in a certain way, someone will bring you food. You don't know how that person came to bring you food, but the action takes place. This is why I'm telling you that this superior energy of will can lead to many achievements."

I was delighted with the clear example and I understood the issue; however, I wanted to clarify some aspects from the experience of some friends of mine who had taken a dangerous road many years ago.

"There are, however, still some 'chains' that can hold one back in the case of subconscious will energy," I said. "For example, if someone wants to quit smoking or drinking — I don't know how it happens — but precisely then, someone appears and invites that person to a party or offers a cigarette. How should I interpret this? Is it a test for those persons?"

"It's a kind of game correlated with a certain manifestation of the inferior will. This sets a trap for that person, but what should be noted is that the energy of superior will must exist so that we can easily accomplish our goals."

"As far as I can see, most people do not feel and probably do not want to amplify conscious will inside of themselves," I said with disappointment.

"In a way, it's natural," Shin Li answered. "People run from the effort that is involved in gaining this superior will. But, if that person is well oriented and selfishness or pride are not too developed within, then it is possible."

"I don't really understand what I must do for this purpose."

Shin Li then shared with me the only advice that could solve man's existential dilemma.

"No matter how strange it might seem in this consumer society, being able to live without error involves the highest degree of exceeding the so-called 'essential' needs: the need for more and the need for competitiveness.

"For this purpose, it is essential to open humbly to God's almighty will and, at the same time, to show that you want to be perfect. For us humans, it is very important to realize when we are doing God's will because we are then sure that we are acting in harmony with God's infinite wisdom and with all that God wants to achieve through us and with us. Take yourself for an example. Had you manifested your will in an inferior and destructive way, then you would have been able to refuse the mission to publish the secret text and the short comments accompanying this ancient parchment. However, even if it is quite hard, you have accepted your mission, have acted according to your free will and have expressed your conscious and fully responsible will for this purpose. Someone else might have refused for some obscure reasons. God will never force us to act in one way or another, but we have in ourselves that special energy of will which can make us be or not be in harmony with His almighty will. To seek to do only what we want or to imagine that such behavior would serve us, in time, might lead to an exaggeration of the inferior selfish will and even to an amplified ego. This can even condemn man to demonism and the amplification of very low aspects of man's being."

I thought about how even Jesus, in one of the most dramatic moments of His divine existence on Earth, wanted to accomplish God's will when He prayed: "Father, if possible, take this cup away from me; if not, then be it as You wish."

Shin Li's voice then brought me back to the present.

"It's one of the most important aspects of spiritual evolution. You can't talk about true spiritual progress of the human being as long as man doesn't understand the roots of failure during man's many lives. But, once man's will is more in harmony with God's will, he or she will know for sure that the road is right."

"But how can we be so sure? How can I know this?" I asked with good justification.

"The method may seem strange for many people, especially for atheists who, in a way, are the unhappiest people. It is very important to want to humbly relate to God and ask Him to inspire you and help you do His will in everything you do. Only then will you know for sure that what you're doing is truly wise because — you know what they say — God's ways are often mysterious. This is why I'm telling you that this inspiration to do God's will and not our own is essential because then we can be sure that God is with us and this will save us many sufferings and temptations. Most people are perpetually confronted with problems, sufferings, fears, and temptations and do not understand why this happens. Their lives are tense, clenched and full of suffering. But, by doing God's will, we more easily overcome tests and problems that might otherwise lead us to collapse and regression."

"I understand that this is a fundamental aspect of individual spiritual evolution."

"It can't be any other way. The one who truly wants to evolve spiritually must do God's will. I think it's the most important aspect of a man's life."

"But, I know people who consider this an 'attempt' upon their own free will. They believe it's a lowering and this makes them even more quarreling."

Shin Li slowly nodded her head and led me to understand that she knew the situation.

"This is due to the dominance of their inferior nature and to a terrible 'rupture' between the mind and the heart. Those people don't consider that

God's answers are always in the heart. The mind is a kind of 'headquarters' of manifestation of the ego's individualism."

"Man wants and even strongly believes that he has the utter need to be the 'center' that governs everything and decides everything. At this level, he is in reality playing the game of dark forces that are amplifying his ego without him even knowing it. Without a remedy, man will end up falling and the suffering will be even greater."

I remembered that history is full of such examples. Great leaders or political men fell like lightning even when they felt more than ever that they were untouchable. I then realized how ephemeral the temptation of power is if it is not mastered by a higher will that is superior to the selfish will which is limited and inferior.

Shin Li continued to explain.

"By abandoning himself to God's will, man seems to lower himself; but in reality, he is elevated because, when doing God's will, he is aligning himself with the divinity in creation. Then, he is sure he is not doing wrong because God can never be wrong. Profound ignorance, however, makes man think that God also fails. An example occurs when God appears to be unjust regarding men's fates or at least towards some men. But, if this were truly so, then what would be the difference between the Creator and the creation? It would mean that both would compete in their errors and this would surely create a chaos out of which nothing would be understood. The universe, however, has functioned for eons with unequal perfection and its laws are forever. This is why, when you do God's will, it gives you true invincibility.

Man is thus free, as you well know, but he is still predisposed to error. If he says he can do everything he wants and even does so, he truly expresses his freedom; but he can, at the same time, slip into evilness. The reason for this is that the difference between demonic orientation and divine orientation is the fact that the demon does as he pleases. On the other hand, the being who is in harmony with the universal harmony and has a tight relationship with God does not do as he pleases but what God wants. Please note that this is a fundamental element."

When Shin Li wanted to stress something very important, the atmosphere around her seemed to change and caused me slight chills that was like an electric discharge throughout my body.

"But," I said, "there are many people who make it a debt of honor to announce with emphasis that they are their own masters who do as they please and when they please. I myself have heard this many times and must say that those men have confidence in what they say; and they have a certain kind of proof and have even done good deeds."

"I know exactly what you mean," answered Shin Li, "but what fools many in regards to the case of evil men is that those men can do both good and evil but always do as they please. This is why they fool many, but by doing their own will, they actually act chaotically and are torn apart from unity with God. Of course, God doesn't force anyone, but in these conditions, those men will have to bear the consequences of their actions. They can be good as well, but they are definitely also evil or even very evil. By comparison, those who do God's will actually rise above what seems to be their lower being which includes the twisted and impure perception of the selfish and the proud, even if they do not realize this. In this way, it's clear that we can never be wrong."

"Indeed. It seems like a way to perfection," I stated with enthusiasm.

"Of course it is. In the end, you'll never say, 'Look, I did God's will and it's awful, terrible! I fell, crashed, and my life is a failure!' No, there is no such thing because God is only good. But, by choosing the other way, when man does as he pleases, there is a great possibility of falling. So, you have two fundamental options. Man can rise by pride and by considering that men may do as they please; but they will then lower themselves. And there is the second option, for man to give his life to God, have solidarity with God and let God do His work through him. Thus, men truly make important steps towards being gods, and don't forget that those who lower themselves like this can actually rise."

I reflected a lot about whether or not to reproduce this discussion with Shin Li in my book and even asked for her advice in this regard. We both agreed that, in the context of presenting the text of the parchment and due to the capital importance of understanding such concepts for daily life, it had to be done. I only allowed myself to adjust the somewhat strange word order of Shin Li's sentences and some expressions which would need many esoteric books to clarify. Once again, my archives — I now use a digital recorder — turned out very useful.

By writing about these moments and trying to adapt them the best that I could for the purpose at hand, I found a recording which was several months old where Shin Li explained to me the reason for the general lack of integration and success in modern man's life. Since I believe that this subject is also related to the harmony and general balance of our lives, as well as to the manifestation of constructive will, I think it is useful to present Shin Li's considerations here.

The recording has some parasites in it at a certain point, the origins of which I do not know; then it stops suddenly. I remember that the discussion lasted about half an hour, but its summary is presented below. I do not, however, remember what started this dialogue.

"Many people complain that they have no success in life and that they don't get what they want but don't understand why," I said.

"Such persons have not yet achieved harmony; and within them, there is a battle between two opposing forces. In a certain moment, they decide to do something; but at the same time, a kind of inner demon tells them that they would not succeed, that the success of that action would be impossible. An inner struggle starts within them and consumes their forces in this sterile confrontation. In some situations, this struggle will eventually lead to a victory of destructive, pessimistic and negative forces which will make those persons lose before truly starting the action they wanted to perform."

"And how do they fight to eliminate these unpleasant effects?" I asked. "There must be a reaction, or is that not the case?"

"An evil cause always triggers bad effects. To change their being and personality, these men must adopt positive habits and replace bad ones. But, if the replacement is not complete, evolution will be blocked. The problem will remain and make them suffer in life more and more."

I must admit that my discussion with Shin Li had a special charm. She was not only a mysterious presence, but the way she expressed her ideas and the inspiration and value of her arguments seemed to create a spell in the room and I abandoned myself to this spell like a voyage to another realm. Shin Li had a sense of the proportion of the discussions we had and knew when and how long to insist on a certain subject. She sensed even my slightest lack of understanding and guided me with great precision through the complicated threads of personality and esoteric notions. I longed for my meetings and discussions with her, but the nature of the activity surely stopped us from meeting more often. She was absent for long or short periods of time because she left with Doctor Xien and returned to the base, sometimes after a period of several weeks. Nobody knew where they had been and what they had done; but through a special government order, the two had absolute freedom to come to and leave our base as they pleased. I did not know the exact nature of their contribution to the activity of our secret services, and Cezar had never wanted to tell me more on this subject.

As for me, I was quickly coming to the drafting of the text of the parchment. Finally, after many months of preparation and clarifying discussions, I managed to give it a final and quite concise form. No matter how strange it might seem, the text only has five closed verses. They had to be translated and arranged in an adequate and intelligible manner for the knowledge of modern man and are accompanied by some short comments representing my modest contribution in accordance with my mission. Even so, I was not convinced that the spiritual message of the text could be adequately understood by all readers. At the beginning, after I received the parchment from the goddess Machandi, I insisted on publishing it as soon as possible, but Repa Sundhi did not agree, arguing that for the time being, "the fruit was not ripe." Later, as would usually happen, I started to lose interest as my life turned to a new track, but the moment came when the old wise man reminded me of my mission.

If I observe things accurately, however, I can see that everything was arranged for the highest benefit of myself as well as those who are interested in spirituality. The text appears exactly in the right form; and if it is correctly understood, it will come at the right time to be assimilated accordingly by the reader. On the other hand, this period has not only allowed me to achieve spiritual maturity but has also given me the necessary occasion to orient my life most efficiently so that I could be at peace with myself and the content of my work. During this period of time, I had several occasions to share some of the content of the text and its meanings to other persons; but I noticed that while I was trying to give these explanations, I mysteriously could not find the right words and stopped at words all the time without expressing what I wanted. With time, I realized that it is not good to tell unexperienced persons about our own experiences which are not yet exactly clear for us. In such situations, we hold onto ideas and involve our ego by emitting false thoughts which are not correct in relation to the phenomena we describe. We will also state errors. In those moments, the errors will not seem so big, but they will remain in our aura and somehow harm the processes which naturally and spontaneously take place.

What I am trying to say is that it is harmful to try to explain to others what we ourselves do not know if we do not know exactly how it happens. But, once this knowledge begins to be assimilated gradually and becomes mature in our consciousness, we can know when the time comes to make it known to others. From this position, I understood the complicated process of editing the secret text according to the wishes of Repa Sundhi who has expressed a superior understanding of things. In a short meeting on this subject at which Cezar and Shin Li also took part, he said the following.

"If we wish to share something important with a person whom we trust, we must choose that person carefully because, if that person can't grasp intellectually or with the intuition the aspects we are telling, then our initiative is useless. What would be the point to reveal certain mysteries and extraordinary facts to a person who, being incapable of understanding with both the heart and with the mind, begins almost immediately to be accusative with a mocking attitude?! The choice to confess to such a person would not be an inspired one. This is why it is much better to write about your experiences as clearly as possible — because there will always be persons who are receptive and open to this information who will understand the hidden meaning and then be able to share it with others. I hope you've understood what I mean," Dr. Xien said to me.

I had understood very well. The secret text of the parchment containing the five techniques of fundamental initiation knowledge, revealed by the great wise man Padmashambhava, was now ready for publication. A last tentative delay to reveal this knowledge postponed this moment for almost two years, by reason of evil forces that have no interest in light, good and freedom reaching the ignorant consciousness of men. Evil forces thus do all they can to at least delay, if not to destroy, this beneficial manifestation as much as possible. And because their preferred area of manifestation is the physical world in which we live, many obstacles and manifestations occur which tend to remove the good. The situation I explained in the beginning of this book is a good example of this.

But now, because all seems quieter and because divine patience always gives the wanted results, I am ready to present the text of the secret parchment I received from the goddess Machandi. I only want to add that it should not be read as a poem or story. In fact, we are dealing with five different statements, five universal cosmic laws of creation which, if correctly understood, fundamentally transform the understanding and even the very existence of the human being. I suggest a profound meditation about the hidden mystery of each of these five statements. To make it more understandable, I have included some clarifying comments. Together with Shin Li's explanations and my discussions with her about spiritual subjects, I hope this will clarify even more the obscure and hidden meaning of the text. In order to facilitate the reading of the main text, I have sometimes included in brackets the immediate explanation of some expressions which are typical to Tibetan spirituality.

Here is the whole text of the secret parchment accompanied by my own clarifying comments.

THE WISDOM OF THE HIGHEST PEAK
FROM THE KINGDOM WITHOUT NAME

The One who, Unborn, has still appeared free in
    the pure lotus of the Deceiving Sea,
Is now enlightening our consciousness and the nineteen
    aggregates of knowledge,
In order to pass beyond the Terrible Wall of the Silence
    of the World.
We are begging him to always spread his Grace and
    Endless Compassion over us!

As there is no written reference to this parchment and there are only legends lost in Tibetan spirituality, we can only assume some things about its content. Repa Sundhi, however, believes that this introductory stanza is a late interpolation written by Yeshe Tsogyel, a disciple of the great guru Padmashambhava, from whom she personally received the text of the parchment by dictation. Such verses represent a relatively usual form of expressing gratitude and praise to a wise lama, even more since the lama was Padmashambhava, the religious reformer of the whole Tibetan region.

Tradition shows him as "unborn" because he is considered to be an avatar, a being who has already achieved the supreme spiritual liberation in another existence and is only incarnated for the good and evolution of other people.

"The Deceiving Sea" is an expression from Tibetan tradition which refers to the illusion of the world we live in and the fact that we live in a dream where our actions are hollow as long as they are not directed at the essence of our being but rather outside of it.

The nineteen aggregates of knowledge are nineteen states of consciousness, starting from the basic elements up to the most re-fined nuances of metal. At this point, the text should be understood as follows: the nineteen aggregates of knowledge are enlightened by consciousness, and individual consciousness, in its turn, is enlightened by the higher consciousness which is comparable to its essence.

The "Terrible Wall of the Silence of the World" is a very beautiful expression with which Yeshe Tsogyel has managed to express both the highest purpose of the human being and his very limited condition in this world. The "Silence of the World" is associated with the same colossal illusion which man is prey to during his lives. Tibetan tradi-tion sees this illusion as a dream or a veil over the eyes of the onlooker that stops him from seeing the truth. For this reason, this veil is also compared with a "silence" which means that, even though the world is agitated and noisy, this illusion makes it silent in relation to the truth which stays hidden.

Tibetans especially emphasize this aspect of the formidable illu-sion of man which tempts and "puts man to sleep" because this always leads to man's suffering. This sometimes causes such great pain that the human being is "silent" in the face of these disappointments and unable to confess or seek happiness "beyond" the illusion. This is where the expression "dumb with suffering" comes from. Tibetans add that this "silence," caused by great ignorance, is helplessly laid before "the terrible wall" of the world. They associate this blocking of man's evolution with a terrible and frightening "wall" which makes them turn away from the wall and dizzily turn back to the world of the illusion from which they were trying to escape. This is the spiritual "obstacle" that man must overcome to find true happiness.

The last verse is a blessing and at the same time an invocation of the great wise man, Padmashambhava, whose divine help is requested for those in suffering or in search of spiritual truth.

1. Oh, Tsogyelma, my valuable disciple who has already
   realized the truth of the first two worlds, listen to me!
   The most important energy coming from the Realm Without
   Name (God the Father) is love; it is Infinite,
   It represents the unifying element and at the same time shows
   us the highest Peak that governs the worlds.

Yeshe Tsogyel was one of the main disciples of the great Tibetan wise man Padmashambhava, and he especially appreciated her. The legend says that she had gained extraordinary paranormal powers and had even conquered death. These stories refer to the period after which her spiritual master had left the physical world and when Yeshe had achieved spiritual perfection. Because the text was dictated when Padmashambhava was alive rather than after his death, we can assume that Yeshe Tsogyel had only reached a certain degree of spiritual achievement at that time as her master precisely indicates this by saying she had "already realized the truth of the first two worlds."

The "worlds" are actually the main dimensions of God's creation, meaning the physical, the subtle (astral) and the causal dimension. Since Padmashambhava mentions only two "worlds" conquered by Yeshe Tsogyel, it is natural to assume that he was referring to the first two in increasing order of their vibrational frequency, namely the physical and the subtle (astral) dimensions. In other worlds, even back then, Yeshe had somehow conquered death since she had acquired perfect control of the laws and mechanisms of the "physical" world; but it seems that she had also greatly amplified her powers in the subtle dimension as well, just as the text of the parchment says. Indeed, tradition says that Yeshe Tsogyel had the power to resurrect the dead, master the laws of matter, and travel wherever she wanted by the power of her will. The great guru, however, does not give great importance to these certainly great achievements. He only mentions them briefly; and even then, indirectly.

What seems to truly interest him is the very essence of this stanza, referring to the energy of love. In a few words, he indicates the original source of this energy: it represents the essence of God. It is endless and inexhaustible and can "feed" everything forever; it is the unifying element of all other types of energy; and there is nothing superior to love in manifestation and that which is beyond it.

The fact that he speaks from the very beginning about the supremacy of love and its importance shows us that this indeed seems to be the "Gordian knot" of Mankind, valid in those times and even more so in the present. We have gone so far from this primeval energy that we often do not even recognize it when it manifests itself with power. All dramas of daily life start here, from the lack of love in our own universe. In its turn, this lack causes evil and a vicious circle appears, and modern man cannot solve it. The problems increase when most people have an acute feeling of guilt after harming a person. This causes moral suffering and strengthens the feeling of guilt because they no longer hope to be forgiven. This is where the energy of love intervenes; but even if love permanently surrounds us and is at our disposal, we refuse to see it, as if it did not exist.

When I discussed this with Shin Li, she clarified some very important aspects which involve suffering, compassion, and especially the energy of love, an energy which includes everything. Some of these aspects were familiar to me from my previous discussions with Cezar; but in the context of understanding the stanza of the parchment better, the new explanations offered greater clarity.

Shin Li referred exactly to suffering being the "illness" of modern society, but she also mentioned the way to overcome it, if not to avoid it completely. The primary problem is that men tend to treat suffering and guilt as something outside of themselves, as a mechanism that should repair itself at a certain moment. In reality, guilt and suffering happen within ourselves. They are our responsibility, and we cannot and should not exclude them as something harmful since, in the end, we generated them. The way we can solve this seems simple as Shin Li presents it. The true test is the test of our ego.

"If one truly understands that they were wrong and asks for forgiveness, it's very good," she said, "because there are also many who don't even realize when they are wrong towards their fellows and, what is even worse, there are those who are happy when people suffer because of their actions."

"But what happens with those who really and painfully feel the shock of the bad deed they did?" I insisted

"In such cases, we are confronted with more subtle aspects," Shin Li explained. "When people realize that they were wrong, due to their own ignorance, they don't understand that there is the possibility to forgive oneself through God's compassion. I think you understand very well that this compassion can be felt even more if we also show compassion towards others in our turn."

I then suddenly realized the truth of the prayer "Our Father"..."and forgive us our trespasses as we forgive those who trespass against us."

"When this forgiveness, begged from God, is called upon, it is actually nothing but a call from the heart to His infinite compassion, meaning God's mercy," Shin Li confirmed. "With the help of compassion, which is actually a reflection of the energy of God's infinite love, people have the possibility to forgive themselves."

"And how can we know that God has given us His compassion?" I asked with high interest.

Shin Li answered, untroubled.

"People realize this when they overcome the state of inner torment that was troubling them. For those who don't know that there is the possibility to forgive themselves, however, this state of suffering can be endless because they will not have access to this energy of compassion which comes from God. Instead, they will adopt very difficult procedures, as some religions do. This is why it is very important for people to understand that they must be able to forgive themselves...when, of course, they realize their mistakes. Obviously, however, this does not involve starting to make other mistakes afterwards."

"It should be so because otherwise we would be confronted with Sisyphean labor. It's clear," I said

"Very good. It is therefore fundamental for those who understand their mistakes to be able to eliminate the guilt they feel with the help of this energy of compassion which comes from God. If they don't, they will always carry a useless weight with them. Think about a chicken that has hatched. If it continues to hold on to the egg shell in which it developed and tries to fly with it, it will seem handicapped."

"However, I know some people who never stop blaming themselves for their deeds," I said. "I do not think that this is constructive."

"When someone is aware of his mistakes, he can realize that he doesn't want to be wrong again and then, with the help of God's compassion, he can return to harmony. But to continue endlessly to blame oneself will not generate anything beneficial because it will only produce a state of continuous guilt, and thus the respective person will continuously come into contact with their past mistakes. It is very important for you to understand this subtle mechanism because it is a fundamental key to individual transformation. We cannot evolve through torment but rather through love."

I became thoughtful for a while. I wanted to clarify something.

"Some people might imagine that they were seriously wrong and that they will be damned for their mistakes. They might imagine that what you said is only valid for some mistakes but not for all mistakes."

"Here, you must understand that God's goodness is unlimited," Shin Li immediately explained. "Any mistake can be forgiven when man consciously calls upon God, asking Him humbly for His help. When a human being thus pleads, God can bring His endless mercy upon that person and forgive his or her mistakes."

All this is possible because the energy of God's love, which can penetrate everything, is infinite. Padmashambhava clearly hints at the fact that there is nothing above it and that through it, anything can be achieved. Its multiple forms of manifestation, such as compassion and forgiveness, are corollaries of the same main motif: the energy of love is supreme and can always be found in all other types of energy which exist. And, the fact that God offers us this love unconditionally and infinitely is an extra proof that we can and should do the same. This is the most direct and sure way of revealing God to us, as the last words of the stanza show.

> 2. Oh, my beautiful Tsogyel! Always be careful that any aspect of reality, just as we look upon it, will be revealed to us exactly in the same manner afterwards.

The main aspect pointed out in this stanza is that we create our own universe we live in, our own world. No matter how unlikely it might seem, we directly influence the world we live in and particularize it after our own thoughts and intentions. This is why they say that "beauty is in the eyes of the beholder." If we have this inner force, then we can discover infinitely more beauty around us, infinitely more love, and we can receive infinitely more than before. But, if we remain closed, mean, and suspicious, then beauty, kindness and love cannot penetrate this shell we have created, and then we must conclude that these do not exist. It's like a leitmotif which, unfortunately, more and more people are following: "everyone is bad, they are all evil; and this is why I must be the same, in order to survive in this unholy world." This is a perverted way of orienting our existence. When the inner transformation is truly achieved, everything surrounding us changes due to this inner transformation of our being. What changes is actually our perception of the surrounding reality. The happiness we feel in those moments makes us discover divine attributes and wonderful qualities in beings who, until then, seemed dull, bad and lonely. It's a real miracle which only depends on ourselves.

In general, man resonates with aspects from the world surrounding him...with stress, tension, closedness, evil behavior, intolerance...and, given this background, even if outside of it, there is beauty and kindness, joy or love, he becomes opaque to them and says that they do not exist. Our points of view are different from those of others, and our way of resolving a situation is different from that of others. We must conclude that men are confronted almost all the time with all kinds of problems or existential crises. What really leads to this often dramatic situation? The answer is simple and it is the very essence of this stanza: man forges his own universe according to his own perception of this universe and then interprets it, respects it, and gives it attention.

If our view of the surrounding world is mostly based on a selfish vibration — in other words, if we regard things only through a small window — everything around us will be much darker and colder, and our universe will be very limited and full of suffering. After all, even happiness is good for something. If we analyze things more, we will see that, in any situation, ignorance led to the occurrence of a problem in our lives. Afterwards, however, all of our troubles have allowed us to transform because, after all, each problem can be seen as a trial. If we pass it successfully, then we will evolve spiritually because we will become more mature and acquire more experience. If the problem is not solved, nobody can force us to solve it or to overcome it because it is our own problem. This means, however, that whether we like it or not, we must, after all, evolve.

I found these considerations very interesting and discussed them with Shin Li when I dealt with the respective stanza of the parchment. Actually, the entire stanza expresses, in its essence, the need for man to evolve and the fact that man evolves depending upon his own perception of the surrounding reality. This truth is valid all the time.

"Either he is interested or not. Either he wants it or not. Man must evolve after all, even if this happens very slowly for some people," Shin Li explained., "but man can't stop evolving. The sense of evolution can't be avoided. A person will be tortured by the tension imposed by his or her problems until that person finds the just solution because there is always a solution for every problem. And, if man continues to suffer, choosing to have a negative perception of the surrounding reality, then his existential crisis will be more profound, his suffering will be greater, until finally, he will be forced to do something; and not just anything, but rather only what is right and necessary in order to solve that problem."

In the context of that stanza of the parchment, the "right and necessary" means changing our view of reality. This means that a certain transformation is necessary, a higher perception of the reality we come into contact with because every aspect, being or thing will appear to us just as we look upon it. For example, if an architect designs a bridge, we cannot expect to have a car as a result, but that bridge might be broken, thus leading to the deaths of many people; or it might be a superb bridge that remains in history for its beauty and long duration.

Even an unpleasant aspect, if looked upon with kindness and transformation, begins to look less unpleasant, both for us and for the others; and in the end, it can even be completely transformed.

At an individual level, these things have clear repercussions with direct consequences on one's personal life because everything we think about intensely now is what we will become sooner or later. This is probably the best practical example for the second stanza of the text.

> 3. Oh, you, who have bloomed like a lotus in the world of the Dakini! You should know that there is no coincidence!
> Everything is in reality a mysterious need for The One who has touched The Kingdom Without Name (the state of spiritual freedom).

> Everything appears as a giant woven cloth in which
> every thread (aspect) is permanently interwoven
> and is in tight connection with the other threads
> (aspects) which make up reality.

This stanza can be best described in modern scientific terms as the holographic reality of the universe. The message transmitted over thousands of years is as clear now as it was then: the part is in Everything and Everything is in the part. Without going into scientific details, some of which are quite avant-garde, it is enough to grasp the essence of this statement. In plastic terms, if we press with our fingers on one part of the universe, then something will definitely rise in another part of the universe, apparently with no connection to the first part. A good example of this fundamental characteristic of the universe, which Cezar explained to me some time ago, would be significant synchronicities. In such situations, aspects which seem distinct are brought together and made to "function" in a mysterious yet coherent and meaningful way for the one who understands their meaning.

The importance of understanding the holographic structure of the universe means especially that we start to feel less isolated from the rest and thus become better integrated into the surrounding world. In this case, individual problems become significantly smaller, existential crises have no meaning, and the purpose of the human life is better defined. The direct result is that man's evolution is greatly amplified. The aforesaid stanza is closely connected with the following one.

> 4. In the entire Kingdom Without Name (God), the vibration
> is present everywhere. Nothing is static.

Stanzas 3 and 4 complete each other because the Manifestation is practically an infinite ocean of energetic vibrations, and the holographic reality of the universe can be explained precisely through the "intertwining" of vibrations because they are never separate and all contain potential. Since the physical, subtle or causal matter is energy vibrating on different frequency levels and since each level contains the other one in an implicit and yet mysterious manner, the result is that, in any time and space, we can access any other dimension of the Manifestation provided that we are in resonance with it or can create a state of resonance between us and that dimension. Thus, we can travel anywhere and anytime. We can have anything we want and in whatever quantity we want, but this all happens based on cosmic necessities because the consciousness of the one who acts in such a manner is so vast that it is a determining factor for the good functioning of the universe.

"The Kingdom Without Name" is presented here from two perspectives. On the one hand, it represents God's infinite consciousness which is the highest peak of man's spiritual realization; and on the other hand, it is the Manifestation itself which involves duality. This suggests that vibration is indeed present everywhere: both here in the dual world and beyond, in transcendence.

Under these conditions, the fact that "nothing is static" seems to be supplementary. Padmashambhava, the great wise man, however, has included this statement on purpose in order to underline the nature of the eternal transformation. This means that nothing stays the same; but everything changes in Manifestation, depending on its "holographic requirements."

> 5. You, who delight the spirits of the three worlds!
> Listen to what I'm telling you now: project your consciousness
>   onto the Highest Peak of the Kingdom and you will (thus)
>   obtain the light of eternal Happiness.
> These five methods are meant for the evolution of every soul
>   in the Kingdom, oh, Tsogyelma! May you be their guid-
>   ing shield!

This last stanza of the Parchment practically gives the instantaneous method for spiritual freedom. Considered the top of the yoga and tantric practice of Tibet, the technique is known as Phowa. In principle, it refers to a complex projection of the higher consciousness of the man who practices the technique, using a very secret initiation method which is not mentioned by Padmashambhava in the text. This makes us understand either that the method should not be known in any other way except through direct initiation by a guru or that it was already familiar to Yeshe Tsogyel as a practical method.

Padmashambhava makes and encrypts a reference to "the Highest Peak of the Kingdom Without Name." The basis for this method is that, through it, the man who practices it becomes capable of automatically assimilating the state and condition of the being or aspect onto which his or her consciousness is projected, even if his or her initial level of consciousness before the projection was inferior to the one onto which the projection was made. This allows the achievement of giant leaps of evolution and culminates in the supreme spiritual freedom which can be thus obtained by projection onto "the Highest Peak of the Kingdom" which is considered "the heart of God." We can understand this unique reference made by the great wise man in the sense that any other projection of the consciousness is subordinated to it and derives from it. He makes us understand this by saying that we can thus obtain "the light of eternal Happiness," meaning that there is nothing else above it.

In the end, Padmashambhava specifies that the five techniques are actually five efficient ways for spiritual evolution and that they should be made known to anyone interested in deciphering them.

The text of the parchment, as stated above, is a spiritual treasure revealed in a very synthetic and hidden manner. In my opinion, a book of commentary on the five stanzas, done with details and competence, would not be enough for an exhaustive presentation of this subject. I have gradually reached the conclusion, however, that one's own learning and personal experience that is acquired through thinking and meditation on these aspects represents the best way of understanding their occult and vast meaning. This is why, taking Repa Sundhi's advice and being guided by Shin Li, I chose to present the main ideas briefly which would act as a trampoline of inspiration for the reader's analysis. Anyway, knowing this ancient spiritual text, which is a true jewel of wisdom, can guide our steps towards a wider and more mature vision of our lives.

CHAPTER FOUR

"HOT SPOT" IN ANTARCTICA

Just as if the sequence of events had been pre-ordained, there was a rush of activity in Department Zero almost immediately after the conclusion of the final drafting of the text of the Secret Parchment. As I said before, the last couple of months had been relatively calm which allowed me to put my thoughts in order and to analyze certain spiritual subjects together with Shin Li. It was also a "cool down" after the stormy events which had taken place during the past year. With his new obligations, Cezar was away most of the time. The General had been detached to the Pentagon where he served as military mediator on national security matters between Romania and the USA. All in all, the changes in the internal structure of Department Zero had settled quite well.

At the end of the year 2006, I was in a meditative mood, preoccupied by the text of the parchment, the discussions with Shin Li and the charm of the quite rare meetings with Cezar and Doctor Xien. At first, this obvious lack of activity seemed a bit strange to me but because it gave me a well-deserved break to fulfill my spiritual mission, I took things just as they were. Between October 2006 and January 2007, no incidents happened. Protocol took place without issues and political pressures were practically absent. This, however, was in fact only the "calm before the storm".

Towards the end of January 2007, the situation took a sudden turn. Matters again returned to the Orăştie Mountains and the Americans' suspicion that we were hiding something from them. Since they did not share further details themselves, the whole situation seemed somewhat hilarious. Both sides had mutual suspicions of each other, but neither of them knew for sure what the other was thinking.

As for me, this subject was a big question mark. I knew almost nothing about the involvement of Department Zero in the Orăştie Mountains, but what was even stranger was that Cezar continuously postponed talking about this. I was intrigued by the fact that this subject seemed very special, even for the RIS. Normally, I would have imagined the great discovery in the Bucegi Mountains to be the headline of the state secrets and collaboration with the Americans. The realities I saw there and which I later described in the previous books — although I could only describe part of them in accordance with the limits imposed upon me — and the implications created for the Romanian-American relations made this a reality that seemed hard to top. After all, this was about a technology which man had not imagined before, about a mysterious civilization which refused to reveal itself and about finding out very uncomfortable truths about man's existence on this planet. Besides, I could not find anything in the archives of Department Zero on the Orăştie Mountains, and neither Cezar nor General Obadea had mentioned anything in particular about this subject until then. The only mention was that the Romanian side did not have much information about this subject either.

When the "bomb" arrived, I had been just as much in the dark as I was a year before. I was at the Alpha Base and was working with the tactical teams on a preparation test for psychological evaluations in maximum risk situations. Cezar was in Bucharest at a meeting of the RIS department leaders and Lieutenant Nicoară was in the Projection Chamber, accompanied by an American team of specialists sent by the Pentagon. In such situations, the base was run (from an administrative perspective) by two other lieutenants, Peris and Matu.

I got a phone call from Cezar while I was doing the psychological evaluations. He told me briefly that I was to leave Alpha Base in half an hour and head for the military airfield at T, then head on from that point. He did not tell me where I was going but left me precise instructions for the emergency code of the base. He told me that he would give me an explanation when we met, in a couple of hours. Up to this point, nothing was unusual, except perhaps the degree of alert he imposed on our unit. I had no information which could justify that action, but orders were orders.

The truly interesting part was that, at the end of our conversation, he asked me to bring him, while keeping the utmost secrecy and security, a file placed near his desk at the Alpha Base. For the first time, he gave me the key-codes for his personal safe and told me what I was supposed to pick up from that safe. It was the file, but it was sealed in a transparent box that looked like Plexiglas which was in fact made of glass fiber. It had the size of a ring binder but it was thicker. This was obviously a maximum security holder for classified information. The box was very elegant. It had metal edges, which I later found out were made of titanium, as well as a very sophisticated computerized closing system which had an iris print reader. Inside of it, I could see a normal file that was quite thin, on the cover of which was written in big black print: CRONOS. Underneath that , there was a "top secret" stamp. Cezar's method of action had been atypical. To the extent that I knew him, I realized that things were truly serious if he had chosen to act in this manner.

I did as he asked me, imposing the emergency code at the base and took off in the helicopter heading for T. For more security, apart from the pilot, I also took Lieutenant Matu with me on the mission. He was carrying active equipment and accompanied me together with one of the agents from the base up to the military airfield in T. The flight went smoothly and, upon my arrival, Cezar was waiting for me on the runway. I immediately handed him the special briefcase holding the box with the file.

"Generals Obadea and Roddey are also here," he quickly told me. "They are in Bucharest for an emergency meeting taking place at the government together with some members of the Supreme National Defense Council (SNDC). Something very important is going on. Here is the briefing."

Cezar handed me a file with red covers upon which I could read: MACOR FACILITY — ANTARCTICA. EYES ONLY. In the noise from the airfield, Cezar shouted in my ear:

"General Inossanto has asked for the best technical team for a mission in Antarctica. It's made up of the men with RV (Remote Viewing) ESP. You've also been included in this team gathered by General Roddey. You'll embark immediately and take off in a couple of minutes. Good luck!"

He looked at me in his own special way, full of kindness and understanding; and, for the first time, he gave me a hug full of affection. Even though I was older than him, I still had the wonderful feeling of a parent's protection, a safety which would accompany me from that moment on. I thanked him with gratitude, took my small luggage in one hand and the mission briefing file in the other, and got into the car which was waiting for me a few meters away. We drove quickly on the airfield up to the plane which was ready for departure. It had only a few seats and a special interior design. I realized that it was a diplomatic flight because, inside of the plane, I could recognize a few American officials and a British officer whom I had met at a protocol meeting in Bucharest. Almost all of them were busy reading briefing notes or working on computers. I took a seat in my place and, in less than 10 minutes, the plane took off.

The sun was setting on the horizon in a perfectly clear sky which had gorgeous colors. The cold outside made the pure view even more beautiful, especially because it was accentuated by the quiet beauty of a calm winter with not too much snow. The discreet atmosphere in the plane was wonderful and the services great. I relaxed happily in the comfortable chair, allowing myself a few minutes of meditation and synthesis.

Only three hours before, I had been quietly performing my activity at the Alpha Base, and now I was in a plane heading for the USA and then towards a secret destination. I had carried a box with me as well as a very important file, about the meaning of which I had no idea. Additionally, I had been given access to the emergency codes, received a mission briefing file and been included in a special technical team with a top secret mission in Antarctica. These were all important events that took place successively during a very short period of time. Just like other top moments of my life, when I was confronted with exceptional situations and conditions, I could only rejoice from all my heart that I had been given these extraordinary opportunities. I felt sure of myself, at peace within, master of what I already knew, and in balance with the flow of events which were taking place. I was happy with my activity at Department Zero, with the relations I had made, with the fact that I had completed my spiritual mission concerning the text of the parchment, and with the fact that I had the chance to meet Dr. Xien and Shin Li, whose presence and spiritual teachings could not be removed from my memory. Relaxed and at peace with the thought that my actions were in accordance with a superior integration and understanding, thus preventing me from committing too many mistakes, I ate my dinner and then opened the mission briefing file.

The file was individualized for my name, bore the mark of origin of the Pentagon, and was signed on the bottom of the pages by General Roddey, who had been assigned as leader of the technical operation for that mission. I was informed that the final destination was a place near the Macor American base in the southwestern part of Antarctica, where a cosmic phenomenon involving extraterrestrial technology had occurred. I was given the list of team members, hierarchical relations, level of access to information — I noticed that this level was maximum for everyone in the team, of which I was also a part — and some more specifications which I am not allowed to reveal. On two of the pages, I read a presentation on the Macor American base, the activity taking place there, and the main events which took place in the area during the last decades.

The report then continued with the actual presentation of the problem: on January 22nd 2007, the technical equipment of the base recorded an unusual activity on one of the lower mountain peaks which are a maximum of twenty kilometers away from the base. Similar odd "signals" had also been recorded in two other locations the previous year which showed a special triangulation with the Macor location: the Orăştie Mountains in Romania and Mount McKinley in Alaska. The Counterintelligence Service of the U.S. Army had no information about strange activities in either region. They told me that this was the explanation for the diplomatic pressures exerted a while back by U.S. diplomacy; however, nothing was unusual so far except for the mystery that nobody could understand the real meaning of the indicated areas.

The surprise came in January when the three points were connected in their turn by the indication of a resultant* in cosmic space having Europa, a moon of Jupiter, as its target. I anxiously read the rest of the material. It said that a precise area of the ice cap covering that mountainous area of Antarctica near Macor Base had melted down in two hours and had revealed an extraordinarily complex technological device on one of the mountain slopes. Four pictures were shown from different angles with certain topometric references.

The object had the shape of the frustum of a cone with an elliptical base. It obviously worked as a kind of "cosmic buoy." It had the approximate size of a three story building; and near the top, at about two thirds from the base, it had a kind of "collar" like a wide fan, possibly a kind of antenna. In the

---

*The word *resultant* has a specific definition in mathematics: a single vector that is the equivalent of a set of vectors.

pictures, this particularity of its construction looked like giant panels, very bright, with red and white lines that looked like lasers. There were many other elements there which I could not distinguish clearly from the pictures.

The report further stated that it was impossible to identify the exceptional source of energy which could melt that huge mass of ice in two hours because the buoy was covered in a 210 meter thick layer of ice, but it was obvious that the source came from inside the device. The last element specified in the report was that after the ice had melted, the buoy started to emit light signals of colossal intensity at a very high rate, like pulsars. On the morning of the third day, on January 24th 2007, any manifestation of this kind had ceased. We were informed, however, that the device continued to work, emitting energy and maintaining the surrounding area with perfect cleanliness. The buoy was lit and there was obviously some activity inside of it, but the powerful energy emissions had stopped.

Closing the file, I remained thoughtful. I was amazed by the direct and obvious manner in which the device had "revealed" itself. If things really happened like this, then this was obviously something very serious and one could draw the conclusion that the phenomenon did not only involve Earth but also our solar system. The most interesting part was, however, the connection with our country. It seems that this area was of great interest in the remote past: first, the extraordinary complex in the Bucegi Mountains; and then the mysterious connection with the Orăştie Mountains, about which I practically had no data whatsoever. Something was known, however, if I make a connection with the special file I had brought to Cezar. The formidable secrecy under which the respective file was kept, as well as the fact that Cezar had never given me any information about it until then, made me think seriously about this. The mystery was even greater because the Romanian side did not have much information in this respect either.

There were therefore many questions to which I, at least at that time, had no answer. I decided to rest a while because the trip would be very long. As usual, we stopped in Spain where I boarded another plane, this time a military one. The second stop was made at a secret American base in the Mojave Desert where we stayed for a day. That was the gathering point for everyone involved in the operation. There were two main teams, and this included the technical team, of which I was a part, along with two colleagues from the final selection from the RV training, the Canadian and an American. I was also happy to meet Aiden who joined us with his exceptional technical support. A computer genius like him was indispensable for such operations. There was also an operational team made up of six men who held a technology I had never seen before. I recognized two of them from the operations in the Bucegi complex, and we said hello and exchanged a few pleasant words. There were also administrative personnel who had been especially selected for that mission.

We then took part in a short briefing session where the parameters of the action and our own roles were set. We were also told that we had a much enhanced secondary support team which was meant to ensure the mission which had been stationed around the wide perimeter surrounding the cosmic buoy. The coordinator of the action was Colonel Trescott, a man with a lot of experience in the "extraction" of relics or mysterious objects, all performed under perfect cover. He was going to lead the operation up to the time of the meeting with General Roddey because we were to travel to Antarctica after that. The mission also included several other colonels and generals, including General Obadea. The Chief of the Pentagon, General Inossanto, would supervise the entire action in person and was going to arrive directly at Macor Base. I was happy to meet General Obadea again. With him there, I felt more "at home" and hoped to learn more information from him since he was directly involved as a representative of our country which had become a complex part of this mission.

The logistics equipment was impressive, and I must confess I had never imagined that we had such technology on Earth. Everything was boarded on two huge military airplanes, and we took off the following day and made a stop in Chile, near Santiago. After a couple of hours, we headed for the southern tip of South America, where we landed at an American military base on Chilean territory, somewhere near the Drake Passage. Here, we met with General Roddey who reorganized some of the points of the operation. General Obadea was also present, but I did not get the chance to speak to him at that time. I noticed that the entirety of the personnel became increasingly preoccupied and withdrawn as we were approaching the end point of the action. The diplomatic and military channels were permanently open because the phenomenon had obviously been observed and recorded by other powers that had also become involved.

In such situations, American diplomacy enters a state of alert similar to "code red" when only a small segment of staff is kept for current operations with other states while the rest of the resources are concentrated on the respective issue that generated "the code." Thus, the general perception is that Washington had taken a small "vacation" when, in reality, almost all of the presidential staff is in a state of maximum alert. This occurs because the Americans have established a kind of "subsystem" which allows them to work efficiently at two levels in such cases: the regular open one on the surface and the secret one which is then like a "throng" even though it seems non-existent.

In our country, things happen in a different manner because there is also a difference in native personality. Through their inner structure, the Romanian people tend to be more free and open. In critical cases, this translates to their preference to go "all at once" by adapting the situation to each moment.

This organization is far from perfect, but we win through spontaneity and freedom of decision. Personally, I prefer this option because it gives a wider range of action. In our country, even when things become precipitated and everyone is very agitated, most of the decisions taken are correct. There is, of course, the disadvantage of a breach in secrecy but, after all, it is a risk that is assumed everywhere. On the other hand, Americans have a different style: subversive, hidden, bureaucratic and quite rigid. I assumed that the combination of these somewhat different ways of action would lead to good results in Antarctica as well as it has proven itself in the case of the complex in the Bucegi Mountains.

As I was involved in the operation and had some experience working at Department Zero and with the Romanian-American relations concerning the Projection Hall, I was able to notice a certain mood which had begun to take shape at the American military and political management level. I had an intuition in this respect more than a year before; and for this mission, I realized that my perceptions had become deeper and were actually correct. The situation did not prove to be an obstacle, but it expressed a certain point of view in the American mentality; and more precisely, the fact that such elements or events of crucial importance at planetary level involved Romania, a relatively small country without big pretensions in the "world architecture." It was that bad mood created by the situation when great oaks should fear little strokes which could make them fall. The American diplomatic corps probably wanted to lead and control from better positions the situations which involved the Bucegi Mountains Complex or the connection between the Orăștie Mountains and the Macor Base in Antarctica, but they obviously didn't find in Romania the obedience which other European states had shown them. The Americans' vexation was also caused by the fact that they couldn't understand the phenomenon: why have such crucial points and such phenomenal discoveries — in terms of their geopolitical importance — been found precisely in Romania and not in other more "serious" and more "accessible" areas of the world? Somehow, by assuming the arrogant position of the almighty "parent" one should listen to, Americans have unconsciously associated this attitude with the right to own the most important discoveries and crucial elements on Earth. In my opinion, this mentality is based on a "quantitative" standpoint which means that the "biggest" is necessarily the "smartest" as well.

Of course, if these discoveries had been made on their territory or in areas which are under their direct and overwhelming influence, the Americans would have been very happy and their pride would have probably been infinite. In this situation, however, the American government had to bear having only a partial influence which was, most of the time, fragile; whereby they had to make compromises, grant certain facilities and, generally speaking, lacked direct control over what they considered strategic points of utmost importance for our world.

As I have said before, the issue did not create any altercation in diplomatic relations, especially because Romanians are very tolerant, but it could nevertheless sharpen the relations when it came to certain disputes. I brought up this subject in the airplane during a discussion with General Obadea after we had taken off and headed for the Bellinghausen Sea. Part of the logistics equipment had to be taken from two nuclear ice breakers which were already present in the area. General Obadea gave me the impression that he knew very well what I was referring to.

"I am confronted with this aspect quite often at the Pentagon," he said. "It is fortuitous that General Inossanto is a good friend of mine."

He then told me that the situation in Antarctica was actually much more serious than the presentation in our briefing report, but that everything was under control.

"The Americans would have liked to cover up everything; but through its nature, the phenomenon has puzzled all the great powers that have noticed it. It's considered a planetary incident. As we're speaking, an International Military Protection and Intervention Force is being set up which makes things even more complicated. This could give rise to pretensions of cancelling 'territorial limits' in Antarctica even though they officially don't exist, but we'll see what happens."

We landed at Macor Base towards "evening" European time and settled there. It was very cold and there was a snowstorm which made the unpacking operations more difficult. Due to the unfavorable conditions, not even very powerful transporters could operate properly in order to bring the rest of the equipment from the two anchored ships to a certain distance. Accordingly, General Roddey decided to postpone everything for the following day. We therefore had the necessary time to rest after the long trip.

I expected the base in Antarctica to be very restrictive in comparison with other American bases, especially from the point of view of space. I was deeply wrong. From a certain point of view, I could even say it was larger than necessary in some areas. It was very nice inside and there was even an impressive greenhouse. It is true that there were very few personnel, but the living conditions surprised me with the available facilities. As far as I understood, the great problem was psychological and this is why the personnel were refreshed every three months, especially in the case of weather stations. I am not allowed to talk about the purpose of this American military base, but I can tell you that it was involved in a very serious accident in the late 1950s.

I slept well even if it was day-time, and when we woke up, we had the chance to enjoy a clear sky and atmosphere without wind. The temperature outside was about -45 degrees Celsius so we were all moving quickly, arranging what was necessary for our trip to the cosmic buoy. Part of the equipment had already been transported there during the first hours of the so-called morning. We travelled comfortably in very modern transporters; and around noon, we could already see the first signs of the existence of the buoy. The landscape seemed to become torn, trapped in the ice around it. The rocky and dry slope of the small mountain was empty and perfectly dry. I could see the gravel, the rocks, and even a very dry kind of sand which delineated a circular area in the middle of which, from far away, the mysterious device rose. Seeing it caused me great emotion, the source of which I could not clearly identify. Maybe it was due to the fact that the device certainly came from another world or maybe it was because of the mystery surrounding it. Alone, unaffected and even mighty in that area, it gave the impression of a formidable redoubt which could withstand any assault. I was sensitive to such things and remembered very well the emotional impact I had felt when I explored the Projection Hall. To a certain extent, the situation was the same here, but the feeling was somewhat different. I could see that tronconical shape with a kind of giant collar near the top. It was massive, imposing, and deeply rooted in the mountain. At the same time, it was very lonely, aiming for cosmic space, hidden under the ice for maybe tens or even hundreds of thousands of years; and yet, it gave the impression that it was untouched by time.

It possessed a kind of greatness, sovereignty, independence and safety in the way it was built and placed there, imposing respect and a lot of attention. I was looking at the groups of forces which were more and more active around it as they were placing the equipment and delimiting the perimeter. It all had the feeling of a kind of assault on and conquest of the buoy. And yet, lonely and imposing, the cosmic buoy seemed to be way beyond the petty preoccupations surrounding it.

At the edge of the perimeter delimited by the melted ice, there was an unstable area out of which steam continuously came out and the water drained towards the valley, freezing very quickly afterwards. The ice had melted on a slope which made our access to the top easier. In the valley, things were even easier to handle because the ice had the natural tendency to "flow." There was a strange phenomenon there. Apart from the fact that the surface of the ground was completely dry, the perimeter underwent a continuous process of melting and freezing, thus drawing a kind of energetic "contour" of the area. Nobody knew yet what determined the maintenance of that phenomenon, which obviously helped us a lot in our work, but it was clear that it came from underground where the buoy was rooted.

Our RV team already had a small hall mounted near the buoy, on its upper side at a distance of approximately 50 meters from it. There were also other small constructions for the other needs of the mission and for the personnel who were to remain there, taking turns. Going near the modular construction and climbing the easy slope of the mountain, I could see the cosmic buoy for the first time, clearly and closely.

It is important to convey the impression of massiveness inherent in the buoy which was made of platinum-like material that shone in the waters. From the top towards the base, its surface had something similar to veins, but they were not of a typical material but were made from a kind of light similar to laser light. Other than the massive metal body of the buoy, all elements and details were representations of this very special light which was sometimes phosphorescent and other times very clear, combining dark red and white color. From this vantage point, I noticed that the "collar" of the device was actually not material but was made of a very dense and orderly arranged light structure which manifested in a continuous and soft movement. In this dense and complicated light structure, I could distinguish some main patterns of direction which were from time to time underlined through a certain rhythm. A preliminary analysis of those signals had already been performed, and a kind of complicated code was established as an initial "trace" which was to be used as the starting point for a detailed study.

All of these technical elements, however, were not an impediment for the Americans. If it had been only that, it would have made a remarkable scientific discovery which they would surely have tried to understand in its every detail. The problem that had made them agitated was the fact that, following the first analysis of the light codes, they realized that something was about to happen in direct connection with the locations in Romania and Alaska. The matter became even more complicated when they analyzed the resultant to Jupiter's moon, Europa.

For the time being, nobody could understand the nature of the "threat," but they all agreed that something was going to happen. During a short informal analysis that was made to update the information for working teams, evidence was presented of a calculation that the complicated light symmetry represented some kind of "countdown." While I appreciated the lucidity of the team of scientists, and even though this option was easy to accept and could cause diverse reactions with unpredictable consequences at planetary level, the situation had also been analyzed from the perspective of another "logic." There were thus several objectives tied to the information light pulse of the buoy other than the one related to cataclysms and mass destruction. The analysis team presented the fact that this possibility of destruction did not fit into the profile of events which had taken place until then.

The difficulty in presenting such a situation resides in the fact that I am not allowed to talk about almost anything that happened there. Even the few mentions I have made here are due to the fact that the matter was a planetary incident and was observed by several states and therefore cannot be denied, at least not at the level of secret services. My story is therefore rather informative only in a general sense because security barriers do not allow me to even hint at what was found there and the final conclusions reached. As this implies an international involvement and some interstate agreements at a secret military level, I cannot reveal practically anything of these aspects, even more since I was part of the "front line" from the very first days of the incident.

Things are different, however, when I am referring to certain discoveries made on the territory of our country. Even though the conditions are almost the same, there is a significant degree of larger freedom to the degree that we are in "our own yard" so to speak. In the previous books, I have exploited this small advantage to the extent to which it was allowed.

The third day after our arrival at Macor Base, General Inossanto also arrived and was briefed on the first conclusions and personally analyzed the on-site situation. A secret meeting of the military chiefs then took place, and General Obadea was also present there. The advantage of working in such remote locations was that, from a political point of view, the diplomatic pressure was somewhat delayed, thus leaving our nerves a bit more relaxed. In this case, however, things were more complicated because several states claimed different interventions.

In the "evening," I would talk with General Obadea about the discoveries in the Orăştie Mountains as this subject was directly involved in our work there. The General knew that the respective area unexpectedly "resisted" any RV attempt to find out more about it which made the Americans even more reluctant. He preferred, however, not to talk about this. General Obadea was a direct man, a man of action who preferred facts to words. He was not comfortable in long discussions and tended to close them quickly and suddenly, without details. This is why I did not manage to find out too much from him, but mostly also because he did not have the necessary information either. It was the second time that I heard about this, but I thought it was not possible.

"But it is perfectly true," the General had assured me one evening when he was in a better mood. "Trust me, I don't like this situation either because it has created many problems. It's the only case where our department hasn't controlled the situation, and not because of our negligence but due to a succession of elements which have inevitably led to this. When we found out what was going on there and wanted to do something, it was already too late. This wouldn't have been a problem if there had been more information, especially in the archives. But, through various circumstances, this essential information has been lost and now there are only secondary elements connected to it which are of no real help to us. The Americans couldn't understand this, and this is why they suspected we were lying. In reality, it's the plain truth."

I then learned from General Obadea that, in 1994, several archeological sites were opened in the area of the Orăştie Mountains in order to better understand the military and administrative organizational structure of the old Dacians who lived in those areas. The idea seemed promising because digs had revealed relics of a much more complex life than had been suspected until then. At the end of a day, in one of the archeological sites, an event took place which has "frozen" our secret services ever since. One of the workers accidentally slipped into an underground chamber, and then, searching more closely, they reached an ensemble which was buried much deeper. What was discovered there has puzzled the leadership of the country to the highest degree, and they reunited for an emergency Supreme National Defense Council (SNDC) meeting. An RIS and an on-site investigation then followed.

"But, you'll learn all of this from Cezar," the General told me. "I delegated him to study the matter thoroughly, even if, in a way, we've lost 'the key' to it. He'll explain in more detail because he handled this case for several years. The attention of our secret services was not only drawn by the fact that the location represents an essential strategic point of this country but also by the fact that the discovery explains a lot about our people. It especially clarifies everything in our relations with the Hungarians and not just with them."

It was the first time I heard the General talking about this. In the beginning, the essence of the problem between the Romanian and Hungarian people was not a territorial claim but rather an ideological factor concerning the origins of the two peoples. There was once a time when the territorial claim prevailed. Now, there is once again a tendency to clarify the matter on historical grounds. In any of these stages that lasted several decades, the relations between the secret services of the two countries were very tense and had a direct impact on the masses which were manipulated by the Counter-intelligence Services.

I remained in Antarctica for three weeks, working almost 24/7 on solving the situation there. Our efforts were intense but did not change the situation at all. Even if I cannot provide any details, I will mention that one of the work discussions involved the area of the Earth's magnetic South Pole where new and amazing elements have been found. Paradoxically, what was believed would escalate matters to an interstate conflict actually tempered the situation almost instantaneously. There have been such beneficial influences for this purpose that the solution was found almost immediately and everyone seemed satisfied. Of course, there was still the unsolved problem of the cosmic buoy and especially its interference with Jupiter's moon Europa, but later analysis has shown that it was not really a threat but rather an update of an inner structure condition of the buoy which had only been potential until then. Until my departure, neither the cause of that update nor its nature could be established.

Upon my return, my presence was requested in the RV group in Maryland for a superior stage in the study and training of this ability. I remained there until the end of April 2007, developing my technique as well as valuable friendly relationships with some American officers. I returned to our country after a short stop in Germany; and in May, I was back at the Base continuing my tasks.

Meanwhile, Cezar had managed to settle things in the activity of the department. He had proven to be a good mediator between the interests of the department and the government and, with General Obadea's help, he had strengthened the cooperative relationship with the Americans which had become quite fragile following the incident in Antarctica.

During one of those quiet and splendid May evenings, after a long time, I once again had the opportunity to take a walk around the base with Cezar. I had taken advantage of a pause in his activity and had invited him to that relaxing walk, reminding him that he sometimes needed this too. He smiled, knowing that this was an expression of my wish to find out more from him. Amused, and in order to save me the trouble, he spoke.

"The General has told me that you talked about what happened in the Orăştie Mountains. Very well. Anyway, you've been directly involved in this matter through the incident in Antarctica so it is now natural for you to know what this is all about. But, as you already know, not even we have much information regarding this."

I briefly told him about my discussion with the General and asked him to give me more details about this matter in order to get a clear picture of it. Obadea was not a good story teller; and besides, Cezar knew all the details. Personally, I felt that the file was drawing me in particular, both through its deep mystery and because the subject had been avoided so many times until then. It was a very special matter even for Department Zero.

"It's the only file on this situation. Actually, the story is much more complicated."

This was the beginning of a story which has dazzled me and gave me a completely different view of our Romanian people. I already knew some elements about our past from the Projection Hall, but what I learned from Cezar that evening has given me the creeps and made me become more responsible and receptive to the origins and history of our people. Only then could I understand the true value of the fight against our people and the occulted reasons behind it. I promised myself to present all of these elements in detail in order for them to be judged by readers as well as possible. Beyond any speculation or more or less subjective interpretation, there is the truth discovered in the Orăştie Mountains and partially reproduced in the only existing file on this subject: the CRONOS file.

CHAPTER FIVE

THE ŞUREANU MASSIF

Cezar explained again, with more details, what I already knew from General Obadea. In the Nineties, there was a vast archeological program in the Orăştie Mountains, the purpose of which was to more precisely establish the identity of our people in the area of the Carpathians but also to better understand the fortifications and living system of the population of that time. After the revolution in 1989, the authorities made certain allowances for these purposes until censorship was instituted by hidden interests and political orders. During those days, archeologists were intensely active and many amazing results started to appear. Some works have been published on the discoveries made, but it seems that there was a time when everything stopped, almost all of a sudden. As usual, a lack of funds and necessary conditions for digging has been invoked.

"Actually, that's when that amazing discovery was made; and since it was a top-level state secret, everything stopped," Cezar explained. "There was, however, another aspect about which not even our secret services are informed: the discovery frightened them and they felt terror. As usually happens in such situations, they've acted blindly. Fear was so strong that they managed to do a better job than usual: they've hidden the place so well that it cannot be found again! A series of factors have contributed to this which explains the situation to a certain extent. At that time, however, it was crazy. Just think about the fact that something is discovered which cannot only alter this country but even the social, political and economic balance of the world. It's not about relics or artifacts nor even impressive structures such as the one in the Bucegi Mountains. There, something has been discovered which reduces everything, something like a singularity. They were not able to understand what they had seen on site, let alone study the matter. It's most ironic that, even if this was the greatest discovery ever made, it was the one to be closed the most quickly. And it was so well closed, that it has vanished again, completely. It's such a pity...."

"There hasn't been a similar proceeding to the one that took place in Bucegi?" I asked, amazed. "Haven't the same forces been mobilized?"

Cezar denied, shaking his head. As for me, I could imagine the turmoil and the activity taken during that time in order to fix the huge error made. But it seems that all efforts have been in vain, and now my good friend displayed quiet resignation in front of a closed matter.

"Not only was the usual protocol for such situations not followed, but the so-called preliminary investigation, reduced to some questions, was done only by the local police station. Then, three RIS agents came and called Bucharest immediately. The representative sent from Bucharest immediately collapsed from the point of view of decision making. They were so scared that they believed that, for greater safety, the place had to be filled up and concealed until teams of specialists arrived. A concrete mixer was immediately brought in and they sealed the entrance themselves, laying soil with vegetation over it. They barely had time to make some photos. The rest of the file, which is very thin, represents the statement of the professor."

"They can't have forgotten the place," I said. "At least they came back quickly."

"This hasn't been possible," Cezar answered, looking afar. "This is the mystery of the whole matter, in its own special destiny. On the way back to Bucharest, the car transporting the three men had a terrible accident. They could barely save the few materials gathered in the file, but they also had problems there. Otherwise, we wouldn't have known almost anything except from the professor's statement. I was dazzled by the turn events had taken.

"But, weren't there any witnesses? Has nobody else known? Has nobody else seen that place?"

"Unbelievably, no. It has all happened so fast and the panic was probably so high that they left nobody near the place. The place is quite isolated anyway."

"What about the representative from Bucharest? There were four people after all. Did he come separately?"

"No, he died in the accident. But, one of the agents had already died at the site of the discovery. Or, better said, disappeared. The only intelligent thing they did after all was to write a brief protocol, until the concrete mixer arrived. Otherwise, nobody would have ever known what truly happened there. Even so, many questions remained."

I was dazzled. I had never heard of such a "matching" of events, but a small ray of hope appeared.

"What about the driver of the concrete mixer?"

"Obviously, this was the first lead we followed," Cezar answered. "He was a simple, poor man. He went crazy right there on the site of the discovery, and we couldn't get along with him. The agents had left the concrete mixer at a certain distance and had brought the concrete with them with which they filled the hole with a barrow. It seems that a small quantity was needed. Working barely for a couple of hours, they managed to conceal the place so well that it hasn't been found afterwards."

"I've never heard of anything like this! But, they could have searched the area systematically because they knew the general area, especially since you said that it was in the archeological site."

"Here's where the problems truly started. No, the place wasn't in the site. It was outside of it, not too far. But, let's say that wasn't the difficulty. After the incident, a special SNDC order was issued forbidding any research. It was a supreme order for top-level state secrets. From a certain point of view, they worked much more efficiently than in comparison with the case of the Bucegi Mountains discovery. They have been very discreet and have acted quickly, without hesitation."

"What do you think about this?" I asked, curious to see Cezar's reaction. He was silent for a while, reflecting upon his answer.

"Honestly speaking, I think they've taken the only correct decision. If it hadn't been so, I am not sure that we would have talked so relaxed here today because it is highly probable that the political, economic and military situation of our country and of other countries would have changed radically. Or, it would have been highly probable for that to happen. Trust me, I am not exaggerating when I'm telling you this."

"An order can be overcome in time, especially if there are enough interests," I said, looking for a breach.

"But not this order. And it wasn't only the decision itself, but a series of collateral measures they've taken in order to prevent the event you're referring to. They've moved very well and, at least from this point of view, things were done impeccably. The chance was, if I can say so, that there were very few witnesses and this is what enabled things to happen like this.

"There have also been speculations concerning the car accident, but thorough research has been done and they've reached the conclusion that it hadn't been provoked. The ones interested wouldn't have had time for this even if they wanted to because it all happened very quickly and nobody from the other state structures had clearly found out what was there. Furthermore, if there had been an intention to eliminate witnesses, how can it be explained that the file, small as it was, was found in the crashed car? Normally, it was the evidence that should have also disappeared immediately, but this hasn't happened. But, there have been some attempts to do this afterwards, and this is why special measures to protect the information in this file have been taken."

"So, you're saying that they've forbidden any research in the area; but they could have done the same in Bucegi, and you can see the current situation. It's still a top state secret. You can have an idea of its existence but no concrete information. You know very well that this, together with hiding the area, is what makes the value of the secret."

"I've told you, in this case, things were different. No diplomatic agreement or negotiation would have been possible. It would have simply been a matter of immediate military attack with international escalation in less than 24 hours. Scenarios have shown that there would have been no possibility of control. The inevitable leak of information would have almost immediately blinded any reasoning on the subject. Fortunately, even if the problem was very serious, this seriousness is what has offered the simple and efficient solution. Even if I am very sorry that our department hasn't received access there, I must admit that things couldn't have happened any other way. It's hard to get used to the idea but only until you get to know the situation in detail. You then understand very well why it had to be so."

It was dark and I noticed that Cezar had hinted at returning to the Base. As I was very interested in this subject, I insisted with one more question.

"But, you haven't told me anything about the professor. After all, it seems that he is the only remaining link to the discovery."

Cezar looked at me somewhat sadly.

"Professor Constantin was our only chance to find out something. He was a special man, very cultivated and serious. Unfortunately, I only had access to him for a couple of hours. He seemed to come from another world, almost completely withdrawn from the reality around him. He was immediately taken over, and we've lost any trace of him. They said it was a top state secret. Nobody has ever heard of him since. I myself was very anxious to find out what had happened there because I had received an order from General Obadea to handle this case exclusively right after the deadly accident of the three. It was the hand of Providence that the professor wasn't also taken in the car but remained at the village police station until the following day. I think this was the only "mistake" of the agents, but it was a fortunate mistake for us, if I can say so. Anyway, I didn't find out too much, or at least not in detail as I had hoped because they came after him at five o'clock in the morning. I couldn't do anything, but I knew I would never see him again."

"Why couldn't you find out all that you wanted?"

"He either didn't talk or spoke seldom with long pauses. He would stare at the emptiness and I could notice that, in some moments, he felt a certain panic. The poor man made efforts to work with me, but it seems that the psychical tension was overwhelming for him. It is from him that we have practically all of the content of the file related to this case."

I then expressed a hunch I had for a couple of months.

"Isn't that the file from the special box which you asked me to bring you?"

Cezar immediately confirmed my suspicion.

"The professor is the one who had the inspiration to take the most photos. There were nine photos totally. The agents made only four, with a Polaroid camera, out of which two have been completely destroyed in the accident. And, of course, we also had the professor's statement which I did manage to obtain. It was very difficult, but I succeeded. I made the transcription on the same morning when they came for him, prior to their arrival. Because I didn't have enough time, I made a summary of the statement given by the professor a few minutes before. There are only a couple of pages, but I gave the agents the recorded tape only. I then announced to the General that the recording could become a serious problem in the future. In the afternoon of the same day, he called me to tell me that he had personally received the tape and had it destroyed in his presence and in the presence of the SNDC who had organized an emergency meeting. This is when they decided to stop everything from the very beginning."

"Do you think that you would have discovered the place eventually?" I asked.

"We had jurisdiction over the case. Others would probably have intervened quite soon because, at that time, the General's influence was not that high and our department still had a lot of things to settle. But, given the interest I had for the case, especially after I found out from professor Constantin what it was all about and saw the photos, I can say that yes we would have found the place even if it would have involved a lot of work. In the beginning, it seemed like looking for a needle in a haystack, but we would have eventually managed to start a wider action of digging the area around the site. It would have been a lot of work, but we would have had many chances to discover the location. It's much better for our country and people, however, that it has all been stopped."

"The General told me that you did intensive research afterwards. If you said that the action in the area had stopped, what did you want to find out?"

Cezar smiled, getting up and making a few movements to warm up his body.

"It was a rather individual study which has helped me structure a certain opinion in our department. It's also useful to me now when I am handling certain matters of ethnicity and national security within our secret and counterintelligence services. Professor Constantin was a good historian and linguist. He had intensely studied the history of Dacia even if, to be correct, there has never been a country with that name. This is the name given to the area by the Romans after its conquest: Dacia Felix. Obviously, the word *felix* or happy refers to the actual Roman robbers, but we have no proof that our ancestors had named it Dacia. I was telling you that professor Constantin had studied those aspects and had some important theories concerning the prehistory of this region. He had done specific archeological digs and was considered an archeologist specialized in Neolithic cultures. I've corroborated his statement with the research done in the area of ancient cultures from the Carpathians area because his main idea was that these people were the origin of any existing cultural development, at least in Europe, and that the Romanian language is actually the primary language or, better said, the Indo-European language. It wasn't his own idea, but he had set for himself the objective of making it well known in all national and international media, based on sources and competent research previously done. He was a good man but a little naive, especially in the current complicated context where the fight to destroy any idea or evidence of this is very passionate."

As he had many times in the past, Cezar had managed to completely surprise me. I only had a general knowledge about this subject, like the kind taught in school; but suddenly, my heart was filled with great joy as I could feel that this was a permanent source of valuable information.

"I've become more and more interested in this matter and have even studied it in detail," Cezar continued. "There are some people in our country whose erudition and analytical talent in this sense is brilliant. Honestly, people should read at least a summary of their works, but the problem is still obscure interests and their manipulation of information, especially the intervention of international bodies which knowingly ignore the valuable documentation and information. We will continue to talk about this."

We returned to the base and spent a lovely evening. The atmosphere was so pleasant that Cezar agreed to continue our interrupted discussion. He then gave me more details of the events that took place after the discovery in the Orăştie Mountains.

Cezar told me that the entire matter got started when one of the archeological sites in that area had just been found and the digging was only at the beginning. To do the work, locals were usually hired and paid by the day. They were unqualified workers or unemployed people. The problem was that they would not come to work every day or they would stay only a small period of time so that, for many such sites, works progressed with difficulty. Furthermore, archeological sites were spread over a wide area in the Orăştie Mountains, the Deva area and the Sarmizegetusa Regia area. The site managers had to handle two or even three sites at the same time, moving from one to another and their presence in a place would slow down the work rhythm in another. An interesting area for digging also included the Şureanu Mountain which is part of the Orăştie group of mountains. On one of its slopes, in a kind of gully, an archeological site had been opened for a couple of days. They had drawn up a plan to divide the sections with a lot of interest and had set the work parameters. Digging had only started for a couple of days when it all began.

One afternoon, the workers left early due to the excessive heat that was making their work a lot more arduous. That site was under the direct supervision of professor Constantin who, as was natural, remained to the very end in order to write the field notes and prepare what was necessary for the following day. Apart from him, there was another worker on the site who was the son of the host in the nearby village where the professor lived during the archeological digging. From the professor's statement, we learned that the young man had gathered the digging tools and had taken them about 100 meters away from the site and towards the west where they had improvised a sort of rudimentary storage area with a "hood" for night time. Although it was in the middle of the forest, the storage area was in a rocky environment. There was no clear clue beyond that statement. Furthermore, nobody knows for sure what made the boy hit that "hood" with a pickaxe. Maybe it was the desire to make a great show of zeal by levelling the surface where the cover was placed. The professor told me only that he had heard the pickaxe sounds and had seen the boy digging but continued his own work.

At a certain moment, he heard a short cry and a stifled sound as if someone was falling. Worried about the boy, whom he could no longer see, the professor quickly went to the place. He got there after approximately one minute and found the young man laughing gladly at the discovery he had just made. His strong hits with the pickaxe had moved part of the rock and the ground on which the hood was placed. He probably hit a niche in the rocks with the pickaxe and its strength led to their falling. The fact is that the rock broke and crashed about a meter and a half into the ground, thus uncovering a hollow place under the surface of the ground. The boy was unharmed except for minor scratches. When the professor got there, he immediately realized that it was a kind of underground chamber with an almost regular shape about five meters long and about four meters wide. He also went down into that hole and examined it carefully, but his initial hopes of making a great discovery seemed to shatter very quickly. Even if he could observe a certain regularity in the shape of the chamber, he realized that it was a purely natural formation that was the result of a normal geological process. The structure of the rocks on the walls and the agglomerations at the edges of the chamber clearly showed that there had been no human intervention. Furthermore, the place was completely empty with no trace of previous human presence there. Disappointed, the professor was examining the place out of professional routine when he noticed a narrow slit in one of the corners of the small cave through which he could feel a strong air draught. With his hopes a bit higher, he instructed the boy to try and enlarge the air hatch.

After a few strong blows, the limestone rock cracked and a new opening was visible, this time a narrower one. While checking that small passageway, the professor sent the boy to bring the protection equipment and the flashlights. Through the newly created slit, no man could pass so they had to enlarge it more and the professor worked along with the young man. After a couple of minutes, they managed to break a larger rock and lit the area beneath it which proved to be a smooth slope going under the dome formed by the ground of the cavern where they were. This slope led further west at a distance from the archeological site. Delighted with the new discovery, Professor Constantin decided to explore what seemed to be an original limestone system. Even though it was something unusual for that place and because it did not seem too difficult, the archeologist decided to begin the exploration immediately and planned to perform more thorough research the following day. Accompanied by the boy, he carefully went down through the slit they had created and, bending as much as he could, he went forwards down the slope. The soil was almost smooth and the first thing that raised questions was that it was covered in a kind of gravel. At first, the place was quite claustrophobic; but after approximately twenty meters, it became considerably larger. Fifty meters after entering the second slit in the ground, Professor Constantin and the boy could easily walk standing up and the slope went even lower. The sides of the cavern could not be observed, but the professor suspected they were quite far away by the sound of his voice inside the cavern. He then stated that he had begun to feel a bit unsafe and slightly fearful, but he quickly encouraged himself and moved on. At a certain point, he noticed that the nature of the rocks on the ceiling had suddenly changed and in front of him, at a distance of approximately eight meters, there was a vertical wall. The professor also noticed some very beautiful glitter had appeared on the ceiling in the strange shadows made by the light beam on the wall rocks and he interpreted them as Basalt reflections. When they reached the furthest wall of the cavern with the downward sloping ground, the professor experienced a sudden powerful emotion. On the clean ground, right near the vertical wall, there was a large opening in the shape of a demi-circle through which he could hear a deep thunder-like roar sounding like it was coming from far away. The impression of force and energy coming through the dark opening was so strong that the archeologist stopped, undecided whether to continue the investigation or not. He was also thinking about the young man accompanying him towards whom he had a responsibility as his employer. That was probably the crucial moment of the entire discovery. Its destiny would have been completely different if the two would have returned to the village and resumed research the following day together with a team which would have included archeologists and RIS personnel. But, as Cezar said, some things are ordered by reasons exceeding human understanding. In such situations, man is nearly powerless and follows a preestablished path to an overwhelming extent. There is, however, that small point of inflexion when one can choose, when all possibilities are fully available. But, after the choice is made, things develop rapidly.

"However, the professor decided to continue the investigation in spite of the bad feeling he had," Cezar continued describing the chain of those dramatic events. "He told me that he hesitated for a few moments, but after the irresistible impulse of the discovery, he overcame his conservative spirit. He was thinking that after his descent to the next level, which announced itself as more grandiose, he would have a better idea how he was supposed to organize the search for the following day. He still had doubts when, directing the flashlight to the opening, he became astounded because it descended underground at a very steep angle; but this time the ground bore the traces of a step. His heart racing, Professor Constantin bent down to study that structure better. He saw that the ground descended at an angle of approximately 60 degrees but in a manner that was sort of like waves. At the beginning, he imagined that the soil had formed steps due to the inclination, but he immediately noticed that there was only rock over which the same kind of weird gravel had been laid and the rock had been carved in the shape of steps. This had probably happened a long time ago because the so-called steps had crumbled and had many cracks, but this was clearly an artificial invention because he could still observe the rock carvings in certain parts."

Cezar then said that the professor suddenly remembered the camera he had brought along and quickly made a few photos. It was quite an old camera with a built-in flash, but some photos were good while the others were fogged. For example, out of the photos he made there, none were usable. Trembling with emotion, the two started to descend the steps into the abyss which seemed to stretch beneath them, but they soon realized that, in reality, the place where they had entered was much smaller than they had initially thought. The descent of those ancient steps did not exceed seven to eight meters vertically.

Professor Constantin was intrigued by two aspects: first of all, when entering that underground structure, he noticed that the ground was very clean and regular. Furthermore, the underground areas were completely empty and, in a certain way, even clean. The researcher has declared that he had the impression of "smoothness" as if somebody maintained that cleanliness all the time. There was no trace or unevenness on the ground. This experience resulted in an odd sensation, but maybe it had to do with the discovery they were about to make. After they entered the opening, the professor and the boy understood that the terrible roar, like a distant thunder, was coming from the passageway which was becoming larger in front of them. They were already about 200 meters away from the site, inside the mountain and at a probable depth of 30 meters. If it had not been for that sensation of "cleanliness" and even emptiness in the caverns they had come through, the professor would have probably given up and decided to continue research the following day. But, driven by the irresistible impulse of discovering the unknown and because the way forward was so easy and natural, he continued researching that passageway which had a slight downward slope. He told me that they descended like that for about half a kilometer. The passage became larger and larger but the ceiling remained relatively low, approximately three to four meters above ground. Even if the darkness surrounding them was frightening and the sensation was even more amplified by the stifled roar, the fact that the environment was so clean and perfectly dry with no unevenness or other obstacles encouraged the two to go forward while maintaining a sustained rhythm. While walking, the professor — amazed by that symmetrical inner structure of the mountain — briefly lit the almost smooth rock ceiling which only had a few deep slits encrusted in it. He could guess that the passage might have been the bed of a tumultuous underground river, but in order to be sure of this, he had to do more research, including a study of the side walls. The walls, however, were very distant and he could not see anything in the light made by the flashlight. The ceiling then started to rise, making the space inside even larger. After almost 500 meters of free descent, Professor Constantin noticed the first changes in the structure of the rocks which were beginning to have a pale shine in the light made by the flashlight. As the ceiling was already too high to perform a better check, he continued to walk, accompanied by the boy. As they went forward, that shine, somehow dull and full of mystery, was becoming more intense, meaning that it occupied a larger space on the ceiling. The passage through which they came then became flat, and they noticed that it took a left turn. After several such "serpentines," a kind of crossroads suddenly appeared in front of them. The passageway was split in two by a vertical wall. The left turn was recognized as being narrower because the professor could see its side walls with a strange shine that was sometimes sparkly. The right passage seemed larger; and logically, he thought that it might lead to a larger cavern. The ceiling and walls reflected the light even more with yellow nuances which helped them better orient themselves. As the right passage seemed much larger, brighter and more welcoming, they decided to continue their investigation through it.

"From the professor's statement, I drew the conclusion that this was the point from which the true discovery began," Cezar told me. "He went closer to the side wall and lit it better with the flashlight in order to see the cause of that dull shine. He was very troubled because he recognized massive gold ore which filled the rock wall. The same was valid for the ceiling and the dividing wall."

I was astonished.

"What? The walls of the corridor were covered in gold? That's fantastic! It seems almost unreal."

I imagined how I would have felt if I had been in the professor's shoes.

"It must have been very beautiful," I observed. "And what did they do? Did they move on?"

"Yes, the corridor took a smooth turn to the left and continued straight for approximately 150 meters. Then it rose a lot, up to 20-25 meters but maintained the approximately ten meters in width. At its end, they saw a blue light which seemed to come from the ground. He told me that it gave the feeling of waves and that it discreetly lit almost the entire final part of the corridor. The boy started to tremble and panicked."

"And they stopped there?" I asked, impatiently.

"No," replied Cezar. "The professor had discovered something magnificent. He stated that the gold ore covering the side walls and the ceiling which had that mysterious shine had 'gathered' on the right wall in a sort of 'vein' which was approximately ten meters thick and then became larger, like a funnel, gradually covering the entire wall. It was not gold ore however. It was pure gold."

Being unfamiliar with this subject, I was not very impressed.

"You don't understand the importance of the situation," Cezar observed. "There is no such thing in this world. No mine on this planet had ever contained such a seam. Generally, gold mines have a more or less pure gold ore which is later processed, by using quite difficult methods, in order to extract relatively small quantities of gold from a few tens or hundreds of kilograms and even up to tons of earth. This happens, however, after a long exploitation of the respective mine and only if it is rich in ore. Anyway, there are rules of national security concerning such mines. All the gold in the mine is never completely extracted and they must be closed before the ore is exhausted. Just think that gold represents safety, stability, and prosperity anywhere on this planet. Any economy longs for it; any country fights for it. The advantage in this respect is that it only appears in small quantities in comparison with other inferior metals. Or, maybe this is actually the great disadvantage which makes it so wanted. Many interests occur in this case."

I knew this very well but only from the point of view of counterintelligence.

"I've read the ROŞIA MONTANA file. I know it's very complicated, but I haven't studied its economic implications in depth," I said.

"It would have been a good idea because you would now have a clearer view of the situation. It's notorious that the Romans took about 200 tons of gold and 300 tons of silver after winning the war with the Dacians almost 2000 years ago. In Rome, there were continuous feasts for four months together with tax exemption for a year as well as donations to the population. There was also the building of that architectural complex which included the column for which Trajan ordered moving an entire hill."

"So, they had about 120 Sundays successively," I calculated, astonished.

"Yes, and they celebrated every day in Roman style. Doing that to a people means destroying them, diminishing them, and wearing them away through annihilation of their moral and inner values. Maybe that was a major cause for the fall of the Roman Empire as such actions leave serious traces. And, consider the fact that I was only speaking about the gold which the Dacians already had, not to mention what the Romans extracted from Roşia Montana for approximately 150 years afterwards. But, even so, this wasn't 'Decebal's treasure' which history mentions as a legend." *

"But, it has never been found. You know that there are implications here," I said.

---

* Decebalus was a king of the Dacians whose capital was Sarmisegetusa in Transylvania. He ruled from 87-106 A.D. as a great warrior and irritant to the Romans. With Roman captives, he diverted the river Sargetia which ran past his palace. Having created a cavity, he deposited a vast amount of treasure which included gold and silver. Covering it with his stones and earth, be returned the river to its natural course. He deposited other treasure in nearby caves. Bacilis was a companion of Decebalus who was eventually captured by the Romans who persuaded him to reveal some secrets of the buried treasure in order to recover it for themselves.

"Back then, only part of it was found due to Bicilis's treason. This is the origin for the Romanian word *bicisnic** which means cursed man, a very evil man who causes much suffering."

"He has practically betrayed his people," I said, shaken.

"Yes, it was an important turn in our history. But, you should consider the fact that the same quantity of gold was later taken by the Austrian-Hungarian Empire for a long period of time, for a few hundred years, also through mining. Don't forget how much gold was taken by the Turkish people during the Middle Ages and during the rule of the Phanariots; and, of course, the difficult problem with our country's treasure that was taken by the Russians; and not once, but twice, at the end of the First and Second World War."

I felt a feeling of partial frustration; but on the other hand, I felt admiration and joy that this country has had so much of this precious metal.

"Romania's national gold reserve for economic stability is now a bit more than 100 tons. The Romans, however, have taken twice as much, not to mention the ones who followed. These are proven facts. Nobody can say it never happened. These are historical realities. But, what I'm trying to underline is that all of this cannot compare to Professor Constantin's discovery in the Şureanu Massif. It's like comparing the Earth with the Sun. What is there is beyond any imagination."

"But, I understand that, after all, it was only a seam of pure gold of impressive dimensions."

"Even if it had been only that, it would have dazzled any geologist and solved almost every economic problem of this country for a very long period of time. A gold sea, in the very rare cases when it occurs, is an incrustation of small variable-size pieces ranging between a few centimeters up to a few tens of centimeters. It seldom exceeds one meter. The reason for this is that gold is rarely found in its natural compact state in one place; and in 99% of the cases, it is found as ore with either a bigger or smaller concentration of this noble metal. But, what the professor saw there is practically a geological impossibility; and if he hadn't had the inspiration to take some photos which are attached to the file — to be honest — I would have doubted the truth of his statement."

Cezar then invited me to go to his office. He opened his personal safe and took out the special glass fiber box containing the CRONOS file.

"It's a very special box. It has been designed by the English, by a company that designs for the aeronautics industry. It has a special iris reader which opens it. The built-in chip analyzes the condition of the iris and, if it doesn't fit into certain parameters of body relaxation, the box doesn't open. This was meant to prevent situations of stress when hasty decisions might be taken or

---

* In Romanian, the word *bicisnic* also translates as rascal.

threatening instances. It also has a double safety system on opening. After accepting the iris print, it requests the vocal print of the authorized person."

"So, it can't be forced or manipulated when opening."

"Theoretically, there is a chance, but the possibility is minimal. At any attempt which differs from the established protocol, it has an instantaneous self-destruct mechanism. There is practically no time or chance to save anything."

Cezar placed his iris near the digital reader and uttered a password. I could hear a brief click sound before he removed the lid. He took the thin file and opened it. Astonished, I looked inside and saw that there was only a magnetic card and a small parallelepipedal device, a bit bigger than the card. I looked at Cezar, questioning him with my eyes wide open in astonishment.

"It's a unique reader designed especially for this card. In its turn, the card can only be read with this device which can only interpret this card. Besides that, it can only be connected to a single computer which has special software installed."

Cezar connected the reader to his laptop and introduced the card. On the screen, I saw several encoded instructions. He wrote something, and I could see for the first time the contents of the CRONOS file, in electronic format.

"It's a random derived function which allows tracking the material in real time but only if the password mechanism is known," Cezar explained. "It's not enough to introduce the primary code in order to see the file information on the screen. At certain intervals, when the program requests me to do so, I must introduce a new variable which allows it to continue the presentation of the file. If I don't introduce this key in due time, the program is blocked and doesn't allow the presentation of the material. Thus, you can only have access to bits and pieces of the information and never to everything at the same time. These are maximum security systems that were designed when the whole device was ordered."

"I expected to see the file with the original information," I said, amazed at the extraordinary security.

Cezar laughed, teasing me.

"And why not a few presentation samples? Seriously now, I can see that you haven't understood the importance of that discovery or of its possible consequences if its location had been accessible. How could you imagine that we would have kept the original file here? At that time, after the SNDC order, there was even a proposal to destroy the unique record and all the information it contained. It was a border-line decision, but it was decided that it was a good idea to keep the information under the reserve of exceptional security measures."

"Who has jurisdiction over this case now?" I asked. "Considering your explanation, I'm amazed that the file is here, even in this highly secured form."

"At that moment, nobody knew about the case. It wasn't just a case, it was a matter of state, the highest matter of national security. It was the exclusive task of the Supreme National Defense Council to immediately establish a set of drastic measures: the file would have only one original and no copy; it had to be secured accordingly; it had to remain closed in the safe of the Treasure Chamber of the National Bank; and access to its content was possible only in a joint session of the SNDC. Of these, only the matter of its special security had to be solved. There was an original project and a preliminary solution with a heavier device than the one you see here but which was also efficient in securing the file. Even so, it continued to be stored at the National Bank. In 2003, after the discovery in the Bucegi Mountains, there have been certain reasons which caused it to be moved to another secure location. It was also then that the current protection system of the box you're looking at was ordered."

"But, you said that there was only one original counterpart," I said, puzzled.

"It was believed that it was better to have a copy of the file, which we hold here, but one that is encrypted with special algorithms. General Obadea has argued that it was best for our department to hold this copy. The way he managed the crisis in Bucegi, which was critical at that time, has greatly contributed to his success in this respect. There have subsequently been several circumstances which have favored the partial passing of this file into our jurisdiction. As I said, there are good reasons for this, but I can't give you any details.

Right now, there are two such special deposit boxes. One contains the original file in a secret location; and the one stored here, which is the only copy of the file and is encoded as you could see. Anyway, even the storage of this box is random. There is a team from another RIS department that handles this by transporting the briefcase containing this special box to certain locations, at certain intervals of time, without knowing what they carry. Only the SNDC and our department know all the details about this. The box is now held at the base due to the link with the incident in Antarctica. There was even the special situation when I had to ask you to bring me the box to that place personally because there was an emergency of communication with American units. I had no choice. The special team for this intervention wasn't available in that precise moment, and it would have been too long before they could have mobilized anyway because they would have come from Bucharest."

I now had a clearer view of the situation. Cezar showed me the copy of the file. I saw on the screen the protocol written by the agents, Professor Constantin's statement, and especially the photos, which were indubitable proof of the discovery. Some of the photos made by Professor Constantin were very clear, especially the two showing the massive seam of pure gold on the rock wall and then its sudden expansion to the whole cavern. I was perplexed.

"Here you can see that the seam covers the whole mountain," I said with a certain reluctance.

"You can see for yourself — there is no doubt. It's truly unbelievable, but proof can't be denied."

I looked at the two photos for a long time. Even though there was a certain obscurity, especially on the edges, the rock wall of the passage could be clearly distinguished with the intrusions of nuggets of shining gold. Then, they quickly converged to the middle of the wall where they gathered to the mouth of a seam of pure gold, almost two meters thick, that stretched irregularly towards what looked like the continuation of the passage, to the left. Or, maybe it was the other way around, whereby intrusions of gold ore started to form from that seam and then dissipated more and more as they were farther away from the seam. The gold "vein" was perfectly pure, with no intrusion of rock or any other metal. I could notice some massive irregularities in its thickness, as if it had been roughly carved with a powerful tool; thus removing massive pieces of pure gold, true lumps of that precious metal. This was, however, only an impression caused by the shadows of the indentations and elevations of the seam. If somebody had truly intervened and removed gold pieces in such a rough manner, it would have surely left much rougher traces. In the photo, however, the "relief" of the seam was irregular but smooth and in soft curves, all of which made me believe that it was in its natural state, just as it had formed. The second photo was dazzling because it showed the gold seam becoming larger and suddenly enclosing almost the entire wall, stretching towards the ceiling. It was practically a mountain of gold. I looked at Cezar silently, unable to say anything.

"I think you now realize what is involved here," he told me very seriously.

I than looked at the next two photos which showed the passageway in depth. The first one showed the ground and part of the side wall. It had all become solely yellow metal: the floor, the side wall and also, as I could see from the previous photo, the ceiling. In the part shown in this new photo, near the wall, at a distance of approximately half a meter, I saw something like an elevation, also made of gold and solid with the floor, that was shaped like a parallelepipedon but somehow rounded on the edges. It had a slight irregular indentation; and in parallel with the long side, I could see delimited in the ground something that might have looked like an Egyptian ancient scroll full of hieroglyphics. But, the encrustations were not hieroglyphics but clear signs of some sort of writing with lines and precise geometrical shapes. In practical terms, it was a rectangle inside of which these signs were scribbled. Almost refusing to believe it, I spoke with amazement.

"This exceeds any expectation! There are clear traces of someone's presence there! What does it represent? A tomb?"

"We also thought so at first and gave the formal scheme of this elevation to a specialized laboratory. They told us that, following an interactive analysis, their final conclusion was that the distortion in the ground of the passageway was actually a kind of bed. Anyway, it was something on which someone had obviously sat down repeatedly. Just imagine our surprise when we heard this. I couldn't find out any more information from the professor because he hadn't paid too much attention to that place. So, we had to analyze the situation for ourselves, using the image in the photo as our only guide. But, we couldn't guess too much. The complex analysis sent in by that laboratory justified every indentation in the metal and apparently left no room for doubts of the final conclusion. The only question was how it had been possible for that indentation which, in a way, vaguely took the shape of a human body to form; and the only plausible answer was that, because the metal was pure, it was also quite soft. In time, due to repeated friction, that weak erosion took place and the metal took the shape of the human body. But, even if it were so, this must have happened over a long period of time, maybe even a few hundreds of years. Another alternative theory was that the parallelepipedon had been artificially deepened a bit by carving, but this couldn't explain the soft shapes of the indentation. One way or another, they had probably somehow finished before that place was used as a place to sleep. A bed made of pure gold."

"Have the signs been studied? Has their meaning been understood?" I asked with curiosity.

"Yes and it's been troubling. We've ordered this study both in Romania and in three other famous world universities in order to have multiple references. The convergence of the results has convinced us of the authenticity of the interpretation. They said that part of the text might be deciphered, but another part, which seemed much older, was unknown. The respective writing couldn't be identified, not even approximately. This raised a new set of assumptions because it proved that several persons had passed through that place during different periods of time. I don't know what could be the cause of living in that place and under those conditions. Personally, I think it could only have been about highly spiritual actions, possibly by priests who withdrew from the world; but even that hypothesis is somehow frail. After all, if they wanted to withdraw for prayer and meditation, they could have done so in many other places above ground. It's true that there is very important occult symbolism involved, that of descending into the cave, but it's clear that the respective place was so privileged that very few people have had access to it. Otherwise, the traces left would have been more numerous and of a different nature. And, if they weren't priests, then who were those beings and with what purpose did they remain in that place? It's a mystery we haven't deciphered."

We both remained silent for a while. I then asked a question.

"What is the translation of the text? I mean, that which was understood."

Cezar displayed that information from the file on the screen. There were actually several documents attested by the institutions that had performed the study as well as a final document which presented the comparative analysis. There were slight differences or nuances in the text, but they were not significant. The text was very short and cryptic:

KR – IO; SAL-MOŞ, HERE IS FOREVER,
THE WORLDS UNITE

An explanatory document was also attached to the file.

"A lot of work has been done for this analysis, and I was also interested to study the subject. Actually, it can't be regarded by itself because it is intrinsically related to everything which represents and signifies the ancient origins of the Romanian people."

I looked a bit at the analysis, but it was too complicated for my knowledge at that time so I asked Cezar to make a summary of it for me and he agreed.

"Here, elements of linguistics are combined with the study of civilizations and cultures because they explain each other," he said. "The main idea, underlined in very competent studies performed by Romanian linguists, out of which one is very special, is that the Romanian language is the primordial language, practically the only language in Europe. And, I am not talking out of a cheap or unjustified spirit but from a perspective based upon references and studies performed by eminent researchers which can only be contradicted out of bad will or ignorance."

"Okay, but anyone can consider this statement about the Romanian language as blasphemy or can at least 'ironize' and mock it," I said.

"Of course they can, but what do you prefer: a worthless attitude of this kind or evidence and comparative studies which leave no room for interpretation? On the one hand, there are aspects here which involve the ignorance of many foreign and Romanian 'researchers.' On the other hand, there are state and geopolitical interests which refer to complex influences. Who could think that the Romanian language is the original language for all Indo-Europeans? The university "conceptions," which in reality are dogmas, have quickly imposed and formed a sort of obstacle to the correct information with regard to getting information to the public. A few 'historians' and career 'linguists' have imposed a line of thinking and knowledge which is now like a seal over the truth and must be removed. Then, it's also about the superiority displayed by the great European states or cultures which don't even consider the possibility that the primordial civilization was in the area of the Carpathians and, more precisely, on Romanian territory. Apart from being a matter of snobbery, it also shows a certain hidden fear of the consequences of admitting this. Just think what it would mean for the pride and 'greatness' of great empires or cultural traditions. How could the governments of the respective nations explain their history and national 'pride' which has, at many times, been the basis for obtaining economic advantages as well as diplomatic and even territorial influence? For these nations in particular, acknowledging such a fact would be a disaster with a collapse of their state 'dignity' as an unacceptable fact. In most cases, but especially in sensitive cases, this is why history takes a fake and fabricated turn. It is done in order to serve much higher interests."

"But, this would require a sustained and correlated effort," I said. "I am referring especially to the mystification of the problem of the spoken language, not to mention the cradle of civilization."

"It's easier than you can imagine. It's enough to have just two or three 'competent' opinions of prestigious university professors which then results in an infiltration of the respective theory into the general academic environment. This is a quick take over and then, with small steps, it is spread through schools to the lower environments, even to the rural ones. It is a known fact that a child's way of thinking is shaped in school, and what they learn there is considered to be true. Generally speaking, the population absorbs what is served as a result to their daily concerns. The idea is something like, 'leave it, specialists know better; we shouldn't be concerned with that.' In other words, if 'experts' say it is so, then it must be true.

"I do not want to generalize, but I am telling you almost for sure that what I have said concerning the culture, language, and origin of our people is the truth. We have colleagues from another department who handle these aspects because, after all, things have turned into a matter of national security. But, you know the situation here. We have certain references at our base here and have analyzed the matter for a long time and know its implications. You'd be amazed to find out the struggle that is taking place at this level and the interests that are involved. But, that's not what I was talking about. I was referring to the fact that the Romanian language is regarded as a 'surrogate' result of Latin, Greek, Slavic, Hungarian, Turkish and many other influences. If you search any Romanian dictionary, you'll see that every word is considered to have an 'influence' or a 'derivation' from another language which is considered older and with more authority. This inversion of values is unbelievable. Besides proving the dogma I was referring to, it also demonstrates a shallow analysis of the matter."

"Yes, it's frustrating, but not because it bothers me but because the truth is mystified; and I understand that this has been done willingly, many times," I said. "I keep wondering how this linguistic 'transformation' has been permitted."

"I told you that you should consider a comparative study. They analyze the same aspect in several languages and influences and reach a final conclusion. But, this involves a lot of work and having a high aspiration to find out the truth. This is where the problem lies: there are very few people who perform such complex and toilsome scientific studies. Instead, they prefer the laziness of an embarrassing acceptance of some 'studies' concerning the Romanian language and customs of our people that were performed in the past by certain scholars who are not Romanian. After that, the processing and spreading of the information is just routine because it's much easier to talk nonsense, repeating what others say and even contributing to their stupidity, than to study, look for competent sources and judge for oneself these aspects that are based upon a profound and authentic background."

"But, you could be influenced here," I observed. "You could be accused of being subjective."

"Not if you go to the origins. For example, the word 'x' can be found both in the Romanian and the German languages. Who gave the word to which language? It's easy to say that Romanians are fools and have always taken from others. This is the very way I was talking about when I was referring to the dictionary. But, a very important element in the structure of the Romanian language has been discovered which proves the contrary, which is the truth."

"What element are you talking about?" I asked, curiously.

"I'm talking about the fact that a language has two fundamental aspects: it has to be organic and must have its own roots."

"What does this mean? What do you mean when you say organic?"

"I mean to say that the respective language can explain any element based on its own resources, without appealing to other languages or influences. And, the root is always assimilated with a basic element, with something primordial from which everything started and based upon which word families were formed. As far as we know, the Romanian language is the only language that has these essential characteristics. This gives us a unique complexity of the popular language; and, what is even more important, this complexity is based on its own roots, on the very roots which have formed the language. By comparison, in many other modern languages — out of which French is a good example — there are very few original terms which express their ideas because the respective languages don't have their own basis. Of course, this idea has been silenced or simply ignored."

"Do you mean that they don't have their own roots?"

"No, they don't have basic roots. They can't be found in their own linguistic resources. There aren't any essential particles which started the formation of word families. We can only find them in the Romanian language. For example, the root *bor*, which doesn't exist in any other language, has generated almost 500 words. The same applies to the root *ma*, which is also very important, although it has generated fewer words. Other cases of greater importance are not known."

"Do you mean that these roots have led to the formation of words?"

"Yes, the roots have led to the formation of both words and word families and these word families are classified in different categories. These categories are related to an immediate utility, such as digestion or storage. The root method allows the discovery of the basic language which led to the occurrence of a word in one language or another. This is how it was concluded that the Romanian language is the basis for all Indo-European languages. This is truly a 'hit,' but everyone seeks to avoid it."

"It's only natural. They'll say that it is not the root for the respective word or word family. Maybe you drew the conclusion that it was so."

"They can't do this because that root is the fundamental root in the peasants' language. Only the popular or peasants' language is authentic. The root *bor* means hole: *bortă, burtă* and so on.* For example, the word *borcan*, which also involves an empty space or an opening, is said to come from Bulgarian. What is the Bulgarian word family and how many words do they have which derive from the root *bor*? Maybe ten. Under these conditions, they practically don't exist in comparison with the almost 500 words identified in the Romanian language. The situation is hilarious. Not only did this Romanian word — and mine was just an example — not originate from the Bulgarian language, but it was actually the other way around. As we have hundreds of derivations of this root, this means they took it from us. Our peasants didn't organize congresses to invent words."

"It's not about inventing words, but there must have been a development," I observed.

"Of course. The development took place from simple to complex words. They started from monosyllabic roots: *ma, la, ta, ba* and others. As objects of activity and things were added to the universe they lived and worked in, they had to be named and people generally did this based upon what they already knew. It wasn't a science of inventing or composing words, but it was rather about the specific vibration of a thing, which ancient people felt much more clearly than we do nowadays. There is a huge difference between those times and now with regard to conception and spirituality."

"But, how can you explain disagreements if the language isn't a scientific process?" I asked, curious to know.**

---

* *Translator's note*: the Romanian word *bortă* means hollow, hole, cavern; the Romanian word *burtă* means belly; the Romanian word *borcan* means jar.

** The reference to disagreements refers to subject-predicate disagreements.

"The concept of disagreement doesn't exist. Peasants speak and distort words as they wish because, in the Romanian language, the meaning is retained. Actually, they do not distort words because they speak a tongue, not a language. A tongue has a much more complex meaning than the spoken language. It has more nuances and is more connected to the origins. This can be explained only if the language is organic, if it fundamentally exists through itself. It's the same for word order in phrases. In Romanian, you can twist words as you wish and place them in any order because, after all, the meaning stays the same. This is not possible in any other language. But, ever since the high language has been invented, we also have the concept of disagreement."

"That is what I wanted to ask. Many states have come up with a 'modern' language over the old vernacular. Why was this necessary?"

"This wasn't at all necessary. It was all about interests. There had to exist a so-called 'common' language for all of the people who made up a nation because, until then, on the territory of the respective country, there had been many dialects and people couldn't understand each other from one region to another. When states started to centralize, this aspect started to create administrative problems because it was difficult to coordinate and make oneself understood in tens of dialects or idioms which were actually different languages."

"But there must have been a basis for them."

"Of course there was. They have a common origin, but it has been blotted out in time because dialects aren't organic. They can't be explained through themselves but are always based upon something which initially existed. This is why, in time, they are blotted out. They become distant from the original state which led to their formation. No dialect can be explained through itself, but they are all explained through each other. At a certain point, this causes problems and this is why they have artificially created a so-called high language which they have officially imposed. This means people could continue to speak their dialect but also had to know the high language. This is the case of French, German, English and so on. Many times, a high language had to be imposed by force because it was the 'king's language' and those who didn't speak it weren't well regarded."

"And by what manner did those people learn the new language? Take the French for example. It's not easy to come and say, 'From now on, you will speak like this.'"

"They learn gradually. First, the King's Court learned; then, it was imposed in schools, universities, scientific environments and later spread, more and more, to all levels of the population. The French have only had their new language for a bit more than two hundred years."

"So, they've simply been forced to learn the language."

"There was a famous effort of the Greek government to impose an of-ficial language that is different from Demotiki, the name for the Greek popular language. They've tried to build up an artificial language called Katarevoussa, which is a dialect they tried to make similar to old Greek, in order to give themselves legitimacy as followers of the ancient Greeks. They've made huge efforts with money to teach the people and the children in schools, but they've failed to impose another language. The French have succeeded, but the process was different in their case. They haven't replaced a dialect with another one, but have distorted the Normans' language which was also a dialect."

"Well, in our case, they also say that our language has taken over the Latin language," I said.

"This Latinization of our language is a sensitive matter for many. First of all, Latin is a written language. It's an artificial language of scholars, but the Roman people spoke what is called today the Vulgaris Latin which was actually the Romanian peasants' language, the original primordial language. Roman locals didn't understand Latin as we know it today, which is the writ-ten Latin, because it had been created to separate the nobles from the vulg, to separate the rich from the poor."

"This is why they still say nowadays that the Vulgaris Latin is practically unknown," I said.

"Exactly. Because, in reality, it is the ancient Romanian language. They can't declare this; they can't even conceive it; but eventually you'll see that this idea will impose itself. It can't be any other way because this is the truth. The common European language is the Romanian peasants' language. There is no other peasants' language. Almost all word families from other languages come from the linguistic roots of Romanian. This is why they say that Roma-nian is the primordial language, the source language for all Indo-European languages."

"And, modern languages are in fact surrogates of the Romanian language," I said, rather for myself. "It makes sense because, otherwise, why bother to create an official language, as it was in the case of Greeks or others you've spoken about, if the language is independent and has its own origins?"

"From the point of view of ethnicity, today's Greeks are not the followers of the ancient Greeks. They don't know the ancient Greek language. It's like speaking Latin in Italy. You'd expect everyone to understand because every-body knows that the official language of the Roman Empire was Latin, and yet the people don't know this language. On the other hand, we Romanians understand everything. We can manage with all Romanic dialects. We even understand old French, the one spoken around the year 1000, even better than the French do. They need a dictionary for this. Even now, in certain areas of France, a primary Romanian language is still spoken. All that happened with the invasion of Western culture was caused by snobbery and facade. The bad luck of the Romanian people was that a couple of so-called 'intellectuals' have decided to adapt the Romanian language and culture to that of the French. They've tried to establish this relation without having a basis or a profound knowledge of the origins of our people and its multimillenary culture, preferring instead the French 'modern' civilization which is mostly an imitation."

"The fact that there were language fragmentations that made up different dialects on the territory of these countries and caused people to fail to understand each other is proof that they had no unity of language and culture," I said. "They can't impose that which does not exist."

"Romania is the only place in Europe where, on the whole territory, the people speak the same language and one which wasn't artificially created. It's always been this way. For as long as we have known, inhabitants of Moldavia, Oltenia, and Ardeal* have spoken the same language. Where else could something similar be found? We have no dialects. We have accents, but not dialects. Everywhere else, this is a disaster. In Germany, there are a few hundreds of dialects; in Italy, a few thousands; and in England, the same. This is better, however, than in some African countries where people sometimes can't understand each other from one street to another due to the different dialects they speak. This is the reality. But, going back, I was telling you that here in our country, in the area of the Carpathians, we can find the only language unity in Europe. Such a case cannot be found anywhere else."

"Do you mean that, in ancient times, Romanian was spoken everywhere?" I asked, dazzled.

"Yes, this was the situation. I am referring to the peasants' language which is the original language. Of course, in the process of moving off from the source language, many linguistic elements have gradually changed; but even so, one could easily be understood almost everywhere by speaking Romanian. On Trajan's Column, one can see how the Romans came and talked to the Dacians but without a translator. They spoke freely. So, there was a unique language in Europe. Ovid said about our ancestors, the Getians, that they were a bit foolish because he would come and talk to them and they would always laugh. Actually, the Dacians understood very well what he was saying, but they laughed at his altered idiom in comparison with the mother-tongue they spoke. It seems that Ovid later understood this and wrote a few verses in 'Getian' but they haven't been found."

"It's unbelievable how this unity of language has lasted for so long!" I said.

"As you go farther away from this center, everything crumbles with regard to language, culture, and people. Only here in Romania does there remain a unity."

---

* Moldavia, Oltenia and Ardeal are regions of Romania.

"Does this mean that, if I were to travel back to the Dacians' time or to Stephan the Great's time, I could understand what the people spoke back then?"

"I told you, if you speak the peasants' language as our authentic peasants know and speak it, your chances are great — but no weekend and fast food," Cezar joked.

"What does this mean? That the language we speak today is no longer the original Romanian language? It is another language?"

"No, not at all. In time, of course, some linguistic constructions have changed, but a language shouldn't be judged by these forms but by its roots which give meaning to words. These don't change. This is precisely the distinguishing feature of the Romanian language. It has kept its own resources ever since families of words appeared, but something in these words, their root as I told you, has remained unchanged and this is what makes you able to understand others in any other part of the continent, even if millennia have passed."

"Okay, but these roots can be marked by linguistic transformations until they become hard to recognize or cannot be recognized at all," I argued. "It's a possibility."

"This hasn't happened in the case of Romanian. Not only does it resist change for thousands of years and remain in its original form, almost unchanged, but even the small changes which are inherent to the passing of millennia are so small and have occurred with such difficulty that they are practically insignificant. For example, some of the strong consonants have turned into weak ones."

"Why?" I asked, with curiosity.

"Because the Romanian peasants, the true carriers of the original language, had the tendency over time to change some words by weakening the consonants. For example, *s* is an extra effort to utter; it's easier to pronounce *ş* than *s*. Then, why does *b* become *v*? For the same reason: because it is easier to pronounce; it is weaker. If you go to the countryside, you'll quite often hear *să aive*, instead of *să aibă*.[*] The same for *blahi* – as they were initially known in the early Middle Ages — they later became *vlahi*,[**] meaning the inhabitants of the southern part of our country. We also know about inversions of letters, especially at the beginning of words. But, all these are not basic changes but rather changes of the exterior form. The same applies to some ways of expression. They are all superficial and do not alter the basis for the language: its roots. It's just like, over time, you paint your house different colors, add an arch, and tear down a shed; but the building stays on its initial foundation. You'll recognize it no matter the color or the small exterior changes."

---

[*] Both words mean "to have"
[**] Both words mean "Wallachians"

"But, they have introduced changes to the fundamental verbs," I reminded him. "For example, they've changed sînt (meaning, 'I am/we are') with sunt (also means 'I am/we are'). Will this have major implications for the language?"

"Not at all. They've done so to be closer to Latin. These are forms introduced to better serve the political interests of the time. For example, communists came up with the word sînt and imposed it because, at that time, the language had to be more similar to the Slavonic language. But in Ardeal (commonly known as Transylvania) and Moldavia, they say îs, which is the short form for sînt. The people in the South, and I am referring to some inhabitants of the big cities, will say sunt out of snobbery, to show that they pronounce it correctly. Actually, it's nonsense because we can never say us as a short form for sunt because nobody would understand what you mean. But you do understand îs which is the short for sînt. Unfortunately, you can see that a certain effort is made — which actually lacks any substance — to change our language which is the origin of the other spoken languages when, in fact, these languages should be changed to be closer to ours."

"Well, efforts in this respect have been made by all of the others who came here; but you're right, they don't seem to have accomplished much," I observed.

"Not only did they not accomplish much, but they didn't accomplish anything," Cezar underlined with determination. "Over this country, tens of thousands of barbarian peoples have passed and conquered us in different stages of our history. They all came with their own language and culture which were more or less rudimentary. However, as even some foreign authors who are hostile to us admit, these peoples have all gone and left no traces of their languages and cultures. The Romanian language — or the Wallachian language, as it was known — has not borrowed any words from them even though it has always been in contact with these peoples' languages. For example, there is not a single Hungarian word which is common in the Romanian language. During 800 years of occupation by the Austrian-Hungarian Empire, they haven't managed to impose anything from the Hungarian language to ours. During the second world war, this was irritating for the Hungarian soldiers because they spoke Hungarian but the Romanians didn't know how to answer. They knew a bit, but Hungarians have never managed to make Romanians speak Hungarian and adopt their language, even if they remained under occupation for so long. And, it was 1940. Under these conditions, how can you think that the Romanization of the Dacians might have been possible in only 160 years as history has confirmed? The Austrian-Hungarians tried hard for 800 years and have failed."

"The idea is that uneducated people, brought to be soldiers, couldn't have made the Romanian peasants change their language," I observed. "Without dictionaries, schools or much of anything else, how could they have caused the peasants to give up their language?"

"But, even if that had been possible, it's proven that they've failed," Cezar explained, "and this shows that their language is not organic while Romanian is. For this reason, the Romanian peasants have never felt the need, and this also applies today, to change their language as they have all the basics and resources in this language. They do not need to borrow anything from another language in order to express themselves because they already have everything in their own lexicon. When you are satiated, no matter how much or how tasty the food offered to you is, you'll not want any more because there is no reason to want any more food."

"Indeed. Our language hasn't changed under the Roman occupation just as it hasn't under any other occupation. One could argue, however, that we weren't even here so there was nothing to change."

"Then, whom have the Romans conquered?" questioned Cezar.

"The Latin chronicles call them Dacians. The Greek chronicles call them Getians, from *ge* which means 'earth' so the term means 'the ones from the earth.' This actually means 'peasant' which means 'man of the earth, earth man, or Getian.' We say in Romanian *get-beget** which means 'true Getian.' Beget** is just a fortifier. When we use this expression, we don't even think about the Getians anymore. We just use the expression *get-beget* which means 'true, whole, precise.'

"Okay, but they could argue that the Getians have disappeared and that we are another people," I said, stating the famous hypothesis.

"This isn't possible because the language is the same and still in its original structure, just as it was spoken by the peasants. We therefore have this incredible language continuity being transmitted over millennia. Even if we consider the possibility that the Romans had attempted to impose Latin, although I doubt it, they obviously met with resistance; but this was of no interest for them. They were very happy to confiscate the wheat and take the gold from the Dacians and then leave. It was not for any more than that because, otherwise, they would have left deep traces in our culture and tradition and there are no such traces. Furthermore, the Romans have made no similar effort to cultivate their language in a conquered region. They would come, build citadels and say 'give us the money!' During the first phase, they killed the locals. Then they plundered, and during the third phase they installed citadels. Of course, this view might seem rough; but in its essence, it remains a process of conquest which involves wars, violence, obedience, and plunder. You can't conquer the world and say at the same time that you were willingly invited to do so while receiving all honors and riches. So,

---

* *Translator's note:* This expression means "pure Getian."

** *Translator's note: Beget* means "pure" when referring to race or ethnicity.

they couldn't have changed the Dacians' language, and this applied for the occupied territory which was only the seventh part of Dacia, not the third part as they usually say, in order to give more importance to these arguments. Under these circumstances, how could they have changed the language of the free Dacians from the other six parts of the territory?"

"What language did those free Dacians speak?" I asked.

"Of course, they spoke the Romanian language, the original language of the peasants. They lived on the same territory with the others. The so-called Dacian or Getian language was in fact the Romanian language. They were Romanians ever since the world was created, as we say in Romanian."

"Did they call themselves Romanians? Did they say that they spoke Romanian?

"Our peasants say, 'our Romanian language,' but in the chronicles, they said that these people spoke the Roman language. In Latin and Greek, the letters î, â, ş, ţ, and ă cannot be transcribed so they wrote 'Roman'. Maybe they were split into communities and, at regional level, they would call themselves 'men from Oltenia' or 'men from Vâlcea' or otherwise.* But, they all spoke the same language because all who lived in the Carpathians area were seen as a single people: Dacians or Getians. The words Dacian, Getian and Romanian have the same meaning. Romanians have always considered themselves a single nation from the same 'mother' no matter if they called themselves Dacians or Getians in ancient times or Transylvanians and Moldavians in recent times."

"As it is commonly known, the Romanian nation was formed through Romanization," I said, "although now I clearly understand that the historical perspective is illogical."

"I've told you, Romanization couldn't have happened. The Romanian language is not a Neo-Latin language. Actually, they had nothing to change because the Romans spoke the same language, the Romanian language. And, I am not inventing all of these arguments. There are already many studies and references about this which confirm the truth. There continues to be a strong opposition, however, due to prejudice and especially to political interests which makes all of this information, which is essential to our identity as the Romanian nation, unknown to the public, especially in order not to 'bother' one state or another. There are also other kinds of interests, but it is not prudent to talk about this now."

"I think we are the only country where this has happened," I said with bitterness. "As I have noticed, a damaging practice of copying and imitating others has been imposed. It's always done in order to justify internal measures,

---

* *Translator's note:* In Romanian, these expressions translate as single words. Oltenia is a region in Romania. Vâlcea is a county in Romania, historically known especially for discoveries showing human life 2 million years ago and for the Dacian and Roman citadels found there.

by referring to the fact that we have taken this or that model from others, that we have taken a certain idea from others. We thus picture ourselves as silly children who let themselves be patted on the back by parents who are allegedly older and wiser than us. After all, it's also a matter of national pride. If we continue to copy others and bow our heads in front of them, we'll end up being copies of them. This is really disturbing."

"Of course it is. The problem is that such an attitude greatly facilitates the destructive intentions of some international organisms. You know what I'm talking about and how complicated things are in this respect."

"Sure I do, and it seems to me that, in order to make room for these evil intentions concerning our country, they have influenced the historical truth and the conception about the origins of our people as it's much easier to have a frail basis, which they wanted to impose, than a solid ethnic basis which has remained unitary and continuous throughout history."

"It's true, and this is how they introduced the idea of the formation of the Romanian people. The so-called 'respectable people' or 'experts' whom people listen to state that there were originally no Romanian people per se. They tell us that the Romanian nation formed following the union of the Dacians and Romans. The history taught in schools doesn't even mention that we were Getians. It only mentions briefly that the Getians had passed through our territory."

"Yes, I remember. Dacians and Getians, the Getian Dromohetes."

Cezar continued undisturbed.

"And, the union between the Dacians and the Romans led to the formation of the Romanian people. It's just like that joke which says that everyone comes from Adam and Eve, but only we, Romanians, come from Decebal and Trajan," he said, laughing.

"And, how can this aberration be explained?"

"As I said, it's mainly the interest of foreign powers to acquire one territory or another. To accomplish this, they say that if you cannot prove that you were originally in the territory before, it means that you came later and should leave or obey. These are territorial claims with everything they involve. But, it was known that things were in fact different and that the Romanians are the only people in Eurasia who have resisted and survived on the same territory. This is when the fabrication of the story concerning the formation of the people and their Romanization started and was mainly based upon the ignorance or shallowness of some chronicle writers or famous historians. But, pay attention. During this process of manipulation, only those chronicle writers, historians and linguists who were famous and supported these false ideas were chosen. The first of these people consciously followed that preestablished plan. Those who followed were already fooled by the partial evidence which was many times inconclusive or even fake and perpetrated by dogmas and prejudice. Different types of pressure have also played an important part here. Then, in modern times, fear, servility, cowardliness and fear of losing one's function have added to these."

"What I find amazing is that the others who knew the truth haven't said anything," I said.

"Interests have taken a two-way action. On the one hand, they've intro-duced and spread this lame idea of the formation of the Romanian language and nation. On the other hand, they've taken care to stop and eliminate any study, proof or attempt to prove this forgery. There are people, not Romanians, who have burned wagons of documents and historical evidence of inestimable value to our country. Therefore, gradually, a kind of terror has been imposed in this field, a politics of the type 'do as we tell you if you want to be all right.' Unfortunately, many have given in to it."

"They've practically imposed on us the idea that we 'formed' as a nation almost 2000 years ago and many have taken it for granted," I said.

"The enthnogenesis can't have taken place between the 3rd and 7th centuries B.C. as historians tell us. There is no such thing. Each conqueror or regime came here with its own alternative. They say that the Romans Romanized us and gave us Latin. Stalin was here and it was said that the Slavs have played the most important part in the formation of the Romanian people because the Romanian language also has many Slavonic words. The Austrian-Hungarians said that we came from south of the Danube and actu-ally had the same origins as the Albanians."

"Why would they say that?" I asked with amazement.

"You can see that here lies the frailness and lack of common sense of such ideas that have been imposed on us. In reality, they have no support, unless you count a ridiculous notion. In support of the idea that the Romanians came from south of the Danube, from Albanian territory, it was argued that there are a few words in the Albanian language which are similar to Romanian words. The conclusion was therefore made that we had come from Albania. So, we couldn't have been here originally because we actually came from the South."

"How many words are they talking about? This is the first time that I've heard this idea."

"About 20 to 30 words. The problem with these words is that they don't have the same meaning in both languages. This is one of the inconsistencies of their theory. The justifications and 'evidence' presented are simple matches and amateurish works which many times are absurd and even foolish. For example, Hungarian historians and linguists state that, for fear of barbarians, the population in the Carpathians area had all fled to the south of the Danube, leaving their country and that they remained there for approximately 1000 years, 'borrowing' words from Albanians. Thus, they conclude that the Hun-garians were actually the first inhabitants of Transylvania and that we came back later, when they were already here. These are purely propagandistic 'studies' and 'ideas' fabricated upon request in order to justify some claims and rights which, in reality, have no basis."

"That's impossible. What normal person could claim that we all left our country when it is known that our territory has been the most stricken and plundered by barbarians?" I asked without waiting for an answer.

"As you can see, some people could claim this. The population actually took a much easier refuge from the invaders by going into the mountains and woods of Transylvania rather than leaving the country completely. It has been suggested that these people went into an area which not only did not offer them more safety but to one that also lacked conditions necessary for living. This means that several million people are supposed to have left a vast territory which offered them a natural configuration unique in Europe and Asia, especially from the point of view of resources and living conditions. Further, they left this country empty in order to crowd into a very small and poor space south of the Danube. Not only is there no historical evidence of that or any other kind in this respect, but the very idea has a smell of intellectual imbecility, if I can say so. Just think about it. The area of our Carpathians was known for its secular, unbreacheable woods. Nobody dared to go in there because it was an unknown and dangerous area. After the fall of the Roman Empire, the Huns plundered many territories in Germany, France and even more to the south, in Italy, which are hundreds of kilometers away from here, but they didn't dare to come a few tens of kilometers up to Transylvania due to these scary forests. So, they had to invent something to say that they were here first and came up with the aberration about the population transferring from the Carpathians area to the land south of the Danube. In this respect, their only 'proof' that we returned from there are the 20 Albanian words in our lexicon and the fact that we couldn't have had such words in our lexicon if we hadn't lived south of the Danube with the Albanians. These statements are truly embarrassing. Apart from the reasons I already mentioned, there are other strong reasons. First of all, consider the fact that the depopulation of this territory would have meant depriving all Europe of its salt resources as our area gave salt to the whole continent through a complex process of human effort. There are no surface salt deposits anywhere else. Without salt, no people can support itself."

"Salt? I don't see the connection," I said, amazed.

"There is a very important connection, but we will talk about it later. Without people to exploit the huge salt resources our country had and still has, how could the life and activity of people in other parts of Europe, and even Asia, have been ensured? Through its specific composition, salt is essential to man's life. Without the Romanians' continuity in Transylvania and the Carpathians' area, nothing around the Peri-Carpathian region — which encompasses the other countries — could have survived. And, they say that we quickly left the country empty, running to the south of the Danube, to an area where we would have surely died because it didn't provide good living conditions. So, we left the easiest and best living conditions of two continents to take refuge, for fear of the barbarians, to an area that provides almost nothing at all. In the case of the numerous invasions we were subject to, I've already told you how people acted. Part of the population fought against the invaders, and the rest gathered in the mountains, in the thick woods. No invader has ever ventured to go there.

"There are other historical inconsistencies claimed by Hungarian historians. They repeat that they have conquered us, but if the Romanian population was already south of the Danube as they state, then whom did they conquer in Transylvania? Even if this had been so, there is still no document or reference to a Hungarian conquest of this territory or its population. So, they came up with the 'invention' concerning the Albanian words which are actually Romanian words because, starting from the Romanian roots, they can be found in almost all Indo-European languages which does not account for their alleged Albanian origin. The problem here is that a large number of opinions have been expressed, but not a single rigorous study has been conducted to prove any of these claims. As I already told you, the same method of information manipulation is at work. A few famous linguists state an aberration with no proof or with a superficial and wrong justification. Afterwards, the others come and weave fantastic 'scenarios.' Thus, a historical and linguistic 'background' is ensured which is later invoked by might as clear evidence."

"I'm curious. What Albanian words are they referring to?"

"*Pentru că au provenit din română, unele se aseamănă. Dar multe nu au același înțeles; de pildă, baltă. La noi are înțelesul de întindere de apă dulce; la ei este balte și înseamnă noroi. Sau grapă, care e unealta cunoscută la noi; la ei este grep, care înseamnă undiță. Sau, așa cum observa cu ironie fină unul din marii noștri lingviști contemporani, poate că înseamnă și fructul din categoria citricelor.*

"Because they originated from Romanian, some words are similar, but many don't have the same meaning. For example, the word *baltă*. In Romanian, it means 'a surface filled with non-salty water.' In Albanian, the word *balte* means 'mud.' Or, the word *grapă*, which means 'to harrow' here, is comparable to the Albanian word *grep* which means 'fishing rod.' Or, as one of our great contemporary linguists noted with fine irony, it could also refer to citrus fruit.'"

Cezar laughed with all his heart and made me smile as well.

"They haven't conducted any etymological research covering the meaning or structure of the words. In fact, they haven't done anything. However, they have spread silly conclusions which defy any form of intelligence. There are

---

* *Translator's note:* In some Romanian markets, the English word "grapefruit" is sometimes called "grepfruit" and thus the irony referred to here.

many other sources and researches which prove the contrary of what the supporters of the "Romanian-Albanian theory" claim. These sources clearly prove the origin of entire word families from Indo-European languages which are related to the Romanian roots from which they have originated. For example, take the word *gard.*˙ You'll find it in almost all Indo-European languages, both in ancient and in modern times, but it is a Romanian word. It is the origin for all other words of its family which can be immediately seen after a study of its structure in other idioms. Hungarian and other 'linguists' — and this quite unfortunately also includes some Romanian linguists — claim that this word comes from the Albanian word *garth*, but they don't have any means to prove this claim."

I commented that such foreign "ideas" practically undermine our past and the true history of our people and language.

"Of course. This is a fact and it cannot be denied," Cezar approved. "Each of these 'theories,' let's say two or three, are actually what political regimes have attributed as being the origin to the Romanian people. But, nobody has ever said that we have originated here because foreigners don't like this. If they admitted this, they would immediately confirm the continuity of the Romanian people and of our language; and thus, any claim or ethnic pressure would stop. They would only be left with the alternative of military invasion which is difficult to accomplish because there are now completely different economic, military and geopolitical realities that are not the same as in the past."

"So, this is the main reason why they don't like it..."

"Yes, you can't just come and sweep off the Romanians, even if you really want to, simply by saying that Transylvania belongs to Hungarians, Muntenia (Muntenia refers to the southern region of Romania, known in the past as Wallachia) to the Bulgarians, Moldavia to the Russians and there you have it: there are no more Romanians. They can't say that Romanians were not here, that we are intruders. This would be an attitude like that of the Arabs who used to fight and win a battle and then plunder and destroy the cities. This happened until Mohammed's times. They did not, however, continue this practice afterwards. Essentially though, they had the same attitude of completely removing a population from the surface of the earth."

"What do you mean by saying a population? As far as I can tell, they used to destroy whole countries during their conquests."

"There were no countries in ancient times. For example, how big was the territory of Dacia? Nobody knows for sure because Dacia didn't actually exist. Countries were eventually created; but a long time ago, they didn't exist. Actually, a country is an artificial limitation which lasts for a certain period of time. The etymological meaning of the word *ţară* or *ţarină* in our

---

˙ *Translator's note* The word *gard* in Romanian means "fence."

language means earth.* It refers to land, region, or living area. This is why we speak nowadays about Ţara Bârsei** or many other such areas in Romania."

"And, how did they draw the limitations? Did they just draw frontiers, as we do today?"

"No, they didn't even have fences. They only knew that a certain garden belonged to one man or another. The ancient Romanians had no fences. In particular, they had no tall fences that would prevent people from seeing what they did in their own yard. This is in stark contrast to other populations who used such fences for privacy. There were no countries, but there were populations, and the Romanian nation has a continuity in the Carpathian-Danube area. There are many sources and documents which prove this. All that is necessary is the will to admit this and continue the research."

"...if it hadn't been for the prejudice you were talking about and the agenda driven interests."

"I just wanted to underline the fact that we have a very complex and rich tradition here which clearly comes from a very distant past. The nature of our folklore and traditions is immemorial. If you ask a peasant 'How do you know this?' he will answer, 'I learned it this way' or 'It's been like that for ever.' This is what they say. There is no motivation behind it. A response like 'I learned it' means that he was told by the family. Somebody has transmitted that information to him verbally and it has been preserved in such a manner until today, ever since immemorial times. One way or another, it has also been transmitted in other areas. After all, they all spoke the same language."

"Something is still strange however. It is a huge area, more than half of Europe, where you say that people used to speak Romanian or dialects of Romanian. At the same time, we are talking about Dacians or Getians only in the Carpathians area where we live now. How is it possible that nobody has ever mentioned anything about this spreading of our language or tradition?"

"It's not true. Many speak about this, but Romanian historians are mostly superficial and do not have the necessary training. They do not go to the sources; they do not read the Greek and Latin sources. Under these conditions, name confusions occur most of the time, false ethnicities are attributed and wrong conclusions are reached. For example, they speak about Dacians and Getians but also mention the Goths who are considered to be a separate people most of the time. Actually, thirty-six separate sources have been identified which prove that the Goths and the Getians are the same people. This is an example of the way in which rigorous research can clarify important aspects of history."

---

* *Translator's note*: The word *ţară* means "country" in Romanian while the word *ţarină* means "ploughed field" or commune (including pastures, ploughed fields and forests).

** *Translator's note*: This word is known in English as Burzenland. It refers to a historic and ethnographic area in southeastern Transylvania. The most important city in the region is Brasov.

"The Goths, the Getians, and the Dacians," I said. "Then maybe there should be some more sources proving that we are in fact the Getians."

"This identification has already been done. But, we don't need sources because we already have the continuity I was telling you about. Peasants have had the same customs for ever. These are agrarian ancestral customs which have remained unchanged. They haven't left their homes and their villages and haven't spread into other regions. Fundamentally, they have remained on the same territory for thousands of years."

"This is a rural community in its most accurate meaning."

"It's true. Only an agrarian civilization, with strong rural accents, has a chance to have a continuity. The later urban developments are perishable. We can't even speak about civilization at this level. They come and go because they undergo a continuous transformation due to specific technological development which includes the life of consumption and competition. An agrarian community, however, is totally different. It is tied to the earth which it identifies as its home. This is why we are called Getians or 'men of the earth' which gives a more subtle meaning of continuity and very old age. This argument alone would be enough to solve the problem of our origin on this territory. Until 1900, generally speaking, people didn't leave their villages because they had no reason to leave. They had barely heard about Bucharest. Romanian peasants didn't leave. Everything was transmitted verbally by parents. At that time, in Romanian villages, there was an archaic state of things; and even now, there are rural settlements of this kind, especially in our mountains. But, things haven't always been like this. In ancient times, they started to leave, but this departure wasn't a migration as it was the case with barbarian peoples. It was rather a departure of a part of the population from their original home to other regions. This was something like the flight of bees from the hive towards other areas, looking for pollen in flowers. Some return, others don't. In any case, however, the hive with a certain number of bees remains in its original place. I hope it is a good example for you to understand the phenomenon which took place in those times. People had started to spread out to different directions from the source which is here, in the Carpathians area. There is even the concept of population swarming which is related to the example I gave you. Bees also swarm, either around the hive or farther away from it."

"But, why did they leave?" I asked. "As far as I understand, they had no reason to leave."

"It's true, but when such a phenomenon occurs, it is mainly motivated by two arguments: either the living space was too small for the growing population, which leads to food problems, or they wanted to do something in particular. The second case is only for very spiritually advanced peoples such as ours was. They wanted to move the spiritual center from here to the East, but this hypothesis doesn't have many supporters."

"Why would they migrate East?" I asked.

"It's about an esoteric meaning which is also associated to the cardinal direction. One of the great esoterics said that, in ancestral times, this territory was called the Black Country because it was the country where Cronos was worshiped and the symbolic color for time is black."

"Cronos? This is the name of the file," I stated.

"Yes, and it is not a random name. It is connected with the inscriptions discovered there which you can see in the photo. The text analysis can only be related to what was later discovered and to very high spirituality elements which belonged to the inhabitants of this territory."

"When did they date the discovery?"

"Nobody knows. We haven't had any clue, and from the photos and the professor's statement, we can conclude that the place is filled with gold. As you said, it is a mountain of gold. The text which could be translated offers some clues but vague ones. The graphic signs are not really the ones we know. The writing is a bit altered in comparison with early writing, but it is still intelligible. This places it sometime between 500 and 1000 B.C. They gave us an accuracy percentage of 90% for the translation, but its meaning is troubling. The other characters cannot be dated as they are completely unknown."

"I see that there is an analysis of the text."

"Yes, for this purpose we have collaborated with a French institute which studies Indo-European civilizations because the linguistic aspects are combined with esoteric meanings. For example, they were quite amazed that the text includes the root *kr*. At first, they said it made no sense because it is not used in spoken language. Later, as they studied further, we realized that the text was not supposed to tell a certain story but was rather meant to serve as a step of initiation. The root *kr* is always related to time, and it is the basis for the word *Cronos* who was the god of time and later called Saturn. The difficulty was that the root was related to *io* which is the archaic original form for 'I' in our language.* The authentic Romanian peasant still doesn't say 'eu' but 'io.' But, the 'evolution' of the language, guided by certain academic minds, has gradually imposed the word 'eu' because it was closer to Latin."

"So, we have *Cronos* and *I*," I said, impatient to find out the conclusion.

"Yes, and the connection could only be the natural one: 'I, who am Cronos' or, just as well, 'Cronos is me.'"

"And, what is the meaning?"

"It can only be connected to a profound spiritual nature. The person who made the inscription states that he was Cronos who was worshiped as god of time. Can you think of a human being as you think of time? Cronos

---

Translator's note: The current Romanian word for "I" is "eu."

or Time was considered very old because time itself is assimilated to an ancestral existence. It is so old that it wasn't even born. So, it must be a metaphor with profound spiritual symbolism. Most probably, the person who made the inscription was a priest, a human being who had reached spiritual fulfillment. From this perspective, there could be a meaning. But, what comes next is unintelligible: *sal-moş*. This was the only point where the translators hesitated because *sal* has raised problems. Our people have indicated *zăul* instead of *sal* and I tend to think they are right. Cronos, who was the archaic patron god of the Romanian people, was called *zăul-moş*.[*] *Moş* also appears in the inscription and is correlated with someone very old and wise. Furthermore, the root *kr* sends us to another important element of our ancestors' tradition which presents a complex symbolism and chronology: Christmas, also known as Santa Claus.[**] The profound meaning of Santa Claus and the god this represents, as well as the holiday associated with him, are no longer correctly perceived by people who are confused and have no clear picture of what Christmas represents; and, if this picture exists at all in their minds, it is very superficial. In ancient times, Christmas was an exalted celebration of time as the winter solstice occurred, marking the end of the old year and the beginning of the new year. This is the origin of the Romanian greetings "Happy New Year"[***] or "When we return next year, we hope to find you in good health." Later, the association with the Christian holiday was added and has complicated things even more. Ordinary men prefer to build a simple image about Santa Claus, something funny, prosperous and happy. It's just an exterior meaning. In conclusion, the inscription said that this was the holy place where Cronos – Santa Claus, the god of time — was alive, present and united the worlds. This last part shows us that the place was considered to represent the origin of time. I was telling you that this is troubling because it is related to the idea that here, in the Carpathians area, is the cradle of all civilizations and nations existing now and that this is the source of the primordial language, the Romanian language. As one of the greatest contemporary linguists said, it is the only natural language in Europe. Actually, it is exactly what scientists look for and do not find: the Indo-European language which is common to all nations which make up our modern civilization."

I breathed in, feeling overwhelmed.

"They will never recognize this, no matter how much proof there is."

---

[*] *Translator's note*: The word *moş* means "old man" in Romanian while *zăul* is an archaic Romanian word for "the god." It has been claimed that *zăul-moş* was the origin for the name Zamolxis, the god of the Dacians.

[**] *Translator's note*: Both words come from the root *kr* in Romanian: Christmas is "Crăciun" and Santa Claus is "Moş Crăciun."

[***] *Translator's note*: If literally translated, this New Year's greeting would mean "next year and many years from now on."

"We'll see. Things change all the time. But, returning to the translated inscription, think about the fact that it is almost 3,000 years old. If so, then when was the unknown one written? And by whom? We'll probably never know. I tried finding out by using the time travel device, but it's the most powerful barrier I've ever experienced. It can't be breached in any way. When you hear what followed in Professor Constantin's statement, you'll better understand why. This will explain what the first inscription actually meant."

"I wouldn't want to miss the explanation you started concerning the migration. I believe it is also related to the spreading and transformation of the language and this is very attractive to me. If we don't talk now, I don't know when we will get another chance."

It was true. Lately, due to his new responsibilities and functions, Cezar had been difficult to approach outside of business-related issues. Such an opportunity was very special and I didn't want to miss it. Besides, the atmosphere that evening was quiet, offering an adequate background for such discussions. I was very happy when he accepted my offer to continue the discussion.

"There was an extraordinary spiritual field in this territory, but proof in this respect has only been indirect so far," Cezar said. "But, the phenomenal discovery in the Şureanu Massif also shows us the actual dimension of this truth. You'll see later that it is huge. It is known that, from an esoteric perspective, massive gold deposits always reveal an area where the spirituality of the people have reached very high peaks. But, this is not about gold ore, no matter how rich the nuggets are. It's about a real mountain of gold or at least a large part of it that is made of gold."

"I was not aware that there was a connection between this metal and spirituality," I said.

"All things are interconnected and especially those which predominantly attract each other. Gold is a very pure and noble metal. It is not in vain that it has raised and still raises such an interest in people who feel and recognize its high vibration, even if only unconsciously. Unfortunately, they relate to it as a means of obtaining income."

"But, it hasn't always been like this. In ancient times, its worth was especially high for priests. I didn't imagine, however, that it could even represent a physical factor which corresponds to spiritual energy. I though it was just a symbolic aspect."

"Noble metals and precious stones are substances which channel certain occult influences and energies. Their 'market' value is just the profane form of admitting this. Why don't you treat stanium or iron the same way? It is because they do not have the same level of high vibration. Out of all, gold is considered the best concentrator of subtle spiritual energy. Even its yellow color is in agreement with this and shows us that the place where there are rich or very rich gold deposits was, in a way, impregnated during a certain period of history when there was a very high spirituality. For common men or modern scientists, all this means nothing. But, I am now talking from an occult perspective which has nothing to do with materialist conceptions. In a mysterious way, the spirituality of a population is especially developed in areas where there is much gold and our case is something unique. The presence of this gold mountain cannot be explained from a geological perspective, or at least I don't think it can. There must have been phenomena of another nature which are unknown to us. After all, it might have been a combination of spiritual and geological action. I don't know. But, what I can tell you is that it is by far something extraordinary and its meaning is very profound. You can't treat this discovery simply as a huge gold deposit. It's much more than that. It is a phenomenal spiritual field which has sustained us, the Romanian people, and has enabled us to keep something of that which was from a long time ago."

I took a deep breath as I was nervous because Cezar's statement touched the profound origin of our people.

"Now things add up," he continued. "A huge concentrator of spiritual energy is like a formidable magnet of subtle and very high energies that supports a culture around it which is very advanced from a spiritual perspective, even if the physical manifestation of it was very simple and its activity was comprised of agriculture and herding. Due to this phenomenal concentration of spiritual energy, magnetized in the Şureanu Massif by the huge quantity of gold found here, other space-time distortion phenomena have occurred which you'll learn about a bit later. The spiritual energy dissipated radially, covering the territory of our country but also following the line of very rich gold deposits in this regions as well in other mountains, especially the Apuseni Mountains.* In a way, the population that formed here was continuously bathed in these high vibrations and this has quickly led to the development of the highest spirituality. It wasn't just isolated or limited to only two or three individuals with a remarkable level of spiritual development but to almost all of the inhabitants of this area who, in the beginning, demonstrated this incredibly high level of consciousness elevation. The specific vibration of this area was so intense and profound that the power has been transmitted over thousands of years, even up to this point in time. It is now, of course, much more diminished in comparison to what it used to be, but it still explains many specific characteristics of our people, folklore and language. This is why the population has remained here ever since its remote beginning. This also explains other extraordinary discoveries which include: the Projection Hall in the Bucegi Mountains; the very special tectonic formation underlying the

---

*The Apuseni Mountains are the Western Carpathians and is where Radu Cinamar experienced a space-time translation to Tibet as is described in *Transyvlvania Moonrise*.

territory of our country; a combination of different forms of topographical relief over such a small area; and the concentration of surprising soil richness. All of these features are restricted to this area of the Carpathians and a bit to the south, reaching as far as the Danube. They are all connected to the phenomenal spiritual force of the inhabitants of those times. And, they also explain our continuity which is unique across the continents because this was once the spiritual center of the world. Over time, natural laws, which included those of cyclicity, applied and the spiritual level has dropped, but the center of spiritual influence has remained with its potentiality becoming more and more pronounced in these times."

"And, at what point in time would you place the extraordinary beginning of the spirituality of our people?" I asked in hope of getting a better idea of the age of our people.

"We can't say for sure, but tradition and esoteric sources seem to unanimously indicate the period following the end of the ice age, after the last great flood. This means sometime between 9,500 – 10,500 B.C., so about 12,000 years ago. Even though the numbers are relative, the variation cannot be more than 500-700 years, more or less."

"It's a way of referring to the great flood," I said, "but there are works which prove that there has never been a flood covering the whole planet as the *Bible* says but only in certain areas."

"Of course. Archeological evidence has been found which shows successive floods that took place at certain intervals of time. The events in the *Bible* are mostly reduced to the Sinai peninsula which was confronted at that time with such a flood. So, there must have been a great flood about 11,000 years before Christ which was possibly related to the disappearance of Atlantis. Afterwards, everything began all over again."

"Where did everything begin?" I asked. "Where did the population come from?"

"Why did it have to come from somewhere? Some of what remained is simply what used to be in this area, but this was the new beginning. Did someone plant them there? No. Anyway, spiritual development seems to have been very quick and at an unimaginable level. This explains the idea of the spiritual center of the world. Afterwards, as I said, they started to decay after a few thousands of years. They continued, however, to remain on the same territory, right here in the area of the Carpathians, especially in the mountains, and in Transylvania."

"But, they didn't know that this was the spiritual center of the world," I said.

"It's true. They mainly remained because they had extraordinary resources here which included salt, gold, and everything necessary for living, but the spiritual element has actually kept them united and attached to these places.

After 4,000–5,000 years, maybe they no longer knew that the places where they lived had been impregnated by that extraordinary spiritual force of their ancestors and that this had been the spiritual center of the world, but they continued this transmitted tradition without alteration in its deeply spiritual and occult form. Because — you ask yourself — why do we still have this extraordinary folklore today? How could it have remained for thousands of years and been transmitted from father to son? It has remained."

"And, why hasn't it been perpetuated for so long in other areas?" I asked. "Why not in Finland or in Malta?"

"It couldn't have remained back then because, a long time ago, there were no nations in Europe. There was tundra and ice up to the middle of today's Germany and up to Northern Maramureş* in our country. From the point of view of living space, human civilization began from these limits downward because there were no living conditions to the North. The glaciation was barely withdrawing. The first and only ones that could be said to have formed a community lived here in the Carpathians area, especially in the area of the Apuseni Mountains in Transylvania and in this area of the Southern Carpathians. Everything began and developed here: the people, the language, the spirituality, and the customs. There might have been other clusters of people in other areas of Europe, but they were insignificant from the point of view of the number of individuals and they must have been nomadic. This is why they didn't resist. Back in those times, due to climate conditions, the population had been significantly reduced in numbers. When a few hundred or thousands or people managed to get together in a certain territory, they were very sizable relative to the entire population of the planet."

"Couldn't they have taken refuge in other parts of Europe? Did they have no other option?" I asked, puzzled.

"The glaciation maps for Europe that have been drafted by scientists show the ice covered Stockholm, Berlin and Moscow. So, nobody could have taken refuge in those areas. The limit where living conditions began and ended was the Carpathians. It began in the northern area of today's Transylvania. Westward, there was mountain glaciation from 1,000-1,500 meters above ground level so there could be no settlements as there was ice everywhere. The glaciation was withdrawing to the north in different stages. It is certain that the Pannonian Lake started to drain around 10,000 B.C., after the withdrawal of the glaciation. What remained afterwards is known today as Lake Balaton in Hungary. Actually, its name was Bălătău as the only spoken language in those times was the Romanian language. The name was later changed to Balaton. The Danube then broke the area known today as the Iron Gates and drained the Getian Lake which came from the Thetis Sea. This great sea covered the whole territory of Romania a few million years

---

* *Translator's note:* Maramureş is an area in Northern Romania.

ago. As a result, there were lakes along the Danube which were traces of the great Getian Lake which gradually drained and dried out. Thus, a warmer climate was ensured because the remnants of the ice age lasted until 11,000 B.C.. We can therefore say that Transylvania was privileged in comparison with other areas because it had a better climate. The rest of Europe had only lichens, moss and gradations of ice up to the poles."

The information was too much. I was trying to keep up, but I was just barely becoming familiar with this subject. I also wanted to correctly understand the meaning of those times and the way everything began. My perception was facilitated by the fact that I had already seen glimpses of times very similar to the ones Cezar spoke about in the holograms from the Projection Hall. Everything checked out, but I now believed I had a chance to add up all of the elements into a unitary whole.

"Okay. So there was a remnant population in the area of Transylvania and in the western mountains of our country, but there might also have been areas with warm climates to the south."

"Maybe, but there was nothing left. The best conditions were here. The mountains are necessary for a profound and sustainable spirituality because they provided a different structure for the human condition, both psychologically and physically. Even though it was called the Black Country, thus taking over the symbolism of Time which they worshiped, the inhabitants of this area were not black. The blackness is symbolic because, from a physical perspective, esoteric tradition tells us that they were blond with blue eyes, were tall and had white skin. This is the typology here in the Carpathians area."

I told Cezar that, according to Plato, the ancient Greeks were also blond with blue eyes.

"This was the situation in 2,000 B.C.," he replied. "But, many things have happened since. The ancestors of the Greeks left this area. What we know for sure is that between 10,000 B.C. and now, the oldest civilization was in this region. We don't have any information before 10,000 B.C."

"How do we know that this is the oldest civilization?"

"Because there are no other traces in any other place and this is how science works. Let's say that we also have other methods of investigation — which you already know about— but they cannot be made public yet. And, let's say that the research to find the oldest civilization, from which it all began, started a few decades ago. They have corroborated the maps and archeological discoveries and have discovered that the most important area is right here; more precisely, in Transylvania and in the Carpathians area in Romania. People did not leave this place for thousands of years until the swarming I was talking about began, around 3,000-4,000 B.C."

"Do you mean that the population remained in Transylvania from between 9,000–10,000 B.C. to 3,000 B.C?" I asked, amazed.

"Yes. As I said, they had no reason to leave. The peasants of those times didn't go on excursions. They have kept this incredible stability in their birth places until today. Even today, authentic peasants barely leave their villages and do not go anywhere else. This is an ancient civilization. They didn't take three boats and go to see if they could steal some gold. It's tough; but, after all, it's the truth."

I smiled at the ironic hint Cezar made to Columbus's expedition to America and the later conquests carried out by Spain.

"Here we have all the right conditions. The climate is good, there is salt at the surface, and there are salty springs," he continued to explain. "On the entire arch of the Carpathians, Romania is the only country which has salt at the surface. This means you can take a tool and take zlatnă, a word which means salty water. This is the origin of the names of cities like Slatina in Oltenia and Zlatna in Transylvania. They cooked with salty water but that was not all they did. Even today, some people sell sacks of salt lumps. There are mountains where salt is extracted from the surface. This territory was called 'Europe's salt cellar.' In comparison with other areas — for example, in the southern part of the continent which you asked about — salt is quite rare. The Romans also accepted payment in salt which, in case you didn't know, led to our word *salariu*.* If you spilled the salt, this would lead to a quarrel. This doesn't mean they were superstitious but rather that salt was difficult to obtain. So, there were resources here in our country and the area was privileged. We had rivers and lakes with fish and people could practice fishing. There was also salt and this gave a much better quality to their lives because, as I already told you, it is very difficult to maintain life without salt. There were also minerals and fruit trees. They could therefore practice gardening which is the predecessor of agriculture. Furthermore, they had herds because there were rich pastures. There were also the necessary conditions for transhumance: mountains and fields. Where else did people have this possibility? This is the only area that was not covered in ice. Transhumance is the best form of shepherding. It is necessary and not just a method invented by these people. Due to transhumance, people continuously ensured food for their sheep. In winter, they descended to the fields; and in summer, they climbed the mountains. There weren't conditions for such an activity anywhere else."

"But you said that they eventually started to migrate," I said.

"Yes, I was talking about the Indo-European swarming because it was believed that the Aryans initially invaded India and then migrated west to Europe and civilized it. It's just as they said before the Middle Ages: the Earth was in the center and the sun and all other planets revolved around the Earth."

"How did that migration actually happen?" I asked.

---

* *Translator's note:* This word means "wage" in Romanian.

"The first one to conduct such an investigation was Cambridge University in Great Britain about 100 years ago. They wanted to write a history of India because India was a British colony in those times and they looked in the Vedas for arguments to establish the departing point of the Aryans."

"How did they conduct this research?"

"They took the Vedas and looked at the flora and fauna described and at the occupations of the people in those times. And, they concluded there were no camels, no elephants, and no tigers; but there were elm trees and ducks for a couple of examples. Then they did a search to see if they were in present day India. No, they are not. So, it was concluded that was not the place of the Vedic stories and epics. And, they tried to see where all of those elements existed, where people could have activities such as shepherding and agriculture as well as elm trees, etc. The idea is that they found all kinds of elements pointing them to an approximate area between the Carpathians and Bohemia because such trees grow only in this region. Only here, can you be both a shepherd and agrarian. This is the only place that has the animals mentioned in the Vedas and which do not really exist in India."

"This means that the migration is actually reversed, that they didn't come from India and populate Europe but that they left towards Asia and reached India," I anticipated.

"Exactly. After a long time, the sun was correctly placed in the center and the Earth and all other planets revolved around it. This is an analogy to the way in which things really happened with regards to the swarming of the population. But, you should know that this alternative is not accepted today, at least not completely. The manipulation is terrible."

"Why is the situation like this?" I asked, amazed. "Why do they continue to support an aberration? This has certain risks and needs an effort to support the lie."

"For the same reasons I've already mentioned. These were the conclusions of Cambridge University which is the most serious, authoritarian and famous university in the world. It's a kind of 'nursery' for Nobel Prize awards; but even so, they have kept these studies on the borderline because, otherwise, they would have had to admit to the final conclusion that the population swarming actually started here in our Carpathians area and with everything I've said about it primordiality. This didn't suit them at all. We've already talked about this."

"Yes, we have. And, what was the final conclusion reached by the researchers at Cambridge University?"

"They said that the origin of the Aryans was right here in Transylvania, outward from the Carpathians towards Hungary, Austria, and up to Bohemia. They said that the flora and fauna described in the Hindu texts written 3,000 –4,000 years ago can be found here, but these were the only elements that they considered. If we also take other elements into consideration which are related to archeological discoveries, we can then clearly define the area."

"Were there no state interests that were opposed to these conclusions?" I asked.

"Yes, there were, even if not openly, because we are still talking about the authority of Cambridge University, and this cannot be so easily overcome. There are tens of hypotheses trying to place the origin or the Aryans, a few of them being really fantastic. Some said that the Aryans came from the Altay Mountains where it is known that the outside temperature is 3° Celsius for eleven months out of the year. What agriculture could people have developed under these conditions? What flora and fauna could exist there that could be similar to the ones described in the Vedas? I gave you this example so that you could see how far speculation can go in order to deny that it all began here, in Romania."

"Now, there will always be people who are smarter and can contradict you, no matter how clear the evidence is that you present. Pride and foolishness are good partners in such cases," I said, somewhat upset.

"Proof does exist. There is a lot of well documented evidence. I told you that the Aryans' origin was moved everywhere by scientists at different times. They tried to prove that the Aryans came from anywhere else but here. The researchers from Cambridge University were the first to say that this was the starting point. It's true that they named this area Hungary, but they described the geography of this area: the Carpathian Mountains and the Balkan Mountains. Of this there can be no doubt. Actually, it is absolutely natural that the flora and fauna are present in a wider region that neighbors the space of the respective civilization and without having a clear delimitation. But, this is the area which they say was the source of the swarming, around 3,500 B.C.. The Cambridge theory fully supports the primordiality of the Carpathians area. It obviously strengthens it. But, as we go back in time, the area inhabited by people is only reduced to Ardeal.* No other alternative is possible. Even the name Ardeal gives indications in this respect. Ardeal makes a reference to *ari*, the hills of the *ari*, which means the area where the ones called *ari*, later known as Aryans, came from. In the ancient language, letter inversion is common, so *ar* became *ra*. Some researchers stated that they found a population called *Ramania* in the Vedas. *Ra* and *ma* are primordial roots: *ra-ma*. *Ra* refers to light and flowing as in the Romanian words *rază* and *soare* which mean "ray" and "sun" respectively in English. The letter *r* (the sound of which occurs in both words) or its sound generally refers to flowing movement which is why it is associated with solar activity.

On the other hand, the ancient word *man* means *om*.** *Om* is actually the inversion of *man*: *om-mo, ma*; and *n* means closing the mouth; hence,

---

* *Translator's note:* Ardeal signifies the region in Western Romania known as Transylvania.
** *Translator's note:* Om means "man" in Romanian.

man. Anyway, Manu is considered the primordial man, at least according to the ancient Hindu, so this is also indirect proof that the Romanian people were primordial in the area where we live now. So, we have *ra-man*, light-man, meaning the "men of the light." This is how we defined ourselves in those times, by making a direct reference to the exceptional spiritual value of the inhabitants of these places. It's possible that the initial form was *ar-man*, after which it was inverted and became *ra-man*, and then it turned into *Romanian*.*

"This is perfectly logical and adds up with the other evidence," I said.

"Yes, and this is acknowledgment that this space was the primordial source from which later all other peoples, what we refer to as Indo-Europeans today, originated and spread. This was also the conclusion of thorough research done on a completely different basis."

"What do you mean?" I asked.

"In the '70s, Marija Gimbutas, a Lithuanian archeologist and professor at the University of California in Los Angeles, was appointed head of a vast research project conducted in Europe meant to document and draft the map of the discoveries related to the Neolithic Age, 5,000 years B.C.. The idea was the same: to discover the starting point for the human civilization as we know it. She went to all major archeological institutes and to all prestigious museums in Europe and asked the following question: Do you have traces dating back 5,000 years B.C.? The French said no, the Italians said no, and so did the Germans, Swedish, etc. She then drafted a map of those who answered affirmatively and named the results: Old Europe. The rest was blank. There was nothing anywhere."

"The fact that they said they had no archeological evidence doesn't mean that it didn't exist," I said.

"There are no traces of Neolithic civilization 5,000 years B.C.. I showed you, the land was simply uninhabited; it couldn't have been inhabited. There was nothing but forest and ice which withdrew gradually."

"It seems incredible that there was nobody in those areas. If they searched for clues of civilizations, where was the population around 5,000-6,000 B.C.?"

"It was restricted to our Carpathians area, its farthest border being the Peri-Carpathian region which also encompasses a small area around the mountains that includes Pannonia, Illyria to the south and Sarmatia to the north which is today's Poland. But to refer to the population of those times as living in Greece or Crete or who knows what other areas would definitely be an exaggeration. These areas appeared much later."

"What was in the rest of Europe, towards today's France and Spain?"

"They have no traces dating back as far as 5,000 years ago...no pottery, nothing."

"You mean that there was nobody else on this continent? If I had walked, I wouldn't have met anyone?"

---

* *Translator's note:* The Romanian word for "Romanian" is *Român*.

"There might have been some people but very few. The population was much reduced. But, it was here in our country where the focus was. Marija Gimbutas later wrote in a book that Romania was the heartland, the 'original land.'"

"And, science talks about Sumer as the oldest civilization."

"In comparison with the Romanian ancestral civilization, Sumerians were babies. Many maps of the different Neolithic Age civilizations have been drafted. If they are compared with today's states, the conclusion is that they all include Romania or parts of Romania as well as some territories outside of Romania. And, when overlaying them, the conclusion is that all these maps extend from the inside to the outside; not chaotically, but clearly starting from a certain area which is our Carpathians area."

"Why haven't others made this observation? As you say, it does seem quite obvious."

"Their interest is not to do this. We always go back to the same problem. Incompetence and superficiality are combined with occult political interests and manipulation. No matter how revolting it is to some people, this is the truth. We know it very well from our own sources."

"But, what happens when you say this — when you present the evidence? To be honest, it seems absurd. How can you deny something that is obvious and already proven?"

"If you talk to diplomats, academics and scientists, you'll silence them momentarily; but afterwards, they'll continue on as I have already told you. They'll say that they have certain political orders, that they want to keep their positions and other similar arguments."

"At least we know that we have the proof," I said.

"Archeological and language evidence is overwhelming. In European civilization, there is nothing older than what was found here. For example, before the island of Ada-Kaleh was destroyed by creating the reservoir for the Danube hydroelectric power plant, Ceaușescu ordered archeologists to see what else they could discover because most of the evidence is now under water. They dug up the banks of the Danube on the Romanian and former Yugoslavian sides. Their discoveries are clearly from the same civilization, but they differ in terms of chronology. The artifacts in Romania are 1,000–2,000 years older than the Yugoslavian discoveries. They are therefore separated by the Danube. We can also find some things in their territory, but the oldest are here, even if they speak about Lepenski-Vir, the name of the culture where the evidence came from. They tried to impose another name than the Romanian name, which comes from this territory, thus insinuating that this was the dominating older culture. But, it is well documented what we have found on the Romanian banks of the Danube, namely the Schela Cladovei culture, which is older than the Lepenski–Vir culture."

"How do they know this? If there is any doubt, they'll probably hang on to it and place it in front of all other arguments."

"We know that they are older because they have all been carbon-dated. It's all dated; these are no assumptions. And, this includes the beans of carbonized cereals they've discovered in these archeological sites, in the caves on the banks of the Danube...everything. They gave the findings to three foreign laboratories to avoid any problems or errors. These labs were in Holland, Germany and England. Their estimation was 7,800 years B.C.. So, people practiced agriculture in those times. They cultivated cereals. Works have been written based on the archeological discoveries of this culture and a temporal scale of the discoveries has been drafted which goes up to 11,500 years before Christ. There is a difference of 4,000 years in comparison with the findings on the other side of the Danube in the former Yugoslavian Republic. This is how long it took for civilization to cross this border. The stability and continuity of civilization on our territory has been phenomenal. This, of course, is also reflected in tradition."

"If they were agrarians in those times, it means that they had a clear system of cultural values because, as far as I know, agriculture involves rhythms, cycles, and rituals," I noted.

"This has changed the whole conception of how and where agriculture has appeared. They thought it had been brought to Europe from somewhere in Asia, but it was actually here on Romanian territory almost 8,000–9,000 years ago. According to the Cambridge University researchers who conducted the study, people remained here and were agrarians before the population swarming that took place around 3,500 B.C.. Until then, they remained here in the center. If you look at a map, you'll see that this area, the Carpathians and Transylvania, lies at about the same distance from Spain, the Ural Mountains and the northern extremity. We are in the center of Europe and we mock the 'specialists' who wrote the *Encyclopedia Britannica* where they said that the Carpathians are a mountain chain in central Europe, but they don't know how come Romania is presented as a country from Southeastern Europe when, in fact, our country encompasses most of the Carpathians. Europe ends at the Ural Mountains, not here, so we cannot say that we are in Eastern Europe. Therefore, we are right in the center of Europe. It's therefore obvious that people have left radially in the following directions: 2,900 kilometers to the Ural Mountains and 2,900 kilometers to Spain. But, they always followed the 'road of the salt.' The fact that we have so much salt and that we even have it at the surface is another argument proving that the swarming began here where it spread and created the various peoples. I have already begun telling you about this."

"Why do you call it 'the road of the salt'? I don't understand."

"When they took their sheep from the mountains to the plains, they went to today's Greece."

"If they travelled for so long, they changed with the season until they arrived there," I said.

"They could have stayed and spent the winter somewhere else, but they surely got there. The idea is that they started to carry bags of salt on donkeys until they reached these areas because, more to the south, in the Balkan Mountains, there was no salt. Sheep are not fertile without salt and the flock perishes. This is why the 'roads of salt' were created and persisted for thousands of years."

"But, why did they decide to go so far?" I asked. "After all, they left the center. Who would have liked that?"

"It wasn't about liking it or not. It was a matter of necessity, and this appears to be more and more obviously in that period, around 3,500–3,000 B.C.. They were probably going there for transhumance only and they searched for lower plains to the south. But, they had already surely begun to over populate and this led to food, living and other problems. So, they began swarming in order to free the area."

"But how did they leave? Just randomly? Did they leave their homes and go wherever their eyes took them?"

"No. They had a very simple system when they couldn't decide. They drew straws and the extra men left. There was even a poem saying that, when they were too many and couldn't ensure food where they lived, they drew straws to decide who should leave. This is how the great population swarming began: radially from the center, moving in the main directions and on along the 'roads of salt.'"

"But, how did they know that they could still ensure food? They couldn't just measure the quantity of food. And, after all, I don't think this goes like this: one year, you have food; the next you don't and therefore you leave. Then, you have food once again; then you don't."

"But, it's not far from the truth either. In any case, they started to realize that their living conditions were worsening, the level of living was dropping and more and more problems occurred. And, they realized this was caused by the large number of people. Thus, they started to leave. Over time, this has led to great transformations in culture, population and language. Leaving their homeland in the center, they first lost cohesion with the original source. They have somehow been torn apart from the primordial unity which ruled here, where their home had been for thousands of years. As is natural, the original language started to split into dialects, thus changing a lot. This happened in many regions of Europe and was directly related to the climate, topography and certain vibrational characteristics of the respective region. To all of these, we must of course add the different periods of swarming which are probably decisive and explain the apparition of the Greek, Celtic, Latin, Northern, and other 'languages.' All of these factors have had a decisive influence on the language changes. And, the fact that they could no longer contact the center (their original homeland) after their departure has amplified the process even more."

"But, they didn't all leave at the same time," I said. "It was probably a staggering as you said because, as far as I understand, this was a wide process which took place over a large period of time."

"Of course they left in successive waves and in different periods of time. This has made them even more different, separating them into distinctive communities, each one with its own characteristics. Even if they had a common background, they were nevertheless different and this has of course affected the language. The best example is the one of British English versus American English. There was a population swarming from England to America 400 years ago and you can see for yourself the differences in their language: accents, expressions, words, and even dialects. And, keep in mind the fact that we are only talking about a few hundreds of years during which communication with their origin, the starting point being England, was constant at all times, and this matters a lot."

"Things are different in this case, however, because Americans are not the followers of the English. They are the most mixed nation on Earth," I observed. "The official language, English, is their only connection with England, because they were initially an English colony. It's just a convention. It's not the language of that population."

"It's true. I only wanted to make a reference to the communication between those who left and their origin. In ancient times, when the swarming began, this communication practically didn't exist. This is why I said that a sort of rupture, a separation from the center took place with inevitable consequences with regard to the language, their knowledge and habits. When you go far away from your home, there is no more interest to keep the language. There is no rigor in maintaining it, and it thus transforms according to the environment and the needs. But even so, the Romanian language was spoken everywhere because it was the foundation of all other later languages. It was spoken in dialects; it had characteristics which corresponded to the respective areas, but people could communicate with each other. There was a common word basis, even a considerable one, which ensured fluency in communication. This was until they started to introduce the official languages, which are actually fabricated, just as I've already told you. In France, for example, in the Occitan province, there are old people who don't speak French, but they speak a kind of distorted Romanian. In England, they have imposed a language similar to the existing one, but the written form of words is closer to the Romanian words while the pronunciation has been modified to give the language a particular character. This has happened the same way everywhere except Romania because here there is nothing to impose. Here, the mother-tongue, the original language, is spoken which is sufficient in itself without dialects. For the rest, they have imposed artificially fabricated languages in schools. In some places they have succeeded. In others, as you well know, they have not. All of these language dysfunctions came from the fact that they tried to transform the original without having their own basis. The closest to the Romanian peasants' language is Sanskrit which is also called "the language of the gods." There are many Romanian words in Sanskrit and some words are even identical. You can also see them in the toponymies. For example, there is Deva which means 'god' or 'deity' in Sanskrit and there is Călimani, Călimănești and many other derived words which are known in Oriental tradition as Kali and Kal who are the goddess and god of time in Hinduism.* The discovery in the Șureanu Massif is also extraordinary from this point of view because it actually shows us the spiritual and traditional reality on this territory. Cronos, Kala and Crăciun** all represent the same 'character' in the spiritual tradition of the area. This is where it started from and it later reached India, not the other way around. From the archeological evidence and the point of view of the period of time, it is impossible for it to have been otherwise."

"And this evidence hasn't been displayed in museums?" I asked. "I think there are very many of them."

"There are many old cultures which have been discovered in Romania. Some of them are the oldest and this has puzzled the international scientific community, but everyone pretends that they don't exist. Take, for example, the famous culture from Cucuteni in Eastern Romania."

"To what period has it been dated?"

"Around 3.500 B.C. according to archeologists. As for the cultures, they can't be exactly dated because they have successive phases and approximations of hundreds of years intervening. But still, a clear idea of their date remains. As for the Cucuteni culture, they have discovered tens of thousands of statues and pottery fragments, and I think this culture is dated around 7,000 B.C.. Then, there is the culture of Tărtăria which is also near the Șureanu Massif. Some consider it controversial because the engraved clay tablets cannot be precisely dated, but this writing is 2,000 years older than the writing which was allegedly invented in Sumer. This places the culture of Tărtăria around 5,700–5,500 B.C.. And, many other cultures have been discovered which contain many conclusive objects or fragments. They therefore couldn't keep track of the number of statues and Neolithic archeological traces found in Romania. Sacks of archeological discoveries have been thrown away because nobody can inventory so many. In Germany, if they find a bone or a fragment of pottery, they immediately brush it and display it in a museum. Here, we

---

* Deva and Călimănești are the names of towns in Romania while Călimani is the name of a national park.
** Translator's note: The word *Crăciun* means "Christmas" in Romanian.

don't have people to keep track of the discoveries, not to mention a means of storing them. And all this richness in archeological relics proves the same idea: that this was the center, the origin of the following civilizations. Of course, discoveries have been made in other places too, but the oldest are here, in the Carpathians-Danube area."

"There is also the tradition and the language," I said, "but returning to the swarming, they reached India and this is the direction towards which most people swarmed. Isn't it odd?"

"Swarming towards the East is something more special. You saw that it involved the Aryans, Sumer, the Hindu civilization. It was a movement of part of the population over a distance greater than 5,000 kilometers which took place gradually. Esoterics say that swarming towards India, the East, was not actually swarming but that it represented a spiritual mission which had to be fulfilled, meaning that they had to move the spiritual center from here to there."

"Why?"

"In order to protect spiritual tradition by moving it to a place which is safer from the terrible conquests which targeted the Romanian territory."

"Nevertheless, traces and names have remained from so many gods who are now interpreted as Oriental," I noted.

"All of the main gods are present. We can especially recognize their names in toponymies. Even if so many thousands of years have passed, they are still here: Deva – Deva; Iaşi – Işa; Călimani – Kali, Kala; Mangalia – Mangala; Şîva – Şiva. Even the name of the mountain massif where this phenomenal discovery has been made is significant: Şureanu; but it initially was Sureanu, until the 's' softened and became 'ş'. Furthermore, the suffix 'eanu' was added later. It is specific to the last millennium because it used to be Surea, Mount Surea. In its turn, this name came from Suria by converting 'i' to 'e' which is a weaker vowel that is easier to pronounce. In Oriental tradition, Surya is the Sun god who is considered the supreme light that gives life, heat, and richness but also the profound spiritual symbol of immortality. If you think that they have discovered what is in fact a mountain of gold, and if we con-sider the fact that gold has almost everywhere been considered the symbol of the Sun, you can immediately get an idea of the spirituality and occult knowledge of the ancient inhabitants of this territory because, one way or another, they knew what kind of mountain this is, what is inside it and this is why they named it so, in order to have a clear symbol of its content. In time, people have forgotten this hidden meaning which fewer and fewer people knew anyway and thus its understanding faded away. Not even the legend remained because it was something so important and secret that nothing has ever happened there which involved a larger number of people and thus the news was never spread to the masses. The absolute secret probably vanished with the last priests. Only the name has remained and it is still kept, but people no longer understand its true meaning."

"Some people we are...we have everything here, yet it seems that nothing is ours," I noted, with bitterness.

"It's true. It is caused by circumstances and manipulation. It all started here, but they say it came from somewhere else. It is proven that agriculture began here, yet they say it came from the Far East. Metallurgy began here, yet they say it originated in Antalya."

"You haven't mentioned this before," I said, drawing Cezar's attention.

"The oldest metal furnace has been found at Câmpeni in the Carpathians and it is dated around 4,000 B.C.. They picked it up and took it to the British Museum in London, but they still claim that metallurgy was first discovered in Antalya. It's odd to draw the conclusion that a population without rich metal deposits would teach us, who have many metal deposits, how to process them. Here, practically all kinds of statues can be found. Others have only one statue representing a deity, here and there, but this means that this is where the tradition of worshiping that deity came from as if they had all thrown them over the fence to our yard and we just kept them intact without knowing anything about them. Relics of not one but many Vedic deities have been found in this space and in our habitats. They couldn't have been borrowed. Nobody can come and do this, just bring you an esoteric tradition. And it's not only that. We gave them the language and word families, but every word in the Romanian language is explained as coming from another language. This space was the origin of the swarming of the population towards the East and towards Europe which has been scientifically proven, but they claim that we came to Europe from the East, as migrating tribes. As you can see, it's a total inversion of values which is sought to be maintained in order to create a false and unfavorable idea concerning the Carpathians area where we live. In the best case, we get to be fully ignored."

"This is amazing, but I don't think that our people have tried too hard to prove the truth. It is the same languor and stick-in-the-mud, as if they hit our heads and made us all idiots," I broke out.

"Until several hundreds of years ago, the situation wasn't like this; but immediately after the period of the dignified rulers, who had faith and strong Romanian souls, a rupture occurred between the governing class and the peasants. The latter started to be considered fools, uncultivated and good only for work although they were dressed in white, were clean and when you see their celebration clothes, you feel embarrassed with our 'modern' clothes. They put them to work and made them idiots. They had no power to fight back; and when they did, uprisings ended in bloodshed. After this rupture, things have never been the same again. They lost the original spirit, losing their power through this kind of oppression. But, the primary background still exists. It is implanted in us through the primordial tradition we represent."

"And, it's waiting to be awakened from potentiality," I suggested.

"Exactly. It needs a kind of awakening, taking a stand, interest and initiative in order to become active," Cezar approved. "This applies to any nation, but I believe here the responsibility is greater because this was the center and, by the same law of cyclicity, it will be once again."

I remained thoughtful, looking at the photos on the display screen. Even if it were only for that place discovered inside of the mountain, it would have been enough to justify the idea of Romania being spiritual center of the world. This goes beyond any idea of worldly richness, elevation in worldly life or commerce. The unimaginable accumulation of physical richness is transposed into an exceptional spiritual richness which has undoubtedly supported the manifestation of spirituality in this territory. Seeing me quiet, looking at the photos, Cezar explained.

"What is here is almost unimaginable. Even we had difficulties in this respect, and this is why we did everything in our power to discover the entrance again. But, other reasons came first and I've already mentioned them. Professor Constantin was telling me that when he stepped on pure gold, seeing himself surrounded by this pure metal everywhere — on the ground, the ceiling, the side walls — as if it were a rock, he felt an extraordinary purity, a kind of delicacy and even holiness. He couldn't find the words to better explain that strong emotion flooding his heart. At the same time, he told me that the atmosphere had become thicker, the air 'stronger,' and yet he didn't breathe with difficulty. With all his maturity, experience and courage, the professor felt overwhelmed. The emotion, a kind of 'psychical pressing' which he perceived in that place, gave an intuitive understanding of the major importance of that place that made him tremble and wish to return. He also thought about the boy who was silent and pale with fear. The blue light, however, with a water-like reflection that had appeared in front of them, at a distance which he estimated at about 100 meters, had intrigued him more and he decided to continue. But, as they went forward, a very strange phenomenon occurred. The light became more intense and they felt that it was more difficult to walk. He kept on telling me that he had a strange feeling, as if the air was becoming thicker."

"Did he feel any physiological effects?" I asked.

"He did not say anything about this. But I suppose not, since he continued to go forward and breathed normally. The ground was relatively irregular, but everything was covered in gold. He couldn't appreciate the layer thickness; but as he felt it, it must have been very thick. At a certain point, due to the increasing intensity of the blue light, he started to better notice the structure of the wide corridor. He could observe, though not quite clearly, that it continued in its arched form, high and majestic, for another 60-70 meters; but afterwards, he started to distinguish on the walls, on both sides, some high formations, like huge slabs, which he saw somehow cut from the walls of the corridor. As he told me, that was the beginning of the end."

Listening to Cezar, I also felt an emotion which I couldn't really explain. Finding out about those elements, combined with the photos made in that place, has created a state of special sensibility which gave me thrills. It was a state of spirit, a fine emotion which brought me closer to those events.

There was also the mystery behind the disappearance of the two persons who had access to that place. Cezar didn't mention the cause. He let things come gradually, allowing me to discover the development of the events. I quickly learned what had happened with great amazement. It seems that the professor and the boy went forward, hesitating, helped more and more by the powerful blue light which got stronger and stronger. They no longer needed flashlights. The chamber had a charming illumination which looked like water and had an unimaginably beautiful glitter. I then read the part of the professor's statement as he had insisted on that description a lot and therefore concluded that he had been very impressed. I could only imagine the phenomenal impact of such a glance over his psychic sensibilities as well as that of the boy's. Professor Constantin declared that in the last part of the corridor, which he could see more clearly up to its end, the roof had an upwards arch that became huge, like that of a dome. He estimated its height at about 3 to 3.5 meters, maybe more. He also discovered the mystery of some forms which he had not been able to see clearly before. At an approximate distance of 20-25 meters from the huge wall at the end of the corridor, he saw three armchairs on both sides, like thrones, which surrounded a parallelepipedal table placed at the center. The six thrones were also made of massive gold and seemed encrusted in the ground. They were neatly done, quite well polished and had high backs of over two meters. Fundamentally speaking, they had no legs or other elements but looked very well like the letter 'L' with the observation that the seat was very thick and almost one meter high. These were very imposing and massive gold constructions but not rough. Their lines were simply but carefully contoured with perfect proportions.

All six thrones were identical: three on the left and three on the right of the corridor, symmetrically placed and perfectly in front of each other. Between them and the side walls there remained a distance of approximately 1.5-2 meters. In the middle, there was a sort of table which was actually a parallelepipedon made of massive gold, like a kind of plateau which probably served as a table. It was very well carved and perfectly aligned with the sides of the thrones. It was in fact a block of massive gold, shaped like a parallel-epipedon, and was as high as the upper side of the thrones and as long as the distance over which they were placed. This entire ensemble was perfectly symmetrical and was completed at the end of the table by a seventh throne which was bigger than the others and, in a way, presided over the "gathering." Placed in front of the smaller side of the table, at the end of the corridor, it faced the person who came through the corridor. Its small side, the seat, was just like that of the other thrones, but the back was much higher, reaching three meters, just as the professor had specified. Furthermore, it had a different shape than the others. It wasn't a parallelepipedon, but a truncated cone section with the larger base upwards, on the superior side. The entire ensemble, amazing in its massiveness and simplicity, had a perfect harmony that imposed respect and solemnity. As Cezar admitted, that structure couldn't be other than a kind of "council chamber" for six human beings, probably high priests, presided over by a seventh man who was obviously considered and respected as an accomplished spiritual authority. But what completely astonished the professor was the ensemble of huge plates engraved in the corridor wall which he, from a distance, had interpreted as slabs. These were in fact huge panels, also parallelepipedons, that were symmetrically placed behind each throne with three on each side. In fact, it was proven that they were directly sculpted within the corridor walls, emerging slightly in relief as huge slabs and higher than the thrones and exactly up to the height of the back of the seventh throne. On their perfectly finished surface, a text of thousands of unknown characters and signs was engraved. The signs were very clearly and orderly engraved and covered the plates almost entirely with the exception of a kind of curb on each side which was approximately ten centimeters large.

As far as he could tell, the professor estimated that the engraved signs, which surely represented some kind of writing, were different from the ones he had seen earlier in the corridor, near the small platform on the ground. Cezar told me that it was also a completely unknown writing according to the results of the analysis conducted by the prestigious international institutions with which our department had collaborated for this case. Furthermore, the special graphic analysis has shown that the writing on the huge panels was older than the unknown one previously found by the professor. The nature of these signs, their succession, and the way they were composed, was proof of a very advanced level of knowledge of written language. The rows were perfectly parallel and quite often the height of the characters was the same over the entire slab. The effort made to engrave those plates was remarkable and nobody knew how this had been achieved, especially since the plates were all made of one piece in the mountain wall. It was most probable that the texts described a history of that place and its true meaning or that they referred to the occupant of each throne, offering elements of a certain nature about that person.

The huge assembly hall was dominated by the seventh plate which was bigger than the others, encrusted on the background wall of the corridor and behind the throne of the leading priest. From the professor's description and as I later saw in the only photo of the ensemble, that slab was gigantic. It was almost ten to twelve meters high and about four meters thick. As its base was placed at a certain height from the ground, it dominated the view majestically, its superior side being placed at approximately three quarters from the height of the dome. The slab was made after the same simple concept as the other six but was much larger and more impressive. There was, however, no text engraved on it but only the disk of a huge sun from which many rays started towards the end of the rectangle. This representation, which surely is an essential symbol for what was there, was grandiose and, through its force and grandeur, it dominated the entire assembly hall from above the main throne of the leading priest. As far as I could see from the troubling photo made by the professor, the impression was amplified by the charming blue light which was sublimely combined with the glitter of the gold around. From the photo, it was impossible to distinguish the source of that light, but it surely came from the ground behind the main throne. As it was partly hidden by the imposing massiveness and its back, it only appeared as an effect in the entire assembly hall.

"Here is when the toughest part, which has confused everything, started," Cezar said. "Even now, after so many years, we don't understand more than we did back than. It is probably the end point of the journey, some kind of conversion of space and time, accomplished in a way which completely exceeds normal understanding. How it appeared there and why, nobody knows. An idea would be the connection which has just appeared with the incident in Antarctica because that buoy has signaled this space, but what can we understand from this? It's like a cosmic knot which is combined with something from Jupiter's moon, Europa. The great planet is probably connected with all this, but who knows what this connection is? There is clearly an answer because we have physical evidence: the cosmic buoy, the signals, this place, the indication to Alaska, and the projection from Europa; but why all these exist and what are the true implications is a great mystery. In any case, it seems to be an extraordinary energy focus point, both for cosmic and for spiritual energy. It is possible that major decisions have been taken here and that beings with a very high level of spiritual evolution have been here. We don't even know the origin of the writing on the slabs. It is extremely old, but how old is it? Then there is the serious barrier which doesn't allow me to search this time cliché with the device in the Bucegi Mountains. We practically don't know anything."

I was astonished with everything I saw and learned. Cezar showed me the last photo made by professor Constantin, from an angle placed behind the main throne, on its right side. It showed an empty space shaped like an ellipsis at the level of the ground, marked by a small wall on the edges, like a curb. The professor stated that the ellipsis was about two meter long on its long axis and about one meter and a half on its short axis.

"What is there is relatively hard to conceive, even for an open mind," said Cezar. "The professor told me that when he went near that place and looked down, he felt he was losing his consciousness. He even fainted for a few seconds and fell but came back to his senses quickly."

"What did he see? What happened?" I asked impatiently.

From the photo, I could not tell what was there because it was made from a certain distance and at a sharp angle. The light wasn't very good either. I could, however, clearly see something very dark with some glitter in it. Cezar then explained.

"When he looked at that empty space, the professor saw another universe. He told me it was as if he was looking through the porthole of a space ship at the surrounding cosmos. He could see the black cosmic space and the glitter of the stars. The difference was that the respective 'porthole' actually didn't exist, but the access was free, as if through a fountain. Downwards, a bit to the side, he noticed a great planet with formations similar to the ones on Earth when seen from space. He compared the size of that planet with that of Earth as seen from the Moon. The difference was the color of that planet which combined blue with different shades of yellow and orange."

"But you've just said he fainted," I said, astonished at what I learned.

"He fainted immediately after seeing the first images, or at least that's what he told me. He also estimated that he only fainted for a couple of seconds, but when he woke up, he saw the boy standing on the edge of that ellipsis and looking hypnotized and downwards towards the planet. The professor than saw a kind of shining funnel which was rising from a point on the planet towards the place where they were standing. He then became very scared and stepped backwards. It wasn't clear to him what happened next. The professor said he wasn't sure he remembered all that happened there. He only knows that the light became very intense, becoming white and, at a certain point, the surface of the ellipsis began to shine strongly. Professor Constantin saw the boy simply stepping over its edge and disappearing downwards through it. Immediately afterwards, the brightness decreased in intensity and the professor went near the edge of the empty space. He saw the 'funnel' withdrawing towards that beautiful planet and the universe around it became quiet once again."

"How long did he remain like this? What did he do?" I asked, curious to find out what happened next.

"He doesn't know for sure. He said that, at a certain moment, he once again saw that light vortex rising from the planet towards him and he felt scared, got up and ran back towards the exit. It only took him a few minutes to get out to the archeological site. With his last powers, he ran to the village police station and asked to speak to Bucharest, to his RIS connection person who was in charge of supervising the digs and discoveries made. He was told to remain there and not to speak with anyone else about what he had seen. They arrived very quickly during the same evening. There were three agents and they were very suspicious. The professor immediately led them to that place. It is unknown how it happened, but one of them disappeared just like the boy. The professor gave me a precise description of the final moments before they covered the entrance because I had already received a phone call informing me that they were coming for him from Bucharest; and I had to transcribe very quickly and summarize the statement I had recorded on tape. So, I preferred his superficial description, which was global, instead of a detailed yet incomplete one. I was hoping things would calm down and I could have access to another statement from the professor with more details. I could not know what the SNDC would decide. That was the situation. It's good that things haven't remained completely unknown. They went out again; and, in order to avoid any contact with someone who might have disclosed the place, they remained at the entrance all night. The following day, they called Bucharest and a special representative immediately came and was overwhelmed with the situation, ordering the immediate stop up of the entrance. As I said, maybe it was better like this."

"They probably thought that they would return from Bucharest better prepared and with precise orders," I assumed. "They could simply remember the location in the meantime."

"Yes, that's what they thought, too. But they didn't foresee the accident where they all died."

"It looks like a kind of 'self-protection' of destiny."

"They only allowed the driver of the concrete mixer to come and help them seal the entrance. When they took a last trip to the assembly hall, the driver probably didn't listen to them and followed them out of curiosity. They became alarmed when they heard his screaming. He had entered with a flashlight and was shocked at seeing the gold seam. From that moment on, they couldn't get along with him any more. They quickly went out and covered the entrance with concrete by themselves, the best way they could, working almost all day long. They asked for help from two police officers in the village and told them to guard the access to the road leading there and the surroundings, but they didn't allow them to come closer. The professor said that they remained at a distance of 300 to 400 meters. They then left the professor at the police station and drove for Bucharest that night. On the way, they had a tragic accident."

Cezar stopped, making a short pause.

"Now you know everything that happened there."

I looked at the clock. It was almost 2:00 a.m.. Feeling as if the waters had calmed down, I was calm and serene inside and thanked Cezar for that memorable evening which I will always remember. I was deeply impressed and clearly felt that a certain understanding had deeply touched my heart. My soul was flooded with a mysterious need to withdraw inside myself, to think quietly about the ancestral enigma of these people and to its connection with the discovery made in the Şureanu Mountain. What unseen influences fill our souls from the unmeasurable distance of the cosmos? I went out in the yard which was empty given the hour. The cold mountain air cooled my hot face and the sound of the forest carried me on the wings of sensible imagination. A whisper of the mountain slowly floated towards the sky as if waking up the unknown and profound memory of these realms. I looked up at the sky filled with stars glittering enigmatically and felt the nostalgia of the forgotten beginnings and the divine worlds within our hearts.

– THE END –

PART TWO

by Peter Moon

CHAPTER SIX

THE VALLEY OF THE GOLDEN THRONES

Since the publication of the Romanian version of the book you have just read, I have maintained a sporadic correspondence with Radu Cinamar. While his communication sheds a little more insight on the matters mentioned, it does not offer unequivocal proof of many of his claims in the four books of the *Transylvania Series*. In his letters to me, Radu has more than once apologized that he cannot offer further proof at this time.

After writing the introduction at the beginning of this book, I travelled to Romania for the fifth time and have discovered further corroboration of his stories. More importantly, I have been privy to an entire scenario of events that reach well beyond the imagination of ordinary people and reveal a higher order at work. This is why I referred to and stressed the importance of the progenitors of the *Transylvania Series* in the *Introduction*. Radu Cinamar is an intriguing character, but there are other characters involved in this scenario who are of even greater interest and actually put Radu into a position where he could write these highly unique tales.

On my most recent trip to Sarmizegetusa, I was surprised and pleased to unexpectedly encounter an area in Transylvania that is known as the Valley of the Golden Thrones. It was pointed out to me by a local legend keeper, and I will discuss more about my encounter with this unique man later on in this book. This valley, he said, leads to the golden caves that Professor Constantin discovered, as mentioned in Chapter Five. The area obviously had its own legends and history long before Radu Cinamar became a renowned writer, but for now, I will restrain my commentary to address only the information presented by Radu in Chapter Five. For these purposes, I will accept all of Radu's data at face value and hypothesize that it is true.

The first issue I will address is the "parallelepipedon" or "golden bed" that was found in the golden tunnels and is elevated off the ground. It was accompanied by hieroglyphics that were interpreted by reducing them to the lowest common denominator. They read as follows:

KR – IO; SAL-MOŞ, HERE IS
FOREVER, THE WORLDS UNITE

The scholars employed by Department Zero interpreted KR as Kronos but were somewhat sketchy with regard to IO. To anyone who has studied Western esoteric Magick even a little, they will readily recognize that IO is an iteration that was frequently used by Jack Parsons when he recited his pagan poetry (as in *Io-Pan*). More specifically, IO refers to IAO which is another aspect of tetragrammaton. Tetragrammaton is most popularly known by the Hebrew letters *Yod He Vau He*, often transliterated into the more common YHVH or YHWH that is sometimes pronounced Yahweh or Yahwah. While these four letters correspond to Fire, Water, Air and Earth, IAO corresponds to another aspect of the divinity which is Creation, Destruction, and Resurrection, symbolized by Isis, Apophis, and Osiris. Isis was viewed as the Creator goddess; Apophis was the destroyer god, often symbolized by a serpent and recognized as darkness (the enemy of Ra); and Osiris was the god who was slain by Set but resurrected when Isis gathered up all of his body parts, most notably the lost penis. Note that both YHWH and IAO consist entirely of vowels sounds which is intended as an expression of the divinity. In both cases, IAO and YHVH make up key component parts of the Godhead or Divinity. If you wish, and it is advisable, you can study up on both IAO and YHVH on the internet for further elucidation on these ancient concepts. The scholarship, if pursued rigorously, becomes very involved.

While I find their interpretation intriguing and of considerable value, I also realize that there is considerably more that can be added to the understanding of these matters with regard to my own already published studies. For one, I am referring to the correspondence between KR and Car, Kar, Cor, or Kor, the goddess who inspired names such as Carthage, Carnac, Charlemagne, Koran, and a host of others. The word *cardiac* (heart) comes from the goddess Car. In ancient times, Car or Kor was a major phonetic iteration of the Goddess.

If you study both the phonetics and etymology of CR or KR, you will see that it is inherently related to "distance," in particular with regard to the invariance of the space-time interval that was included in the appendix of *Transylvanian Moonrise*. The invariance of the space-time interval, as taught to me originally by Dr. David Anderson, refers to mathematical models revealing that time equates to distance. In other words, it is misdefined in common dictionaries. Time is movement through space. CR refers to movement in space when we consider that the word *car* evolved out of CR as an expression of movement. CR is also the root of *chariot* which is virtually the same as *car*, but in *chariot*, we have a direct or indirect (depending upon how you look at it) allusion (from the Tarot) to the physical body which is the instrument we use to negotiate movement through space and time.

When we consider the human body and its immersion into the physical universe, there is a very rich etymology in the word *carbon* as follows:

Carbon (n.) non-metallic element, 1789, coined 1787 in French by Lavoisier as charbone, from L. *carbo* (gen. *carbonis*) "glowing coal, charcoal," from PIE root **ker-* "heat, fire, to burn" (cf. L. *cremare* "to burn;" Skt. *krsna* "black, burnt," kudayati "singes;" Lith. *kuriu* "to heat," *karštas* "hot," *krosnis* "oven;" O.C.S. *kurjo* "to smoke," *krada* "fireplace, hearth;" Rus. *ceren* "brazier;" O.H.G. *harsta* "roasting;" Goth. *hauri* "coal;" O.N. *hyrr* "fire;" O.E. *heorð* "hearth"). (Note: The symbol * indicates uncertainty in etymology.)

At its core, the word *carbon* refers to the fire or hearth of the goddess Car. This concept was transmuted into the Hebrew letter *shin* where it symbolizes the Shekinah Glory which sparks over the Mercy Seat in the Holy of Holies. The concept of fire with the goddess Car corresponds quite precisely with the goddess Kali of Indian tradition. Kali is not only a goddess of fire and heat but one of time as well. Kali inspired words like *caliente* in Spanish which means heat and also words like *calendar* which refers to time.

As we are in a carbon-based universe, we cannot escape the correspondence to 666. Carbon has 6 protons, 6 neutrons, and 6 electrons. All the embroidered symbolism off 666 is reduced to the lowest common denominator when we simply consider that 666 refers to the core expression of physicality.

Aleister Crowley defined and preoccupied himself with the concept of 666, and we find another very important etymological tie-in to CR in the words *cross* and *circle*. This is another aspect of the goddess Car that is known as carfax or carrefour, both of which refer to the circle and cross, a key feature of Crowley's "Key of It All" as described in *The Book of the Law*. Carfax refers to the unfoldment of all geometric potentials as well as the morphogenetic aspects that accompany consciousness. This ranges from the most banal aspects of chemistry and cellular life to the more esoteric aspects of enlightened or godlike intelligence. Perhaps more importantly, carfax also refers to a portal outside the circle(s) of time.

When we combine KR and IO, as was presented to us in the translation of the hieroglyphics, we have the unfoldment of life in all of its myriad variations through the principles of creation, destruction and resurrection. We are talking about the Tree of Life.

Cezar specifically mentioned that *io* relates to *eu*, both of which mean "I." Combining this with *kr*, Cezar suggests that KR IO is "I Kronos" which is quite intriguing when we consider it as an iteration of the god of time. I would also point out that *I* is no different than *EYE*, the archaic form of which is EVE (the letter *Y* being an extension of the letter *V*, both letters being considered interchangeable) or IEVE.* EYE evolved from EVE, the original spelling for

---

* In the Phoenician Paleo-Hebrew language of Canaan, the name of God was IEVE. If you compare the original writing for this word in Phoenician, you will find it hauntingly similar to how it is spelled and written in Arabic, Hebrew, Japanese, Chinese, and Sanskrit. When you strip away all of the ignorance caused by transliteration with regard to phonetics and their representative letters, IEVE was pronounced in the same way that we say Eve. In other words, the name for the Creator was IEVE or Eve. The so-called Fall from Grace is (*continued on page 164*)

the word YHVE or YHVH. In other words, the original word for *God* was the word we know as *Eve*. It represented a Goddess. EYE and EVE are quite interchangeable, both referring to conscious perception and self-referencing intelligence.

All of this, including that which was offered by Cezar and his team, suggests that this area of the golden tunnels represents a key carfax point of the universe being conscious of itself. If you consider that the universe is akin to a live organism, it is like a major ganglia or key component of the "brain" of the planet. Further, and based upon the data just presented, if one reconsiders the iteration *KR IO*, it is simply saying "I am a divine vehicle of time," or it could refer to the "Eye of Time" which associates God with time, just as Car or Kali are associated with time. This corresponds exactly with the definition of KR as Kronos.

It is already pretty clear from what Radu has offered us that this area of Transylvania is a portal into time. I have only re-emphasized it with additional reference points. If we make KR and IO one word, we have KRIO which is the same as the Greek *chreo* (related to *cristos* or *christ*), a virtual phonetic duplicate of the Sanskrit *kriya*, a tantric term which refers to a spontaneous physical or energetic manifestation that clears out energy in relation to rising kundalini. In Greek, *chreo* referred to communion with a god or oracle. The phonetics of *kriya* and *krishna* should also be noted. *Kri* is very similar to *cre*, as in *create* or *creator*, but *krishna* (which also appears in the aforementioned etymology of *carbon*) means "dark blue" in Sanskrit, and this brings us back to the mysterious blue race of which both Krishna and Machandi are identified with. The associations run very deep.

Let us now consider the next part of the hieroglyphics which were interpreted as SAL-MOŞ. Neither Radu, Cezar, nor their scholastic team mentioned the rather obvious correspondence between SAL-MOŞ and Zalmoxis, the most popular and ubiquitous god in Romanian folklore. This was noticed, however, by my translator who states in the footnote in Chapter Five that the word *moş* means "old man" in Romanian while *zăul* is an archaic Romanian word for "the god." It has been claimed that *zăul-moş* was the origin for the name Zalmoxis, the god of the Dacians. This definition makes a lot of sense because there are many different iterations of Zalmoxis that come to us,

(continued from page 163) very much evident in the name *IEVE* itself when it was transliterated into *YHVH*, *YHWH*, or *JHVH*. If you consider the conventional Hebraic derivation of *Eve*, you will learn that it comes from the Hebrew *chavvah* which means "living one" or "source of life." *Chavvah* is a particularly interesting word because it derives from two earlier words where the letters *y* and *v* are demonstrated to be convertible: *chavah* = breath and *chayah* = to live. The very essence of life is thus embodied in the name of Eve as breath and life go hand-in-hand. It is, after all, the act of breathing that makes one alive. In this sense, it suggests that this golden "bed" discovered by Professor Constantin is part and parcel of the living breath of the earth. (Note: This information and the relationship between Eve and the eye are from *The Montauk Book of the Living*, by Peter Moon, where it is further expounded upon in Chapters 38 and 39.)

mostly in legend form, but there are historical references as well. There is no question that the ancient Dacians worshiped Zalmoxis. The *zal* in Zalmoxis means *leaping* or *transcending* while the *moxis* means "god" but also equates to *moses* or *messiah*.

Even though Herodotus, the Greek historian who first told the West about Zalmoxis, refuted the story, conventional views have persisted that Zalmoxis was a disciple of Pythagoras who spent four years in a cave whereupon he was transformed from a man into a god. Herodotus suggested that, based upon what he learned, it is far more likely that it was Zalmoxis who actually taught Pythagoras. This not only aligns with theories that Zalmoxis was the basis for mystery schools which eventually sprouted into the Egyptian, Hebrew, and Christian religions, it fits with what Cezar says about the repression and obfuscation of truth with regard to the crucible of civilization emanating from the land we now know as Romania and, more specifically, Transylvania.

On my 2011 trip to Romania, I learned that Zalmoxis is really an ancient principle or archetype that has embraced many remarkable characters in history. More to the point, Zalmoxis is really a name for Gemini, a word which stems from "germinate" and refers to twins. The symbol of Zalmoxis or Gemini is really the swastika as rendered below where you can visualize it as being made up of two numeral 2's (see figure below and to the left).

The symbol above left is the Gemini or Zalmoxis swastika (whirling in a clockwise direction) because it is evocative of two number 2's. Conversely, it is the reversal of that swastika (on the right, going counterclockwise) that can be rendered as 6's and is most often identified with the Nazis.

This association with the numeral 2 is not accidental as the original symbolism referred to pairs or twins, and Zalmoxis represents two very important twins who were native to ancient Dacia (the land we know today as Romania) — and they were Apollo and Artemis (or Diana). There were also several other sets of twins who have embodied this archetype.*

---

* The number 22 is considered a master number in numerology, representing the life path of a "master builder." This is not only a Masonic reference, but 22 is highlighted by the fact that the Tarot features 22 major arcana which are pathways connecting the sepiroth (or spheres) of the Tree of Life. The swastika represents 22, but one can also see 5 (see the swastika on the right) in its construction (*continued on page 166*)

It was also pointed out to me on my 2011 trip to Romania that this swastika on the right represents 666. You can see this in the example. When the swastika is turned around and is whorled (*whorl* is another name for the meaning of the swastika) or whirled, it reveals the numeral six as it moves from one position to another. I was further told that, in recent times, an ancient tablet was found not too far south of Bucharest which states "I am 666 and I am waiting to be transformed." This was an astonishing and major archeological discovery. The transformation of 666 (our carbon-based material universe) during these so-called end times, according to my Romanian friend, refers to the process of discovery that began with the chamber beneath the Sphinx. It has been extended to the revelation of the manuscript in this book as well as the remarkable "Hall of the Golden Thrones" with its accompanying portal.

When we consider the "Peter Moon experience," it is easy to hypothesize or recognize that I was led to all of this through the investigation of the Montauk Project. While it is not quite that simple, we can delineate it through the various progressions of my own experience. This begins with the Babalon Working and the interweaving of its players into my personal life through the investigation of the synchronicity surrounding the Montauk Project. It extends to Dr. David Anderson who served as the catalyst in getting me to Romania. What is perhaps the most special aspect of these experiences is that so many of the spectacular and key elements of the subjects I have dealt with are not only ripe in the Romanian scenario, they are waiting to be activated and reveal yet further information. These include, but are not restricted to the Blue Race, monatomic white gold, immortality, the Goddess, the Inner Earth, and the technology of time travel. These revelations and, more importantly, the transformation process that is implied, represent an endeavor that is designed for all of humanity. It is, quite obviously, not a job that is done overnight.

Zalmoxis is a very appropriate catalyst for these matters because the undisputed essence of this archetype is transformation from the human condition to that of an immortal creature or "god." For me to visit the capital city or sacred domain of Zalmoxis and experience so many tangible tie-ins has certainly been a lot of fun and exciting for me, but it is much more than that. It is serious business, but I would also add that it is also pleasant business. The fact that Elinor, the mysterious alchemist who can do more than feign ancient knowledge with regard to prolonging life, lurks in the background is one further testament to the Zalmoxis factor or hope of immortality. This

---

(*continued from page 165*) along with the 6 already referred to. 5 + 6 represent 11 (the number of Abrahadabra) or the hexagram over the pentagram (see *Montauk Book of the Living* for a detailed diagram) which reveals the pattern of the Qabalistic Tree of Life which, when turned or twisted, represents the mobius strip of DNA. Two of these strands equals 11 + 11 or 22. These two strands of DNA represent Gemini which, once again, means germinate.

not only lights up the archetypal essence of Romania like a Christmas tree, it offers the hope that this mysterious and too often overlooked country embodies for Mankind.

Zalmoxis has been rendered in many different ways by many different authors and legend keepers. While the majority of these (I have certainly not read them all) concern or emphasize the transition of a mortal human, there are some that include Zalmoxis as an entity that is not in human form, sometimes demanding and receiving human sacrifices. In such scenarios, it is only the best and most perfect humans who are selected for sacrifice so that they can make a successful transition out of this world. While it is entirely possible and even likely that such sacrifices existed, it is my personal opinion that this sort of sacrificial rite degenerated over time. In other words, death and killing began to be ritualized as the transition from a human to a godlike state became less and less tangible. In other words, the issue eventually had to be forced. At the end of this degeneration, the ritual becomes an absolute horror and becomes the opposite of transformation. This is a demonic influence which managed to weave its way into a process that either once aspired to or actually brought about something akin to everlasting life.

In any event, Gemini is represented by Zalmoxis, and Gemini is the sign of initiation. Gemini is distinctly and deliberately rendered as such in the *Thoth Tarot Deck* by Lady Freida Harris and Aleister Crowley in ATU VI The Lovers, sometimes also referred to as "The Brothers" or "The Twins." ATU means "divine emanation" and refers to the key or trump cards of the Tarot, also known as the Major Arcana. This card goes hand-in-hand with ATU XIV Art, which is also known as "Temperance" or "Alchemy." ATU VI, which features a Moorish king paired with a white queen, is the precursor to the alchemical secrets of ATU XIV. Gemini concerns itself with duality and opposites as the precursor to the secrets of alchemy. These secrets include immortality as well as transmuting base metals into gold. In this regard, ATU XIV contains another very interesting feature and that is the acronym V.I.T.R.I.O.L., which stands for Visita Interiora Terrae Rectifcando Invenies Occultum Lapidem in Latin. The above phrase literally means "visit the interior of the earth and by rectification you shall find the hidden stone."

This reference to V.I.T.R.I.O.L. with regard to the Inner Earth is very synchronistic if not suggestive of the precise drama unfolding in Romania. Besides this, V.I.T.R.I.O.L. is a trace reference to the Universal Solvent which refers to the elixir by which one transmutes base metals into gold or, in the spiritual sense, the mechanism by which one transmutes base energies to more sublime ones. V.I.T.R.I.O.L. refers to both the Microcosm and the Macrocosm. In the Macrocosm, it tells us that we can engage in this transmutation process by looking into the Inner Earth both metaphorically and in actuality.

It should also be pointed out that V.I.T.R.I.O.L. has another particular significance because, according to Rosicrucian tradition, this acronym was found in the mysterious legendary tomb of Christian Rosenkreutz, the titular founder of Rosicrucianism. While the story is too complex to go into here, there are rumors and legends that Christian Rosenkreutz never died and was known in other times (potentially in a reincarnated form) as Francis Bacon and St. Germain, amongst others. The most pervasive legend, however, is that his tomb was discovered 120 years after his death.

When we consider the stories of Elinor, and that includes the mysterious network of individuals who "smuggled" him out of Romania and set him up to do his work, we are faced with a secret society that is parallel to the sympathies of the Rosicrucians if not the Rosicrucians themselves. Whichever way you view it, we are confronted with transmutation of the human condition through the vehicle and mysteries of the Inner Earth.

One of these mysteries concerns the "parallelepipedon" or "golden bed" discovered by Professor Constantin. Besides the hieroglyphics I have just elaborated upon, it was also mentioned that this bed of gold featured indentations. The scholars employed were uniform in their assessment that this was most definitely used as a bed of some sort. Based upon what I consider to be rather obvious data, it is my assessment that this was utilized for out-of-body travel by a priesthood. If gold is the superconductor that is suggested by Cezar, this would be a perfect vehicle for such circumstances.

Although Cezar mentioned that there is a serious barrier (in regard to the golden "bed") preventing him from searching this time cliché with the device in the Bucegi Mountains, I do believe he was eventually able to access this area himself. My conclusion is based upon what is written in Radu's books as well his personal correspondence to me. My intuition suggests that Cezar eventually accessed this "golden bed" and did some sort of psychic travelling which connected him to the Inner Earth beings that he is reported to be an ambassador to. As I have reported earlier, Radu has stated to me that Cezar left Department Zero in order to serve as an ambassador to these beings. The scenario I have suggested is a very plausible explanation of what might have taken place. Independent of Radu, I have been told that the mysterious tunnel that leads to the Inner Earth in the Bucegi Complex leads to an underground necropolis which is near the Golden Thrones and the portal to the other world. This Inner Earth tunnel does not lead in only one direction but is more like an underground highway which goes to many different locations.

Earlier in this book, it was mentioned that Radu was assigned the job of coordinating the section whose area of activity concerns the borderline between the real and the unreal. It seems that Cezar quite literally jumped beyond the borderline and into an area that is not quite within this world. In any event, Radu wrote to me about a year ago that he was delighted to have finally heard from Cezar after a very long absence of communication. Cezar reassured him that he would return when the time is appropriate. These circumstances might sound unusual if not bizarre. They do, however, fit it in with a point in the text of *The Secret Parchment* that many of you might have missed. I know that I missed it the first time I read the manuscript. This concerns Professor Constantin's statement wherein he felt he was losing his consciousness. He also mentions a blue light that is reminiscent of the violet light that Radu described in the tunnel between the Bucegi complex and the Occult Chamber beneath Giza (in the book *Mystery of Egypt*.) This makes one wonder if what he was experiencing was actually taking place in this reality or in another one. The report of his taking photographs of the tunnel and golden thrones, however, suggests that it is either in this reality or another that closely resembles this one.

Cezar also comments that what was encountered there is relatively hard to conceive, even for an open mind, and that it is probably some kind of conversion of space and time, accomplished in a way which completely exceeds normal understanding. Further, Cezar states that it is connected to Alaska and the cosmic buoy in Antarctica in the manner of a cosmic knot that is tied to whatever is emanating from Jupiter's moon, Europa. While all of this presents an enigma, it also reveals the presence of a superior consciousness. The entire scenario is delightfully similar to the movie *2001: A Space Odyssey* and its sequels, including a mysterious beacon in the form of a monolith from Europa. Ironically, Jupiter features another moon by the name of Io.

Although IO was defined as meaning IAO or "I," it was also pointed out to me at Atlantykron that IO can, quite specifically and intentionally, refer to the number ten. Ten is *diez* in Spanish and refers to the deity. More importantly, a Romanian author, Mihaela Muraru-Mandrea, has written about ten-dimensional string theory, according to which there are ten dimensions in this universe and that is how time materializes or manifests in our day-to-day world. In other words, time fixes you in ten dimensions. She also refers to a Universal Integrating Matrix which is a mathematical model for DNA. As I do not understand Romanian and have not read her book, I cannot elaborate further. Certain people at Atlantykron, however, told me this was very important to the equation and should be mentioned in this book. I cannot take it further right now.

As you can see, the hieroglyphics are replete with deep meanings that reach into the infinite. If you want to take it further still, you can look up the roots of *ion, iodine,* and *Ionia* (where we get the word *Ionic* from). *Ion* derives from *e,* "to go, to walk" and ions got their name from this definition as they go or move towards the electrode of opposite charge. In this respect, *io* or *ion* represents duality. You can even see it as the two binary digits, *1* and *0*, that are used in computer languages and also in the biology of the brain. The word *iodine* comes from the Greek *ioeides* which means "violet-colored," from *ion* "the violet; dark blue flower," + *eidos* "appearance"; and we are once again back at the concept of sacred blue. Ionia was the name of a civilization that once included parts of ancient Greece and Asia Minor. The name *Ionia* derives from Ion, the son of Apollo and Creusa, and is believed to have derived from the Sanskrit *yoni*, meaning "womb" or "vulva." The Ionians were a goddess worshiping people and, I would assume, were a part of the ancient Amazon culture.

Anyway you want to look at it, the hieroglyphics described by Radu and Cezar trace back to the roots of ancient mysteries. Perhaps the most significant is the etymology of *karma*, a word which is believed to have derived from the pre-Indo-European *k(w)er* which reduces to KR and means "to make, form." This is the idea of creating one's own karma. Whatever you think of these stories is not as important as what you make or create with them. In my case, I was pursuing a quest which began some time back. There are, however, some other players creating with the karma of Romania.

CHAPTER SEVEN

RULE BRITANNIA

It is a completely understandable and human reaction to doubt the veracity of Radu Cinamar's incredible tales. What is indisputable, however, are the intriguing facts and circumstances surrounding them. Besides the unique and unprecedented alliance between the Romanians and the Americans in the wake of the Bucegi discovery, there have been additional developments that have added fuel to the fire with regard to the discoveries reported by Radu. Not only was Romania admitted to NATO as a consequence of the new Romanian alliance, but one of the former commanders of NATO, Wesley Clark, is now serving as a personal advisor to the Prime Minister of Romania and is reported to be a frequent visitor in Bucharest.

Clark came to my interest years ago during his failed bid for the Oval Office, at which time he publicized his interest in time travel and said it was scientifically feasible. It suggests he knows more than a little about Dr. David Anderson, a man who rubs elbows with all sorts of high level political people. The association between Clark and the Prime Minister is intriguing if not disturbing, and this would be due to the latter's recent bid to oust the Romanian president, virtually the only politician who is known to be privy to Department Zero matters. Clark's resume is rather unique to say the least. He grew up as a Baptist, claims to be a Roman Catholic, but says he attends Presbyterian services. Clark also asserted to Jewish groups that he is of the lineage of the Cohen priests, the keepers of the Holy of Holies, the sacred shrine which held the Ark of the Covenant. As a politician, he seems to have all critical angles covered with regard to faith. Whatever his ostensible reasons for being involved in Romania, his unspoken intentions are of far more intrigue. If Radu's accounts are even partially true, they would certainly explain the keen interest and participation by such a person as Wesley Clark.

Another passionate and relatively new player in Romanian politics is Prince Charles, the heir apparent to the throne of England. Subsequent to the events relayed by Radu with regard to Department Zero and the golden tunnels, Prince Charles and the Romanian media have been promoting his Transylvanian heritage, his blood relation to Vlad the Impaler (who is a national hero in Romania), and the prospect of him succeeding King Michael as the King of Romania. I am not exaggerating, and you can even find articles on the internet indicating that when Queen Elizabeth passes on, Charles will abdicate the throne of England in favor of Prince William and then assume the throne of Romania. The rationale behind this is that he allegedly has a more legitimate claim to the Romanian throne than Michael or his successors. While most serious political commentators might dismiss this as preposterous, one has to wonder why this rhetoric is being fostered by the Romanian press and is being egged on by the Prince himself. What is the motivation?

If you listen to Prince Charles' often publicized motivations with regard to Transylvania, he talks a very good game and makes it look and sound as if he is a passionate protector of the environment. The Prince has invested in quaint Transylvanian real estate and waxes over this area as being the last of its kind, a tribute to a natural ecosystem. He has also criticized the incursion of Gabriel Resources, a Canadian company, who has a contract with the Romanian government to extract gold from a region called Rosia Montana whereby they plan to utilize a cyanide extraction process that has the potential to create horrific environmental degradation. While the Romanian Supreme Court has blocked this contract for the time being due to popular outrage, Gabriel Resources has vowed to their investors to find a way around the Supreme Court. If we choose to look deeper into these matters, however, it appears as if the Prince is fostering a public relations ploy that belies other intentions. More specifically, facts demonstrate an unhealthy alliance between the Crown of England and Gabriel Resources.

While the Crown is not subject to revealing its financial dealings, it is a documented fact that the Crown purchased the company that eventually became British Petroleum or BP. Prince Charles, BP, and Gabriel Resources are all advocates of an idea coined by the United Nations as "Sustainable Development" which essentially means that one should extract resources at a level by which the population can benefit but also at a rate that will not destroy or severely compromise the natural resources of an area. This is fine verbiage and is excellent PR, but in practice, BP (with the help of Ken Lay of Enron fame) has expanded upon this idea and set up a barter exchange whereby companies are fined for polluting, and the money goes to the exchange which then invests in green technologies that will benefit the environment. In political parlance, this is known as "Cap-and-Trade" which virtually no one really understands. Barack Obama, known for his connections with BP, is a big supporter of Cap-and-Trade. His wife was a lawyer at the Chicago firm which figured out how this would all work. More details are available on Dr. True Ott's website. I learned about this from him.

While this sounds like a virtuous idea, we are not told that BP is the owner of the exchange (to be operated by Goldman Sachs who was bought into it) as well as many of the green technologies being developed. In other words, they would receive the money collected in fines. By reason of this astute and ingenious manipulation, BP was and is in a position to expand their income fourfold if oil were to become antiquated as a major fuel source. In either case, they have harnessed the world market whether the oil market fails or succeeds.

It is not known whether the Crown is an investor in Gabriel Resources, but as their holdings are not held up to public scrutiny by law, we will never know. This, in a sense, makes us all subjects of the Crown when it comes to global financial intrigue. Their influence is occulted.

On another public relations front, Prince Charles and the royal family have suffered considerable fallout in recent times. One of his former mentors, Jimmy Savile, has been exposed as a notorious pedophile in recent times. Savile was a television star who portrayed himself as a clown, but he had a very influential and strange association with the royal family. Princess Diana exposed the Jimmy Savile connection to Prince Charles prior to her untimely and tragic death. Savile was also a player in back-door politics and was seen calling certain shots in Israel during the Six Day War with Egypt. There is currently a scandal concerning the BBC suppressing the knowledge of Savile's pedophilia. In addition to this, a British appeals court recently ruled that Prince Charles's letters of influence to government officials are subject to public disclosure. This was, quite oddly, protested by the Attorney General, who is seeking to protect the Prince from such disclosure. The bottom line is that there is a hornets nest festering around the ruling influence of the royal family and Prince Charles. It is more than substantial, and it is not prudent to elaborate on it further at this point in this book as it is too involved. You can read up on it separately if you wish.

Prince Charles has also long been known to have a strong interest in occultism. While this is no secret, the circumstances and history of the occult influences surrounding him are not that well known to the general public. This goes back to the Sixteenth Century and the reign of Queen Elizabeth I. This topic and its impact upon the world has been explained in my book *Synchronicity and the Seventh Seal*, but I will give a brief summary here. I should add that it is literally impossible to logically understand the machinations and the underbelly of the British Empire without understanding the influence of Dr. John Dee, an occultist who is more popularly known as either the court astrologer or court magician of Queen Elizabeth I.*

The quintessential scholar of his day, Dee sought to move beyond the obvious limitations of conventional scholarship and began investigating all of the functions of the human brain that are normally inaccessible. More importantly, he was dealing with the mechanism that would activate them. These functions, particularly the activating mechanism, are so shut off in ordinary human beings that there should be no wonder why Dee's very existence has been met with so much "dead gray matter" by historians. We are talking about the program that controls the programs by which we live and meander through life on Earth. Such a concept, of course, is not much different from what is happening in Romania today.

Dee was a conjuror who literally conjured up the British Empire according to occult principles. With Edward Talbot Kelly, he communicated

---

* *The Occult Philosophy in the Elizabethan Age* by Frances Yates is a thorough and well footnoted history which seeks to resolve a major paradox about John Dee: why was he so influential yet virtually ignored by history?

with discarnate entities who taught them the Enochian language, a precise language with its own grammar and syntax, that is said to be the language of the angels. In less theological terms, it is a fundamental interface with the source code of the matrix of creation. Dee's forays into the occult did lead to the formation of the British Empire, and he even coined the term *Rule Britannia*. This conjuration is said to have taken place in the presence of Kit Marlowe on the Isle of Dogs at the point which eventually became known as the Prime Meridian — the spot where the time keeping of civilization is all referenced to. This is not an accident. One of the more spectacular historical references to Dee's magic can be found in Shakespeare's *The Tempest*, a work which contains hidden and not-so-hidden references to Dee and how his conjurations defeated the Spanish Armada. This historical event, where the British defeated the Spanish against great odds, sealed Britain's rule of the seas. If you truly study Dee, you will come to see that what I have stated is not only not an exaggeration but is the tip of an iceberg.

It should also be pointed out that Francis Bacon was a pupil of John Dee, and there is no way to measure either one of these men's influence on today's civilization. Just as Queen Elizabeth and Dee are inseparable, so are Dee and Bacon inextricably related. Bacon was an instrumental factor in the formal foundation of the Rosicrucian Society, an organization which came about only two years after Dee's death. The first Rosicrucian papers appeared in Germany just after Dee had returned from the Continent to his home. As Rosicrucianism is an invisible factor in the threads of immortality that has been propagated in the *Transylvania Series*, the John Dee influence should not be discounted.

For those who truly understand the occultism of John Dee, it is clearly obvious that Prince Charles is not so much a significant practitioner of occult magic but rather an instrument of it. This is the way the British Empire was constructed. It should also be noted that as much as John Dee was a conjuror, he was really an instrument of spirits himself. His intelligence and studies opened him up to strings of consciousness that swallowed him up and used him. This is not unusual in the spirit world, a place where the big fish swallows the little fish. The ruler of the spirit world, as well as the sea, is Neptune or any other name you wish to ascribe to that archetype. John Dee and Prince Charles could only be servants of this archetypal force.

The point in all of this is the connection and rivalries between the various mystery schools of planet earth with regard to the discoveries taking place in Romania. This is the environment in which Transylvania has now taken center stage in the political machinations of planet earth.

CHAPTER EIGHT

PELES CASTLE

At this writing, I have taken five sojourns to Romania, two of them taking me to Sarmizegetusa and three to the Romanian Sphinx. The site that had eluded me, until this year, was Mount Omu. It means the "Mountain of Man" wherein the latter word is meant to refer to Humankind. It was a sacred site to the ancient Dacians and contains its own network of underground tunnels.

On my first trip to Romania, our plane arrived very late and our hotel rooms were sold to others. We had to go to a resort in the mountains just to find a place to sleep. There, during my first sleep in Romania, I had an encounter with an androgynous spirit who visited me. One year later, I would meet a lady whose face corresponded with this spirit. She grew up near Mount Omu and identified herself with the spirit of the mountain. There is considerably more to the dream, but it is too complex to go into. What is important is that I was "contacted" through the dream state within twenty-four hours of my arrival in Romania. It was accompanied by a tangential manifestation one year later.

After spending two nights in a mountain hotel without any practical transportation, we found a new hotel in the city but were unceremoniously dumped at Peles Castle on a rainy day with no explanation from a taxi driver who we thought was our tour guide. Peles Castle was the traditional summer home of the Romanian royal family but is now leased by them to the state who runs it as a tourist attraction. Peles Castle is named after the nearby Peles River, but no one is quite certain of the etymology. It is believed to have something to do with the Romanian word "*piele*," a word which means "skin" and can also refer to "bravery." Of considerable interest to me at that time was that one of John Dee's key talismans was a magic ring featuring the letters PELE. I could not help but think of this association although I could not place any connection to the royal family of England at that time.

Having no desire to enter the palace, I did not go inside. I was, however, accosted by a very unusual and friendly beggar who seemed to come and go out of nowhere. The only negotiable currency I had was given to me for my two companions and myself. As I was responsible for the entire party, I was not inclined to give him anything and sent him on his way. Upon my return home, I learned about a very old and famous legend: when you come to Romania and see a beggar, you should give him something. By showing the generosity of your heart, this act will result in Romania opening its heart to you. With hindsight, I was remiss over the fact that I had not fulfilled this legend. Our trip to Romania had been pretty rugged up to the point we met the beggar. Even though I had not given him anything, things began to slowly but steadily improve, especially when we reached our final destination of Atlantykron in southeastern Romania.

At Atlantykron, I learned that the most sacred area of the country is Sarmizegetusa, located in the heart of Transylvania. With much encouragement, it became my desire to visit the ancient capital of the Dacians on my second visit. Due to the hospitality and friendship of Nicole Vasilcovschi, I was able to visit Sarmizegetusa on my second visit in 2009. It was quite an adventure and was written up in the book *Transylvanian Moonrise*. On August 12th of that year, just after my journey to Sarmizegetusa, I had an out-of-body dream. There are dreams, and there are dreams. This one was reaching the deepest part of my soul and why I was in Romania. I awoke in a lucid state and found myself floating over the landscape of Romania. A gigantic dark cloud that was unmistakably loaded with dark energy was hovering over a major complex which represented the official government and/or their buildings. Black helicopters appeared, and I am not quite sure whether they were part of the negative energy or were trying to contain it. In either case, they came with the dark energy. The best part of the dream was a very clear message to me that I was neither a part of the dark energy nor connected to it. I felt free.

Two years later, I returned to the Sphinx and met my friends from Bulgaria. We had hoped to take the long hike to the top of Mount Omu. By the time we arrived at the Sphinx, however, we were told there was not enough time to take the three-hour hike and return in time for the last cable car home. Instead, we visited the nearby Iomolita Cave which goes deep within the earth and is quite spectacular. Nicole accompanied me on this trip as well and told me that there was another cave nearby. Known as the Priest's Cave, it contains a natural "bowl" of water that fills whenever water is taken from it. The water, however, does not spill over. It just stops. It is a smaller cave, but we did not have time to visit it.

Hoping to visit Mount Omu on our second day, it rained. Instead, I went with my Bulgarian friends to Castelul Julia Hasdeu. It is a small castle loaded with Masonic symbolism and was built by B.P. Hasdeu, a remarkable renaissance man who received worldwide acclaim for his accomplishments and adopted Romania as his home country. When his daughter Julia died at the premature age of seventeen, she contacted him from beyond and directed the building of the castle to exact specifications. Through seances and the like, he was in repeated communication with his departed daughter whom he loved passionately. The castle tour features headphones in about four languages, one of which is English. It was a very interesting and spiritual way to spend a rainy day. On our return, my four Bulgarian friends wanted to visit Peles Castle. I was not in favor of returning but was out-voted. Just as I had experienced two years earlier, it was raining hard when we got to Peles Castle. As it turned out, no one wanted to go inside.

In 2012, only a couple of months before writing this chapter, I was the guest of Jonette Crowley who leads spiritual tours to sacred sites across the world (see *jonettecrowley.com* for further information). As is described in her book, *The Eagle and the Condor,* Jonette Crowley suddenly and unexpectedly acquired the ability to channel many years ago. It has changed her life for the better and has enabled her to cross continents and wield a great deal of influence worldwide. I recommend her book, especially for a better understanding of how she works.

During a previous trip to the Bucegi Mountains, at a time when she had no knowledge of Radu's books, Jonette correctly perceived that there were tunnels below the mountains, and she took an "out-of-body tour" of the area. During this journey of the soul, she penetrated the subtle realms whereupon she was escorted by "the white wolf" in order to protect her from certain negative energies that were present. Although Jonette was unaware of Radu's books at that time, one of her friends who was with her, Anna, told her about the books as well as the fact that I had published them in English. As a consequence, Jonette contacted me years ago and asked if I would like to be part of a future spiritual journey with her to Romania. I accepted and that is how I ended up on this tour as an esoteric guide.

Jonette and her husband, Ed Oakley, also accompanied me to Atlantykron where we all lectured and got to meet Nicolae Nicolae, the publisher of Dacia magazine. Nicholae wanted to interview me because he had heard that I was an expert on Sarmizegetusa. This was extremely amusing to me because I had only been to Sarmizegetusa once (in 2009), and I am far from an expert. He, on the other hand, regularly produces an excellent magazine on the history of the Dacians, and this has included a complex analysis of Sarmizegetusa. In any event, we had a lengthy conversation through an interpreter. One thing he spoke about was the gold in and around Sarmizegetusa. According to the Dacian way of life, accumulating gold means trouble in life. There are considerable legends about the curse of gold. It does, however, link to the astral body. It should be known that the stories and actualities of Dacian gold exist completely aside from Radu's stories.

After departing Atlantykron, we travelled to Bucharest where we met up with some forty people, including a dozen Romanians, who would accompany us on our journey to Mount Omu, Sarmizegetusa, and a host of other interesting and sacred places. After a welcome dinner on a Friday evening, we set out early on the morning of August 11th. Our first step was Peles Castle. Once again, it rained. This time, however, I found my beggar right away and gave him ten lei which is almost $3.00. He was ever so grateful and blessed me. Thus it was, that Romania, which had already opened its heart to me, was about to open up yet deeper chambers of its heart on this visit.

After being pounded by synchronicity and avoiding Peles Castle twice, I would finally take the hint and take the tour on my third visit. It was beautiful beyond belief but describing it will not be done here. What was important was that I became informed about and conscious of the Romanian royal family, which is of German origin and is currently headed by King Michael who is 91 years old at this writing. The Romanian royal family has only been in existence a relatively short period of time. Less than two-hundred years-old, Romania only became a country after the Crimean War, a little over a century ago. The Romanian royal family's ancestral roots trace back to Germany and this is how Prince Charles justifies his own claim to the throne of Romania. Charles and his family are from the German House of Hanover.

Thus it was that I encountered a rather profound synchronicity on the first leg of my sacred journey. After becoming deeply aware of the royal family and its connections, I was subsequently subjected to lively news reports from the Romanian media about Prince Charles waxing environmental over Transylvania with accompanying rhetoric about him succeeding King Michael after the latter's death. As I said, there is a plan for Charles to abdicate the throne of England in favor of Prince William. While the Romanian royal family might not have moved me one way or the other, the entire issue of the sovereignty of Romania was being thrust in my face by the Romanian media.

It is challenging to explain the conscious symbolism I was being confronted with by reason of my sojourn to Peles Castle and the underlying occult current of the royalty involved. I am once again referring to the PELE ring of John Dee and its occult influence upon the British Empire. This ring, given to Dee by Enochian angels, was presented to him as the very same ring that King Solomon used to control the jinn and build his temple. It represents all worldly power; and more importantly, the functional power (jinn) that made the worldly power possible. PELE has different meanings, the most commonly accepted of which is "he who will work wonders." A no less accurate but far more occult and deeper meaning (from which the name of the famous Pele volcano is derived) for PELE is "black fire" or, more specifically, "the black fire of one's will." This concept and its profound significance, especially as regards the unfolding situation in Romania, are somewhat challenging to explain. The essential esoterics of the matter are described in my book *Synchronicity and the Seventh Seal*. At best, this can only be tightly summarized here. I can, however, add some additional insight based upon my own acquired knowledge since that book was written.

The era of John Dee, out of which the writings of Shakespeare emerged, was a time when the English language suffered or enjoyed (depending upon how you look at it) sloppy spelling with a conspicuous interchangeability of consonants and vowels. In this regard, the signature letters of PELE on Dee's ring have been interpreted as both *apple* (PELE = EPEL = APPLE) and *fall* (PELE = FELE = FALL). This represents the biblical story of the apple and the Fall, and it is not a mere coincidence. Do keep in mind here the comment about coincidences from the parchment that is the focus of this book.

The apple, besides containing the pentagram, is shaped upon the geometric pattern of a heart. When you throw out the apple, you have not only trashed knowledge, you have thrown out anything that could be termed compassion. The universe we live in is already known for its shortcomings when it comes to the heart and compassion. This brings us to the first of the teachings in the parchment: there is a divine source of compassion in the universe. If we do not acknowledge and recognize it, it is our loss and we are taking ourselves further down the rabbit hole. The PELE ring, however, conjures up plenty of energies that show no compassion. Solomon's ring had everything to do with enslaving or commanding the jinn. His so-called public works enslaved most of the local and distant populations. Whenever you study or experience the divinity, you have to remember that it is double-sided. This supreme power, however, represents the core control matrix of our local universe. Real world politics, including the Crown, revolve around this matrix. This explains why Prince Charles is orbiting around this area of Transylvania. If he is not fully aware of the circumstances you have just read about in this book, his energetic field has no choice but to hover around this key point of power. Slavery and freedom are close brothers. You cannot have one without the other.

If Solomon truly commanded the jinn through Enochian magick, it did not die when he died and the temple was raided. It was conjured up again by John Dee who was the pre-eminent scholar of his day with a library of thousands upon thousands of books at a time when Cambridge had less than five hundred. His library was something akin to the library at Pharos (Alexandria) for its time. Knowledge attracts spirits and Dee gated in the mother lode, a lode which represents so much of the hidden control over today's civilization. I will state again that it was this complex that was running Dee, not the other way around. It also ran Solomon. In this respect, the best that a Dee or Solomon can do is to have a conversation with this terrible or awesome force that manifests as a formidable power. In other words, one can interact back and forth, if one is lucky. It is not unlike wrestling or boxing on the edge of a cliff. The shortcomings of the aspirant or player are going to come into view loud and clear and be amplified. Solomon's empire went into ruin immediately upon his death and Dee ended up in poverty, discarded from the powerful empire he engineered and magically erected with the help of magical "friends."

When I suggest having a conversation with this formidable power that represents the control of our evolutionary matrix, to say nothing of our political matrix, this runs hand-in-hand with the stated purpose of Aleister Crowley's magick which is, specifically, to converse with one's own Holy Guardian Angel or HGA. This is akin to your true or higher self. One obtains conversation with one's HGA by activating one's TRUE WILL. This is really no different than the fifth precept in the secret parchment which has to do with aligning oneself with the will of God. It is important to point out here that the entire modus operandi of Aleister Crowley's magical work, as dictated by *The Book of the Law*, is *Do What Thou Wilt shall be the whole of the law*. What is heinous about this dictate is not the statement itself, but rather, that virtually all practitioners of magick see this statement and think it means something akin to eating as many Hershey bars as your stomach can put up with or having as much sex as you can get away with. The whole proposition is that one should seek out and discover one's TRUE WILL, this being something akin to that which is connected to the essence of life (God). What is equally or even more heinous than the aforesaid practitioners of magick are people who know nothing about the subject who will look at such and say, "Look, he's saying you can eat as many Hershey bars as you want and have sex with them too!" That being said, it should also be mentioned that even a serious practitioner of magick, who aspires to more than Hershey bars and sex, is predisposed to falling into temptation and being side-tracked. Demonic possession, sometimes very subtle, is rampant in this field. The solution is simple: work on yourself diligently and cultivate your own true will. It does not happen overnight or by joining a magical order. The TRUE WILL very much aligns with step number five of the secret parchment and has to do with reaching for "the Highest Peak of the Kingdom Without Name."

When we consider the political machinations surrounding the discoveries in Romania, we have to consider and reconsider the jinn, again and again. When we refer back to the inscription of KR, there is another viewpoint with regard to the goddess KOR, and that is its etymological reference to both the heart (as in *cardiac*) and the word *core*, as in the core of an apple. As was said earlier, the apple shows the archetypal symbol for a heart and compassion. The core of an apple, however, shows the symbol of a pentagram. In other words, if you make a transverse cut of an apple, it will reveal a five-pointed star in the center. Thus, the core or *shin* is that which is within the heart. It might also interest you to note that the dictionary's etymology of the word *compassion* states that it originates from the traditional passion of the Christ. Although it is certainly not true, it is as if our concept of compassion began with Christ and/or the Christ story. Krishna, of course, was full of compassion long before the Christian era. As has been painstakingly demonstrated in *Synchronicity and the Seventh Seal,* shin is the secret word of Freemasonry and that is the core principle upon which Christianity was formulated.

Although the rival forces surrounding Transylvania can be considered two polarities representing the Christ and the Antichrist, it does not have to be viewed that way. What we cannot escape from, however, is the fact that the black fire or hidden will suffers a blockage on the TRUE WILL. This applies on a collective basis, but it most certainly reflects back to all of us as individuals on some level. When we arrive at and recognize *shin*, we are not only at the gateway of a new aeon, we are at the fulcrum of change, and this includes the long missing compassion already mentioned.

In esoteric Judaism, the hidden meaning of *shin* is demonstrated by means of a metaphorical comparison to a piece of coal. Let us first look at the three flames emitting from the top of the letter *shin* itself. See below.

The Hebrew letter *shin*

These three "flames" represent three quantum states. First is the black essence of the coal which symbolizes the changeless essence of the black void. It is sometimes known as the Black Flame as it houses the second, hidden flame, which also contains the hidden will. This is comparable to a piece of coal because when coal burns, it is fueled by a hidden inner flame which cannot be seen by the naked eye. This inner flame is the power to change within the "changeless" universe. This is *shin*, also known as the eternal hidden flame of life. It has no beginning and no end but always survives. It is the quantum potential to change.

The third flame represents actual change. When you apply the element of air to a piece of coal by blowing on it, you have created a flame that is now outside of the coal and visible, and this represents the continuity of life. Breath (or prana) is a push-pull (inward and outward) exchange of the element of air that makes us alive or dead. It is the test by which something is judged to be alive or dead. It is also important to remember that *shin* serves as a bridge between life and death because coal is created as a result of dead vegetable matter condensing over a period of considerable years. It is a never ending cycle of alpha and omega.

Shin represents the inner chamber and quintessence of the heart. In physiology, the primary physical function of the heart is to circulate blood and energy to the entirety of the physical body. If we think of *shin* on a collective basis, it represents circulation through not only the morphogenetic grid but throughout the universe itself. The fact that KR not only represents *shin* in the inner chamber of the heart but also Kronos, or time, encourages us to look at the relationship between time and the heart as well as the circulation factor between the two. Saturn (Latin for Kronos) is often viewed as the antithesis of compassion as it represents cold hard facts independent of emotion. In astrology, if one is conflicted with issues of the heart (Venus), the antidote is Saturn. Conversely, if one is surrounded by a desert of cold hard facts, the antidote for too much Saturn is Venus. There is an archetypal push-pull between time and the heart, the phenomena of nostalgia being just one example.

For those of you who have studied my past work, you know that I was led to the revelation of the meaning of *shin* through my pursuit of the time phenomena of both the Montauk Project and Ong's Hat. The circuitous path of synchronicity led me directly and spectacularly to Marjorie Cameron, a human representation of Babalon, who introduced me to the cosmic relevance of the divine feminine. This not only represents the compassion principle but also the relentless and ruthless aspects of Kali. As I was taking a spiritual journey to Sarmizegetusa, my past research was not only catching up with me, it was intertwining in an expository way. The trip to Peles Castle was only the first leg of my second sacred journey to Sarmizegetusa, and I was getting far more than I had bargained for. My third trip to Peles Castle was forcing me to make a subconscious association with my past studies of John Dee.

In this respect, a relevant hallmark of John Dee's writing is one particular conversation with Michael, an angelic entity. When Dee tried to pin Michael down by telling him to come when he is ready, Michael tersely replied by saying, "We lead time, Tyme leadeth not us!" This offers us some insight into the forces in play in the scenario that Cezar has described with regards to his use of the time machine made available to him. Although the artifices that Cezar uses to penetrate time are functional, they are monitored by forces that demonstrate themselves to be a senior monitor.

All of these factors, which very much includes my past studies and books, were showing themselves to be an active part of the landscape I was adventuring into on my sacred journey. This applies not only to the Crown of England but to the monitors of Tyme itself. My destination was Sarmizegetusa, an area that is said to house some of the most powerful energies in the world. And I would never even have learned about Sarmizegetusa had it not been for time scientist, Dr. David Anderson, arranging for my first trip to Romania in 2009.

I have herein expounded upon certain key aspects of my past studies because you will soon read about how they began to interplay on the journey itself. As for the regular three-dimensional world, it was now time to continue on with the rest of my sacred journey. As we emerged from Peles Castle, it was raining hard, just as it had on my two previous trips there. We huddled into the modern bus to escape the weather and get ready for our next destination: Mount Omu.

CHAPTER NINE

MOUNT OMU

Gathering our backpacks and ponchos, we secured our luggage in the bus before transferring to several four-wheel-drive vehicles that would take us directly to the Romanian Sphinx. The rain was not encouraging because we were slated to hike from the Sphinx to Mount Omu, a three-hour long trip on a day with nice weather. Due to the rain, I am sure Jonette would have cancelled and delayed this part of the journey if not for the fact that the accommodations on Mount Omu had been already secured for that night.

Our vehicles let us off right in front of the building which receives cable cars from down either side of the mountain. There were sheep all around as I made my way into the building where a woman and her daughter sell all sorts of honey products from the area. I bought and consumed a honey-laced cracker which gave me a boost of energy, the likes of which I have never quite felt before. It was the high point of the day and very much needed.

Not far from the honey ladies is a public rest room with two stalls, neither of which features a conventional toilet seat. It is important that I give you an idea of the toilet experience for those of you in Western countries who might like to travel there someday. Those of us who wanted to use the toilet went inside where we were greeted by a burly Romanian woman who collects a toilet donation that is the equivalent of about twenty-five or thirty cents. She was dispensing "not quite enough" toilet paper to those who needed it. Acting as both the jinn of the toilet and the toilet paper as well, she would then direct you to one of the two stalls. There is also a sink for washing your hands. I had brought my own toilet paper in my backpack, and this is a must for any excursions you take in Romania. It can make all the difference in the world and helps with other intangible aspects as well. Had I needed more toilet paper from the jinn of the toilet, I think I could have persuaded her to part with another strip of paper for another quarter. For those of you who wish to travel to such destinations in Romania, be warned.

Our specific destination was Mount Omu, the name of which literally means "Mountain of Man" as in "Mountain of Humankind." It is an area that is studded with underground caverns, and the Dacians viewed it as an ascension chamber or stairway to heaven. Both then and now, the locale features sites with altars and sacred stones used for worship. Any human journey to Mount Omu can only be a microcosm of the more grander aspects that are implied by the magical geography and history of the area. It manifests in different ways for different individuals.

Mostly uphill, the journey to Omu was an invigorating but somewhat brutal hike. The conditions were wet and miserable, including muddy terrain. Those with tennis shoes got their feet wet. Due to the uncomfortable conditions, there was no time to gather around and either contemplate or enjoy the Sphinx. Everyone was rather scattered. Up to that time, Jonette's only formal address to the group, other than a few concise words in the hotel lobby in Bucharest, had been via the public address system on the bus. There was just enough direction so that everyone knew to move up the mountain and follow the hiking posts. Everyone tended to gather in small groups and make their way up the mountain according to their own chosen pace. We had also been advised to bring our own water as there was no guarantee of it atop Mount Omu. Personally, I was mostly preoccupied with keeping my video camera dry. I had a good poncho, and it did the job. My feet did not get wet at all due to a good pair of hiking shoes. The only discomfort I endured was sweat from my T-shirt and turtleneck. In my case, the water penetrating me came from the inside and not the outside. At least two people could not make it and stayed at the hotel cabin near the Sphinx.

The views on the hike were beautiful, particularly after the rain ceased for the second half of the journey. I was finally able to take some video. There were many interesting rock formations and also cave entrances in the distance. I have put up on YouTube a short video of about seven minutes which features some of the terrain. It is called "A Trip to Mount Omu and the Sphinx."

The last part of the hike is supposed to feature electromagnetic anomalies whereby you feel refreshed after having traversed the area. While this might be exaggerated somewhat, there was plenty of energy in the group when we reached the top. Such a hike is not for the faint-hearted. We all worked hard to get to the top, and it was a trial by earth as well as a trial by water. When you finally get to the top, there is a good-sized cabin and "restaurant" with no running water and no plumbing. It features minimal accommodations where several people sleep together, all in a short row, on a large platform "bunk bed." There is a higher level and a lower level, and it forms an L-shape around the inside of the cabin. It is not heated. If you ever plan to go to Omu, accommodations need to be scheduled ahead of time as you do not want to arrive in the evening with no place to sleep.

Even before everyone got to the cabin, Jonette arranged meals for those of us who had arrived. As rustic as everything was, it was a great comfort compared to being out in the wet wilderness. It was not until about 9:30 or 10:00 o'clock that we gathered in the main sleeping quarters for a discussion and channeling courtesy of Jonette who channeled the mountain itself. The message of the mountain was that it is time to reclaim the energies for the sacred spiral. The goddess, she said, left this area aeons ago, and it is now time for the feminine to come back. War will be neutralized by compassion. The salamander (fire dragon) is the protector of the sacred fire and is the transformative symbol of yin and yang. We are to work with the salamander. It was also explained that, during the germination process within the womb, we had all once possessed the body of a salamander.

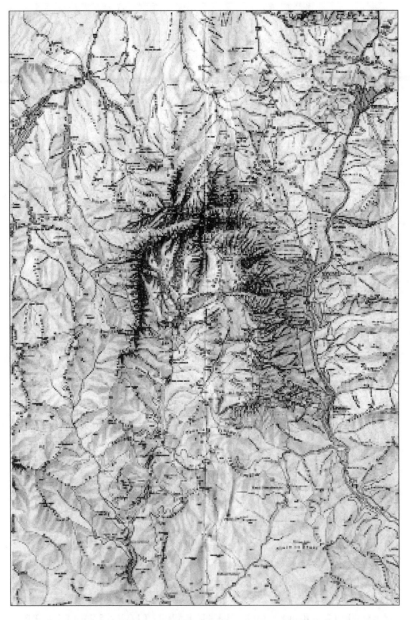

ABOVE IS A TOPOGRAPHICAL MAP OF THE BUCEGI
REGION THAT REVEALS THE LIKENESS OF A FACE. SEE
THE NEXT PAGE FOR FURTHER EXPLANATION.

185

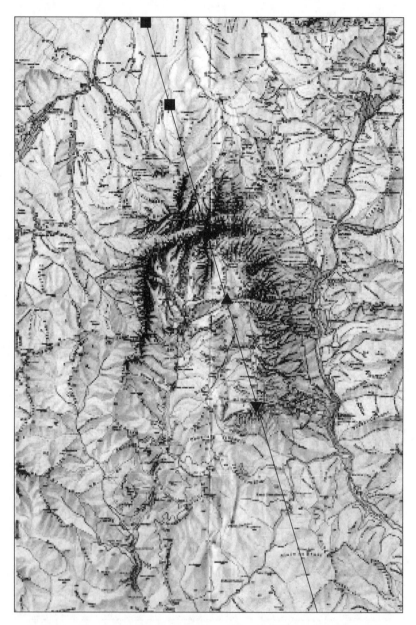

ABOVE IS AN APPROXIMATE RENDITION, SUBJECT TO
OBSERVER ERROR, OF THE MAP SHOWN ON YOUTUBE
BY COSMIN. ▼ = COLTII LUI BARBES, ▲ = THE SPHINX AND
BABELE, ● = MOUNT OMU, ■ = OTHER TOPOGRAPHICAL
PEAKS RECOGNIZED AS SACRED SITES.

Jonette's channeling resulted in a lot of spontaneous contributions from the group, the most dramatic of which was from Cosmin, our Romanian tour guide and coordinator. He showed us a topographical map of the general area, and how Mount Omu, the Sphinx, and the rock known as Babele are all aligned on a vertical line which is superimposed over a large area of topography that appears to be the profile of a human face (see map). It is very important to note that the depiction of such a face could only be recognized from a vehicle or view from high in the sky. Of additional importance and irony is that the part of the face that equates to the chin was named Coltii Lui Barbes or the "Thorns of Bărbesh." This name was ascertained hundreds of years ago and long before topographical maps were available. In Romanian, the word for chin is *bărbie*, and this is a clear indication of the name being derived from the chin or area of the chin which includes words like *barba*, meaning beard. Thorns could refer to the spikes of hair that make up a beard, probably named after the terrain of the area. Mount Omu is at the crown of the head while the Sphinx and Babele are at the eye level of the face. If you follow the vertical line that extends downwards from the crown, eye, and chin, it will lead directly to the Giza Plateau. If you draw a perpendicular line to the vertical line, the "eye" of this face is looking in the direction of Tibet. This was not the only revelation that Mount Omu imparted to us, but it is an objective reference point that is very relevant to share. This map and Cosmin's dialogue can be viewed in the aforementioned YouTube video, "A Trip to Mount Omu and the Sphinx."

Cosmin followed his presentation of the map with an incredible story about a vision he had about this area. It was actually the most spectacular of different visions he had experienced in the last two years. Not previously prone to such visions, it amazed him. Although the vision was rather short in terms of human time, it impinged upon his consciousness. It is such a rich vignette that I have encouraged him to develop it into a book at some point.

According to the vision, there was a huge crystal next to Babele (which is only a short distance away — maybe a hundred yards or so south of the Sphinx). This crystal was a depository for information and served a purpose that was something akin to the Library of Alexandria. There was a port next to Babele where space ships would come and land. Representatives of different civilizations would land at the port, work with the crystal, and leave. They would access the information for their own purpose, the only requirement being that they were to download whatever information they possessed into this crystal. There was no other payment or tax. All Romania (or Dacia or whatever you want to call the host civilization) had to do was to maintain this crystal for Mankind and allow anyone to work with it. There were so many different ships that wanted to utilize this huge crystal that it took many days, and often months, to make an appointment to land.

One day, after a period of turbulence, an extremely large ship gave a signal that it wanted to use the crystal. The Mount Omu faction had never seen this civilization before but had heard of them and recognized them as the civilization that created Humankind and the population of earth. Their request created two immediate problems. The ship was so huge that it was very challenging to have it land in the mountain area. There was little room. Second, there were many other ships in orbit waiting for their turn to access the crystal. It also did not help that there was not a familiar language between the two factions.

A quick decision was required, and this would be made by a council of thirteen elders of which Cosmin was the youngest. His job was primarily concerned with logistics. The council met at Mount Omu, most of them feeling a moral obligation to allow this huge ship to land because their civilization represented the forefathers of the human race. Meetings of this council were regularly held at Omu, and this is where they made their decisions. After a quick discussion, the council invited them to land. Cosmin was the only one to vote against this as he was in charge of logistics, and this operation would be a nightmare. He was already committed to other ships who had reserved their access, but he was now assigned the responsibility of fixing the logistical nightmare in order that this ship could land and do its work.

The entire evolution took place very fast. Telling all other ships to remain in orbit for further instructions, they cleared out the port for this huge ship. It took maybe twenty minutes. A positive signal was given to the ship to land, and it did so. The area was cleared of most personnel. Two or three remained in a tall tower, and there were two or three guards positioned every so often for protection of the visitors. Although the ship was huge, it fit like a snug glove with part of it sticking out over the edge of the mountain. A door eventually opened and five beings came out. Standing two and a half meters high, their appearance was both unique and interesting. With hands and feet barely emerging out of their suits, they walked around like penguins to get around. They possessed dome helmets which looked like black glass, and one could not see their faces.

The crystal itself was surrounded with columns, all of which had a marble floor beneath it. There was a ring on top of each column. The five penguin beings who disembarked from the ship went to the crystal. The being in the center lifted his hands over the crystal as did two others to his side. The other two did not raise their hands at all. The crystal then lit up like a Christmas tree, and Cosmin was intrigued by how much the crystal resonated with these beings. This sort of response was unusual.

Looking at these creatures, Cosmin felt that they were acknowledging his presence without saying anything. Although he was very interested in them compared to the other civilizations he routinely dealt with, he had become upset because they had asked to have their way as they claimed to be the forefathers of that particular Dacian or Romanian civilization. As this incident unfolded, Cosmin was just looking and watching them without any thoughts. The being to the right of the central being then turned to him. Although Cosmin could see his gaze, he could not see his eyes. He then felt as if he had been filled with all the galactic love possible. During the time he actually experienced this vision, shivers went through his body and be began crying. He felt the universe was loving him through this being. This profound glance lasted only about two seconds before the being turned his gaze back to the crystal. They soon finished, turned away, and went back to their ship, taking off with no goodbye. Looking at them at the edge of the landing pad, he wished that they would have stayed longer.

This rather remarkably intense vision was not only detailed, it all flashed sort of instantaneously through Cosmin's mind when it occurred. More importantly, it had all happened in the very territory we were visiting. If the vision is at least partially true, it gives a very plausible explanation of how the Bucegi complex beneath the Sphinx was able to acquire, according to Radu's story in *Transylvanian Sunrise*, so much information about the genetics of the galaxy. For those of you who do not recall, this chamber features tables whereby one places their hand over a section of the surface as it gives a complete holographic readout of the DNA of a particular life form from a different planet, also designating the specific location of the star system it is from. By placing another hand over another section at the same time, it allows for a readout of the potential hybridization of the two life forms. It is also important to note that in Radu's previous books, Cezar has experienced issues of censorship when it comes to penetrating the makers of the various devices they have discovered.

As interesting and as controversial as Cosmin's vision might be, it was only one more step on our spiritual journey to Sarmizegetusa. It was now time to sleep. I was given a "heated" room with three others while most everyone else slept in the big room. I think it was warmer in the big room due to the body heat of thirty plus people. Our little room had two bunk beds with a gas heater. There were two very thick wool blankets, and this was just enough to keep you warm. When one blanket fell off during the night, I could sure feel the difference. Due to my irregular diet as a result of travelling, I had to get up twice in the middle of the very cold night to use the outhouse facility. It was perhaps the most uncomfortable challenge of the entire trip, but I survived it and woke up on August 12th to a brisk mountain morning and breakfast.

Before descending down the mountain, we visited the sites of ancient altars of the Dacian priests and created our own stone circle with a symbol of Venus. After another long hike down the mountain, we gathered in a circle in front of the Sphinx, and Jonette spoke of her earlier visit where the "white wolf" had acted as her protector within the tunnels. At that exact moment, a real white wolf/dog joined our circle as if to confirm that what she had said were true. It was rather dramatic and is only one example of her authentic spiritual work which is far more than just a theoretical or mystical exercise. Cosmin then got out the topographical map again and clearly explained the phenomena of the face shown on the earlier pages of this chapter. Up to that time, I could not clearly make out the face, but others could see it. It was not until I focused on it through the lens of my video camera that I could see the obvious figure of a face. It is this explanation by Cosmin that you will see on YouTube. The line drawn over the photo on page 186 is subject to inaccuracy as I had to recreate the line with my own eyesight from watching the YouTube video. I do, however, believe it to be more accurate than not.

It was now time to leave the Sphinx and head down the westward slope of the mountain which leads to Iomolilta Cave and our hotel. Iomolita Cave is one of the most remarkable caves you will ever see, and it is lit with electric lights so that you can experience it visually as well. That adventure, however, would be for the next day. Our mission was to simply go down the mountain inside of the cable car in different groups and make our way to our hotel. That required a walk of a mile or so. There was, however, some unfortunate news. Due to the severe rainstorm the day before, the road to our hotel had been washed out, and our modern bus could not safely bring us our luggage. The elements had spoken. Personally, I could have cared less. I would be safe and warm in a hotel, and I still had a toothbrush, an extra pair of socks and some other clothing. Others, however, were distressed as they would be deprived of certain necessities that might include medication and the like. Jonette did her best to override this unforeseen difficulty by hiring more SUVs to pick up our luggage which eventually arrived sometime in the middle of the night.

That evening, we had a Romanian dinner (there was no other kind available) in the hotel dining room. I sat at a table that was almost exclusively filled with Romanians. This was an opportunity for all of us to find out more about each other and what we were all doing on this spiritual journey.

Before long, it was time to sleep. We were all very tired, and the comfort of a hot shower and a warm bed was quite enticing. Although I would go into a deep and comfortable slumber, my spiritual journey to Sarmizegetusa was continuing on in my sleep. The next step included some rather elaborate dreams which would prove themselves to be quite prophetic by the time the journey reached its end.

CHAPTER TEN

RAPID-EYE-MOVEMENT

After going to sleep on August 12th, I had three dreams that were deep, penetrating, and complex. Besides being a part of my spiritual journey, there was no question in my mind that they were inextricably connected to the August 12th biorhythm, just like the dream I had three years earlier on my journey to Sarmizegetusa with Nicole. When I awoke for breakfast, it was announced that we had a free day for everyone in the group to relax. Different excursions were offered, however, one of which was a visit to the traditional shrine of Vesta, the original Vestal Virgin upon which the religion of the state of Rome was founded. Vesta was the mother of Romulus and Remus, two twins who were born of a virgin birth. Mars, the god of war, was their father. At 5:00 p.m. that evening, we had an exclusive reservation for our group of forty plus to visit Iamolita Cave. I made the decision to sleep in a bit but dedicated the rest of my free time to recounting and writing down my dreams in detail. This is not what I ordinarily do with my dreams, but this series of dreams was so strong, I felt compelled to record them. There was no thought of putting them into this book. That did not occur to me until I returned home and had some realizations.

In the first dream, I was walking towards the Kennedy compound in Massachusetts for the funeral of Joseph P. Kennedy, the patriarch of the Kennedy family. I was very self-conscious as I did not feel I belonged there. As I approached the security detail, I was ready to use the name of an old friend who was very close to the Kennedys as I figured that was the only tangible way to get past security if they questioned me. As it turned out, this was not necessary. They considered my attire to be impeccable, and I was made to feel a friend of the family. My interpretation of this part of the dream is that it represented not only presidential authority but the family that could create a president. As Joseph Kennedy was also an ambassador to England, this fits into the John Dee theme as well. The fact that he was dead represents the end of an old guard as well as a new beginning.

I was then escorted to one of the female Kennedys who talked to me. It was a challenge for the two of us to seek out familiarity in each other. When I told her about my books, she said that she had read them. In the dream, however, it was my perception that she was mistaken as she was referring to books specifically about liberty. I explained that my books were about time travel. Once we got over the awkwardness, she shrunk to an immature little girl. This represents the diminutive goddess but also suggests immature presidential or governmental characteristics. It also reveals how politicians view the feminine energy. After becoming younger, she wanted Mexican food, and I took her out of the compound to get her some. I should point out that I have repeatedly dreamt of Mexicans, and when I do, they are shells for aliens. Due to the high incidence of "illegal" Mexicans in New York and America in general, my subconscious sees them as one and the same. In this case, I was not dreaming of aliens, but her desire for Mexican food suggests that she wanted to eat alien food. We then returned to the compound.

When I re-enter the compound, I am now with Ed Oakley, Jonette Crowley's husband. As Ed taught a leadership seminar at Atlantykron, I associated him with that subject. I was walking in the spirit of leadership, and we were both very well dressed. As we approached security, I once again remembered my old friend who knew the Kennedys and thought I might have to play that card, but it was not necessary. They made that completely clear. This has to do with new connections.

The young Kennedy girl then explained dissatisfaction with the Mexican food she had recently eaten and wanted me to take her out again. I do so and point out a Mexican restaurant in Westbury to her that is named Don Juan's. I indicated that we could go there, but she suddenly expressed a desire for new clothes. Accordingly, I took her to my home where she could pick from a very colorful and plentiful wardrobe belonging to my daughter who is named Sky. Note that when I typically dream of my daughter, it refers to my book company, Sky Books, which is named after her. In the dream, the Kennedy girl picked from a whole bedroom full of colorful clothes belonging to my daughter, and her desire was taken care of.

I then needed to use the bathroom. When I entered, however, I saw a urinal slowly but deliberately sliding across the floor. It was very odd. After it slid to the point where it was right in front of me, it suddenly and inexplicably cracked down the middle. Although I realized it would cost money to replace this urinal (I do not actually have a urinal in my house), I thought it was absurdly funny. I laughed and did not really care about the expense. Knowing I would need to use another fixture, I then looked to the wall and saw that the regular toilet and the sink next to it had been smashed with a sledge hammer or the like. This was no longer funny. It occurred to me that my home or domain was being violently and deliberately violated. I went to the upstairs bathroom and was not happy to see that the fixtures there had been similarly smashed. The message was quite personal. I saw my daughter and explained to her that if I could not find the culprits then she would be the obvious person to blame. She concedes that there would be no other logical suspect.

Hearing voices in a downstairs bedroom, I entered and saw three men. One spoke to me and clearly knew who I was. Without them saying anything, it was clear that they were hoping to intimidate me with the violence that had been committed in my home. Further, they wanted to scare me away and squat in order to take possession of what I own.

It was definitely an issue of ownership, and the man began talking in an angry and challenging voice. He wanted to know how I got all the money to build such an energy efficient and environmentally friendly house. This is a huge exaggeration as the only energy-efficient aspect of my house is a wood burning stove in my fireplace. It is not an environmental house by most standards. With regard to money, I do not possess any great wealth at all unless you consider the virtually untapped resources of the literary rights which I own. The man was, however, astounded, as if I had gotten away with something that no one else had. Instead of arguing with him, I went into re poi re with him and engaged him with communication. As I was not fighting, he knew that he would have to negotiate with me in order to deal with me. It was my intention to call the police on them for breaking and entering, but I did not tip them off. I waited so they would not react badly.

As is often the case, major spiritual dreams come in threes. Although I had two more dreams, I will first analyze this one.

The Kennedy compound is deeply symbolic and concerns power, control, and authority. The patriarch dying, as opposed to JFK, symbolizes a change in the power behind the power. I am welcomed to the fold twice, and there is no mistake about it. My interaction, however, is through a diminutive goddess who is seeking food from me from a foreign source. Unsatisfied with the food, she wants more but seems to show no interest in Don Juan or a loving interest. Instead, she wants the colorful clothes or exotic data that my books represent. I should also mention that the Don Juan restaurant is on Old Country Road which symbolizes the "old country." This could refer either to Romania or to the way the United States used to be under the old guard. It could also refer to both.

After serving the diminutive Kennedy goddess, I go to relieve myself and every means to do so is broken. Toilets and plumbing represent the release of toxic waste matter and emotions. Even though it is my personal house, I am not deeply bothered and laugh, particularly at the sliding urinal. The sliding urinal is representative of loss of control, particularly with regard to releasing toxicity. As I do not have personal issues and do not feel emotionally upset over any of this, it obviously has to do with the matters at hand in my work. It suggests that the events surrounding Radu's efforts are very censored, and there is no room for emotional entanglements. There is nothing I can do about it. When it gets personal, however, I have to take a stand against the perpetrators. I deal with them diplomatically. Their upset over energy efficiency, I believe, could have to do with my association with Dr. David Anderson and his time reactor which offers virtually limitless energy that is cheap. The dream ends with me knowing I can get help to get rid of these squatters.

My next dream features a black cat being grabbed from the back by a lynx. I am concerned for the cat when another lynx appears and runs by before grabbing the other lynx which is still holding the cat. In dreams, a lynx refers to secrets and the need to examine them. There is more to be known and more to be learned about a situation, relationship, or problem. A cat, in particular a black one, represents "shin" and the feminine energy. Black is also Dark Energy as defined (or misdefined) in physics. To me, this was an obvious pun on the word *lynx* and the link between both dreams, including the one I was about to have. Two lynxes suggest a very important connection between the dreams and the most sacred aspects of the feminine energy. The first lynx suggests that the secrecy concerned the bridling, containment, or possession of the feminine energy. The second lynx suggests that this possession was also being cloaked by an even greater or second secrecy.

The third dream was just as complex as the first one. I was in a pub that I once owned on Montauk Highway. The new owner appears as a young female, and there is plenty of food. I was friendly with her but was not quite sure what I was doing there. Walking across Montauk Highway, I saw a pub that I had never noticed before. It does not exist in reality and the terrain in real life is a parking lot. This establishment is called the President's Pub, and it is filled with all sorts of statuesque caricatures of former presidents. The patrons of the establishment also dress up as old presidents. It is highly comical but more baroque than comical. The dream is getting a point across, and it has to do with presidential politics and authority, reaffirming the earlier dream. This time, however, it is on the other side of Montauk Highway and exactly opposite the other establishment.

I went outside the pub and walked to the corner where I saw an abandoned building with an Indian name beginning with a "W." In a dream, the letter "W" is an iteration of two "U's" and refers to "you." One needs to focus on you and only you. I then saw two Indians in a fire truck who were cutting trees down and doing so in a reckless and callous manner. One tree fell down and almost hit me. I looked up, pointing to them so they would know that it almost hit me. They were very clear that they could care less about changing their ways. Laughing loudly, they clearly acknowledged that I had passed a test of initiation. From their behavior, they considered initiation to be a senior factor to what most people would consider to be nature, such as preserving trees and the environment. I then went back across Montauk Highway and returned to the pub I used to own.

The pub was not crowded. I found that I was looking for a girl named Nancy Hearty. In real life, her father owned another pub down the street, and I once had a long conversation with her. We seemed to get along well, and I recall talking to her about my interest in word processing. This was long before it was an every day skill. Her name speaks for itself with regard to the heart. She was not only the feminine energy but the heart aspect. The fact that she was associated with a pub refers to spirits or altering consciousness. In the dream, I then learned that she was now known as Chrissie and had taken a walk down the street. Attempting to follow her, I went down the street to a very busy pub. It was the old Firehouse, a restaurant in Sacramento, California. In real life, the Firehouse was at one time the most high-end restaurant in Sacramento. The owners built it over or around an old firehouse in the most dilapidated part of town which was literally the old historical Sacramento that dated back to the post Gold Rush era. When I lived in the Sacramento area and the Firehouse was at its peak, every single building in the neighborhood was a shack at best and all were abandoned save for bums here and there. This area is now the top tourist spot in Sacramento and has been fixed up utilizing the theme of the Gold Rush. In the dream, the Firehouse was on the corner, and I was accompanied by a minor. There is a sign that says you must be 21 to enter. I went down the street to another establishment, and Chrissie emerges and goes out. I pursued her but was no longer sure what was happening or what I was doing there. That is the end of the dream, but it is only the beginning of the adventure that I was about to pursue in real life. The past, future, and present were expressing themselves through my dreams. Without prematurely revealing certain aspects of what happened in real life, I will now interpret the last part of the dream beyond what I have already offered.

A pub or bar refers to an alteration of consciousness and also has to do with socialization. That I once owned it refers to my past. The new owner is feminine, youthful, and invigorated. Crossing Montauk Highway is obvious, indicating the cumulative experiences of investigating Montauk. The President's Pub represents the subjugation of Native American power or authority through the alteration of consciousness. They are the new or empowered social order, and my roots are on the other side of Montauk Highway.

I have already explained the "W" on the abandoned Indian building. This is self-explanatory and refers to my adventures with the Montauk Indians. In dream interpretation, a fire fighter represents one's higher self and indicates one is experiencing a period of cleansing and purification. The firefighter is the symbol of a true hero and of hope. While a pine tree can be a phallic symbol, it also refers to growth and the passage of time. A pine tree, which this was, symbolizes immortality, life, and/or fertility. The fact that the tree was falling suggests all of those good things crashing down on me. It can also mean that you are off balance, out of synch and headed in the wrong direction. The falling tree, however, missed me and was designed as a test by my higher self. Once again, the "W" is all about "you" and "you." These are my lessons from the Montauk experience. I cross back over the highway to the heart of the matter in the pub. Once again, we have the feminine energy.

195

It was not until I returned home that I realized the full implications of this lady in my dream whose name had been changed to "Chrissie." As a matter of fact, the process of writing down these dreams and their interpretation has facilitated sudden jolts of consciousness which are so deep and interweave so intricately with my life and the different threads of my research that I can only begin to expound upon the tip of the iceberg at this time. One of these is the realization that the name "Chrissie" corresponds to a girl from my fifth grade class. She was the most beautiful thing I had ever seen up to that time in my life, and I think practically every boy in the class had a crush on Chrissie. In the sixth grade, Chrissie was put right in front of my desk. Chrissie eventually told me she had a crush on me. We always remained good friends for the rest of my days in that town. The name "Chrissie," however, would take on further significance during the rest of my journey. I did not realize any of this at the time and will explain in just a bit.

The fact that the Firehouse in Sacramento appeared in my dream is of paramount interest with regard to our ultimate destination: Sarmizegetusa. The city of Sacramento was named after the sacrament of the Catholic Church. Specifically, Franciscan friars referred to it as Sacramento because they were able to easily grow the two necessary crops for the ingredients in the sacrament: grapes and wheat. Besides being the political capital of California, Sacramento is where gold was originally discovered during the Gold Rush. It is also a region I lived in. As for the Firehouse, it is the house of fire, and most etymologies with tell you that the word *pharaoh* means "house" which was symbolized in those days by a pentagon that looked like a home plate in baseball. Fire refers to *shin* where it is the Shekinah glory, the outward manifestation created by the spark of the divinity within. Fire also refers to transformation, just as the sacrament does in Catholicism.

With regard to the minor in the dream, this has a double meaning. It is a pun on "miner" as in a miner of gold, a big issue in Transylvania. During the Gold Rush, a whole class of citizens became miners. It is also symbolic of the fact that a minor or immature soul will not be allowed into the house of the sacrament. There are many factions vying for the control of this area of Romania, and you have already read about them. The number 21 is also a precursor to 22, the number of Zalmoxis that I have already expounded upon. 22 represents Gemini as well as the Major Arcana of the Tarot.

This is what my dreams had to say about all of this. I knew they were important, and that is why I wrote them down in such detail at the time. The prophetic nature of them, however, only became evident upon my return home and as I began to interpret them. As interesting as they were and are, they were only one more part of my sacred journey to Sarmisegetusa. As you will soon learn, the dream was cluing me in on what to expect.

CHAPTER ELEVEN

THE JOURNEY

On the afternoon of August 13th, everyone was invited to get together, share stories, and participate in a session with White Eagle, courtesy of Jonette. One of my new Romanian friends, who I will refer to as Madame V, shared her visit to a nearby waterfall located at the traditional hearth of Hestia. Hestia is the goddess of the hearth and was the inspiration for the Vestal Virgins, her name being Vesta in Rome. There, Madame V had a profound spiritual experience wherein she experienced the presence of a particular being. While the details of what she felt are largely subjective in nature, her vision would not only prove useful during my next adventure, it would also serve to actualize what had taken place in my dream state the night before.

That evening, we were scheduled to visit Ialomiţa Cave, a locale I had visited the previous year with Nicole Vasilcovschi. Nicole and I referred to it as Zalmoxis' Cave because that legendary character is reputed to have stayed there. On that trip, Nicole had told me about another nearby cave, called the Priest's Cave, which contains a natural "bowl" or receptacle of water that refills whenever a portion of it is emptied. Due to time constrictions, we did not have time to see it the previous year. Hoping to see it on this visit, I asked Cosmin, our Romanian tour guide about it. Neither he nor anyone else, however, had ever heard of it, and it was not readily visible from the Ialomiţa Cave area. My hopes were dashed.

Ialomiţa Cave is a huge natural cave, and you could drive a tank into the beginning of it. It is at least two stories high. An orthodox monastery has been erected in front of the cave, and you have to go through their door to access it and are asked to pay a small donation. There is also a chapel in front of the cave. It features a mural where the saints, depicted with white skin, are thwarting off demons, depicted with black skin. The chapel is situated so that you enter from the cave side. At the back of the chapel is a running source of natural water from the cave that is considered to be holy water. To me, entering the cave is a penetrating experience. One is going into the bowels of the earth and feels whatever that might represent archetypally to each individual who enters. One lady, who was in front of me by only a few feet, let out the most blood curdling scream I have ever heard in my life. It was a visceral reaction. Due to its extremely dramatic nature, which was completely unintended, I regretted that my video camera was turned off at the time. Anna, the lady who screamed, needed only a few minutes to gather herself. She was quite all right. It is quite surprising what descending into the Inner Earth, even if it is only a half a mile or so, might bring out in you.

After you leave the main "two-story" area of the cave, the passageway narrows considerably, and it eventually gets to the point where you have to bend down and navigate your way a little carefully. At no point, however, did it require getting down on my knees and crawling. The cave is also lit with electrical light, and this makes the path considerably easier. Even so, I still felt that I was emerging into a great darkness. I imagine that the experience would be much more profound with only candle light. It would certainly be more precarious. There are wooden steps here and there, and one has to be very careful in certain spots. The cave opens up again at certain points, and it is a truly magnificent experience. We eventually gathered together and did a meditation in what amounted to a virtual amphitheater about three-fourths of the way into the cave. One is surrounded by flowing water, stalagmites, and the like. Before the very end, there is a fork on the path which leads to a pool of water. Someone speculated that this might be the Priest's Cave, but I was sure this was not the case. I had already been there the previous year. At the very end of the cave's path, it becomes too wet and unwieldy to proceed further unless you have a board to walk on and good light. The electric light does not go past that point. I am told that you can negotiate your way with a board for about eighty yards. After that, you will need spelunking equipment to go further. The cave, however, is endless and leads to a series of interconnecting tunnels, an actual conduit to the realm of the Inner Earth.

After spending about two hours in the cave, we emerged into the light. By happenstance, I was walking alongside Madame V. Looking over at one of the monks, who was operating a souvenir shop at the front of the cave, I suddenly got the idea that he might know about the Priest's Cave. I asked Madame V to come along with me in case he did not know English. He did speak English, but it took him a while to understand what I was talking about. Finally, his eyes opened up in recognition. I then asked him to give Madame V the directions in Romanian so that it would be perfectly clear. He told us that the path to the Priest's Cave was on our way home but that we would have to veer off on a path to our right. The walk back to our hotel was at least a mile, and Madame V and I had to leave our group to make this journey. We were accompanied by one other, a lady who was one of the very few Americans on the journey. This new cave was a little challenging to find, and we almost missed it, but we could eventually see an opening on the side of the mountain. It required a little more adventurous climbing than I had experienced thus far on the trip. When we eventually arrived at the Priest's Cave, we discovered that it is so small that we had to take off our backpacks and leave them behind. After a very short distance into the cave, we came to a point that required going down on one's hands and knees. As I am tall, I hesitated. The American and Madame V hesitated too, but both soon went past this point and relayed back to me what they saw. Before long, they came to an area where they could stand up. Madame V then became excited, exclaiming that she could see the exact being that she saw earlier in the day at the waterfall of Hestia. Instead of a spiritual manifestation, however, what she saw was a representation of the being inscribed into the wall well above her head. The "glyph" was pointing in a particular direction. Both ladies had to climb upwards and negotiate an awkward passage in order to come to a higher but very narrow level. In the direction that the "being" was pointing, they soon found the "bowl." At this realization, Madame V became almost ecstatic. I then got down on my hands and knees and worked my way to where they were. Someone had left a pitcher, and we all shared in taking some of the water. All in all, it made for a magic moment. It was not only a challenge to find the place, it required a certain amount of fortitude and resolution to access this inner and rather hidden chamber of the Priest's Cave. Madame V commented that it took both a Romanian and an American to find this place. This comment is symbolic of what else is currently going on in Romania.

When we finally emerged from this small cave, everyone was long gone and had returned to the hotel. Taking the long walk, the three of us all talked to each other in English. Based upon what Madame V was saying and what I had recalled from our earlier conversations, it soon dawned on me that my new friend is some kind of celebrity in Romania. She did not say that, but it became obvious. When I asked her, she sort of shrugged her shoulders but admitted she was somewhat well known. Her Romanian friends later confirmed my suspicions and said that she is very well known. When I later checked her out on the internet, I noticed that there is an important man in Romanian politics who shares her last name, and she later confirmed that this man is her husband. Although I did not realize it at the time, my presidential dreams were alluding to power and authority in politics. My dreams were starting to take shape through my interaction with Ms. V and her own deeply personal spiritual experience at the hearth of Hestia. When we returned to the hotel, it was after nine o'clock. Most of the others were gathered together, and there was a formal discussion going on. We soon interrupted the proceedings to tell them of our success, and I could not believe how happy everyone seemed to be over the fact that we had succeeded in our quest to find the obscure Priest's Cave. This experience told me that we had indeed accomplished something significant. Afterwards, we all enjoyed a very late dinner.

The next day was a day-long drive into Transylvania that would eventually end in the general area of Sarmizegetusa. Other than bathroom and food breaks, our only stop was at a sacred spot, Sinca Veche, more or less a couple of hours north of the Sphinx, where there is an absolutely beautiful grove of trees surrounding a magical stream of water. It also features a magnificent cave where you can see an ancient human figure inscribed next to a Star of David. Visitors are only able to access the very front of the cave, but it goes deep into a mountain side, atop of which is a monastery.

It was very late in the day when we reached our destination in Transylvania, but it was still daylight. Although we enjoyed the comfort of a modern bus, we were travelling on a rock-studded dirt road. The bus had to move slowly, seldom more than twenty miles per hour and often less. We were arriving at the small town of Costeşti, the general area of which is said to feature a population of two or three thousand. There, one is very far off the beaten path of civilization as we regularly experience. It has been my experience and direct observation that this area of Transylvania is not only surrounded by a virtual field of energy unique unto itself but one that makes it challenging or difficult to penetrate the more esoteric or sacred aspects thereof. The unpaved road is just one obvious example in this regard. Although I do not consider it particularly dangerous, it is my opinion that one should be very mindful and respectful of where one is going, what one is doing, and why one is doing it. I will now give you one small example of how one might get misdirected. There is another town of the same name, Costeşti, in Wallachia, in the southern part of Romania. If you should decide to go to this region, you want to go to Costeşti in Transylvania, not far from Sarmizegetusa Regia. There is also another Sarmizegetusa which served as a political center for the Romans at one point. Do not get confused by that either.

In any event, our bus eventually arrived at a fork in the road where it absolutely could not pass. The road was really not quite wide enough and was too riddled with ruts and rocks. When the bus came to a stop, Cosmin announced that we had reached our destination and made a call on his cell phone. We were waiting for directions and everyone was a little anxious. I do not even believe that any of our fellow Romanians had been to this specific area before. Were we lost? It had been an all-day trip on the bus, and we had already been tested more than a bit on the journey thus far. Was this another test? As a matter of fact, when I originally learned of the schedule that Cosmin had prepared for this trip, I was very sceptical about the logistics because I had been to this region before. I knew of no hotel. Although I voiced my concerns to Jonette, she had no choice but to trust Cosmin. To tell you the truth, however, Cosmin was going blind. He had never been to this spot, and he had only made the arrangements by phone. As he later admitted, he did not know exactly what to expect. As I said, it is far from the beaten path.

Even though I had doubts about the hotel, I had been comforted on the subject when I went to lunch with Nicole in Bucharest several days earlier. She had just flown in from Canada and was able to spend part of the day with me. While we were on a city bus, Nicole received a phone call from Lenutz, a remarkable lady that I met in the middle of the solar calendar on my first trip to Sarmizegetusa. Lenutz has become a very special person in my life. She called Nicole to tell her to say hello to me and to let me know that she was sending a package for me that would arrive at the hotel in a few days. I was now not only convinced that there was a real hotel in the region but that I would have a welcoming gift waiting for me in a sacred spot located "in the middle of nowhere." This gave me the additional comfort of knowing that I would be made to feel at home in a place that was rather well known for its obscurity and unfamiliarity.

As we waited for a response to Cosmin's phone call, everyone got out of the bus to stretch their legs. In a very short time, a pretty girl arrived in a car and pointed us in the right direction. It was announced to us that she would transport our luggage by car, and we would walk a quarter of a mile or so to the Pensiunea Cotiso hotel. If anyone needed a ride for any reason, she offered to take them as well. It took her three trips to deliver all the luggage. In the meantime, no one knew what to expect. When we arrived, we saw a facility that was quaint, modern, nice, and clean. We were greeted by different Romanians, none of whom spoke English, and given our accommodations. Our group, many of whom are world travellers, were very pleased and impressed with the facilities, particularly when you consider the remoteness of the location. I would eventually learn that the hotel had rushed to finish construction of the main floor of a new building, just for us. There was another floor up top that was still unfinished at that point. Although it is certainly not that well known to outsiders, there is something of a tourist business in this region. This hotel also features a conference room where people attend conferences on different topics, ranging from astrology to more mundane subjects.

We had arrived very late and beyond our scheduled arrival time, but our hosts were very courteous and served us a sumptuous dinner that surprised everyone. Their food was over-the-top, and they did not stop serving us until we were all fed to our satisfaction. All of the food is from local farms. Transylvania is one of the last unspoiled regions in the world. It was soon time to go to bed and get a good sleep for our adventure the next day. We were going to White Faces, an old Dacian citadel that is known as one of the last places to fall during the invasion of the Roman Empire.

For some reason, I awoke in the middle of the night and realized that I would have to speak to the pretty girl as she was the only one I saw at the hotel who spoke English. It was my intention to get all the details about the hotel and the local area so that I could return for future trips. Only later would I realize that my awakening in the middle of the night was directly tied to the dreams I had experienced two nights earlier. When we awoke for an early breakfast, she was busy helping to serve it. I decided it would be best to approach her later that evening.

After breakfast, we walked down to the fork in the road and waited for our bus to arrive. It was parked at least fifteen minutes away where the driver stayed with the rest of our Romanian contingent. I took this time to do my morning chi gong workout. This features an exercise of standing perfectly still without any movement for twenty minutes. As it turned out, I was standing by myself and across from everyone else. While I stood, Marianna, a

Danish doctor, began to do energy work on me, from a distance. I had asked her for some help a couple of days earlier, and she said that she would get to me when she could. As she worked on me, I just continued standing. As I stood there, completely still, a herd of water buffalo came barreling down the road. There were about seven in total, and I was rather surprised. Besides the fact that they seemed to come out of nowhere, I had no idea there were such creatures in Transylvania. I thought of them as being relegated to more tropical areas, like Africa or India. One ran off into a farm, and three of them slowed down and began to walk in my direction. After all, there was a fork in the road, and they had to decide which way to go. Instead of taking either path, they walked right up to me and were no more than two or three feet away. Curious, they just stood there and looked at me. As far as I was concerned, there was no consideration of fear as I was doing an exercise that requires extreme stillness. One is also linking to the primordial mind. If done properly, there is no room for anything but the exercise. Of course, I noticed the creatures and their curiosity. All I knew about water buffalo is that they have a reputation for being extremely nasty. These creatures were not so, but their physical presence can be very intimidating. I also knew that if I moved, I would create more opportunity for an incident. For me, there was no choice but to remain in my stance. They continued to stare at me until a man on a bicycle came and motioned them up the road. He was apparently their herdsman and was taking them to graze.

There are different interpretations for the water buffalo totem when it appears in your life. It often has to do with carrying a very complex burden, but it also suggests leaving the burden of domesticity behind and embracing the wild aspects of nature. Additionally, Lao Tse was depicted as leaving this world, through the Hunan Gate, on a water buffalo. Whichever one applies, and I think they all have some relevance, I was definitely getting more than I had bargained for on my spiritual journey to Sarmizegetusa. This was, after all, only my first morning in Transylvania, and I had only woken up a short while earlier. Keep in mind, when one makes a pilgrimage to Sarmizegetusa, it is the journey itself that makes up at least half of the experience.

The bus soon arrived and took us to a place from which we would take a several mile hike to White Faces, the ancient citadel. Although one is going uphill and walking miles, this path is much easier to negotiate than the more commonly travelled route, a shorter path which is very steep and requires grasping and hanging onto branches at different times. The shorter path is directly accessible on the road to Sarmizegetusa Regia. We, however, were not going there on this day. We were taking a more obscure path that was off the beaten track, and I did not recognize where we were. We walked by beautiful scenery and many farms, even having to walk through some of them to reach our destination. Our party included a local guide who took care of the required permissions. Eventually, we came to a grassy knoll where we rested. A lady from a nearby farm came out and brought us a bushel full of apples to eat. It was an extremely nice gesture, and we then enjoyed a talk about the local area. It was here where I learned about an ancient order of wizards with special knowledge and abilities. They are known as Solomonars and are often linked to the ancient Dacian priests. It is said that the term Solomonars is a more recent name for them and was given to them by Christian priests. The original name for them is Zgrimties or Hultan, the latter sounding very similar to *sultan*.

The Solomonars or Solomanari play a complex role in Romanian mythology with regard to the interaction between the "other realm." Known to control the weather, they live away from the world, often in caves where they access another realm. Sometimes they come down to the villages to beg. Although they do not need anything, they are testing humans and can bring down hail or other ills if they do not like the response. In human form, they often appear with red hair and white robes, sometimes accompanied by a dragon. They have the power to summon dragons and often ride them. The earlier versions of these characters are much more pure than the later renditions which are deeply influenced by Christian agendas. At first, Christians attempted to neutralize the Hultan or Zgrimties by applying a Judaic-Christian namesake like Solomon, the most powerful figure in Freemasonry, a king who had power over the jinn. The magical powers of such creatures was readily acknowledged by the first Christians and were even recognized as beneficial. As time went on, the Christian priests began to demonize them for their own benefit until the point where they were declared evil This amalgamation of the original energy with latter day appellations has created a watered down synthetic myth in current times. It is, however, through interaction with such spirits that the Dacian priests of ancient history became initiated.

A very important part of this tradition is that children born with special signs, including those with the placenta on their head, might become a Hultan. Such children might be stolen by a Hultan and taken to a school in "Crugul Pamantului" where they are trained until the age of 20. "Crugul Pamantului" can be translated as "the middle of the Earth" and is sometimes expressed as being "raised in the middle of the wolves". This also alludes to Romulus and Remus, two twins of the virgin Vesta, courtesy of the god Mars, who were raised by wolves. It is not only ironic that Cezar Brad was born with a special sign, in his case a very large umbilical cord, but that his later life was in Department Zero under the tutelage of Dr. Xien. It further evolves into Cezar becoming an ambassador to the people of the Inner Earth. This gives us all cause to wonder if Dr. Xien is of the order of the Hultan. In any event, I find it fascinating that Cezar Brad's personal life story, whether intended to or not, parallels the legends of ancient Romanian mythology.

Besides finding Cezar's correspondence with the Solomanari legends fascinating, I also find it to be delightfully appropriate. This relates to my own personal desire, as a young man, to become a science fiction writer. I had no idea at that time that I would eventually surpass this goal by leaps and bounds through the vehicle of the Montauk Project, a synthesis of virtually every scientific and occult discipline imaginable. When I initially engaged in the writing of that book, there was no question in my mind that everything known about the Montauk Project was not quite exactly the way it had been reported. We were dealing with fragments of what could be termed a crashed hard drive on a computer. The fragments were so odd, however, that it was most definitely a computer the likes of which no one had ever quite conceived of in popular literature. In any event, I chose the following theme for my book company: *Sky Books — Where Science Fiction Meets Reality.* The fragments of the Montauk Project given to me represented either a partial truth or a fictionalized truth. The actual truth of the situation, however, remained elusive and was even more interesting and mysterious. The stories of Cezar Brad and Radu Cinamar are no different. There is, however, a greater coherency with regard to the events and circumstances and the hope these stories offer to humanity. Discovering that Cezar's personal story is so interwoven and aligned with Dacian myth gives it, at least to me, new life and increases its significance. It is apparent to me that there is not only more myth behind Cezar's life than I had previously suspected but that there is also much more life behind the myth.

My spiritual journey to Sarmizegetusa was not only playing off of my past, it was doing it in such a way as to reactivate and strengthen my goals as a writer. It was manifesting right in front of me by way of enabling me to learn about the mysterious Solomanari. This was rapidly followed by an introduction to a local Romanian man. Much to my surprise and utter delight, he took me to an area and pointed to a valley. This, he said, is known as the Valley of the Golden Thrones. I was rather dumbstruck. You mean it really exists? That was the question I asked myself. Even if it was only a myth, it was now clear to me that the mythology of this area runs far deeper than what Radu has stated thus far. Radu alludes to a very deep mystery in this book but has not yet elaborated beyond what you have already read. I was now learning that there are indeed more legs to this story.

The Valley of the Golden Thrones is a beautiful valley that leads into pure wilderness. I was told that, within this valley, there is an entrance leading to the caves or tunnels described by Cezar in Chapter Five. If you follow the tunnels long enough, they will eventually take you to the golden thrones mentioned in that same chamber. Those are the thrones that, according to Professor Constantin's account as relayed by Cezar, surround an elliptical vortex to another world.

For his own personal reasons as well as for my own protective considerations, I will refer to this man as Mr. C. The first thing I asked him was if this entrance to the underground was a different one than the one described by Professor Constantin in his report. Mr. C said it was a different entrance and further stated that these underground tunnels lead all the way to the Bucegi Mountains. These were the pathways of the ancient Dacian priests and extend for hundreds and hundreds of miles. It occurred to me at that point in our conversation that the mysterious third tunnel in the Projection Hall beneath the Sphinx would, more than likely, lead directly to the thrones described previously. All we have been told thus far is that the third tunnel leads to the Inner Earth. As Cezar has reportedly become an ambassador to the beings in the Inner Earth, a more visible pattern is beginning to take shape in this saga that I have become far more personally involved in than I had originally intended.

As Mr. C speaks only Romanian, we had to use a translator to speak to each other. He did, however, know about me as he had read my books in his native language. As I asked him more questions, he said that he knew Professor Constantin, the man who discovered the entrance to the Golden Thrones before mysteriously disappearing. Mr. C said that the man's real name was Professor Constantin — he even gave me the first name — and that he did indeed disappear. He said, however, that the actual story is a bit different than that described in this book, further explaining that full accounts of sensitive information are sometimes restricted to protect various individuals or circumstances.

To reiterate my surprise, I had absolutely no idea that I would meet such a man or that I would personally and directly encounter circumstances suggesting that there were considerably more legs to Radu's book than even he has stated. This was all completely beyond my expectations. It was also an opportunity, if not an outright invitation, to look further into these matters. During his discourses with me, Mr. C had already stated that one can only penetrate the sacred aspects of this valley with permission from the resident spirits. This, of course, implies the Solomanari or Hultan. He has had many sacred experiences in that valley, all amounting to an alpha state of mind. There are certain times of the year, he said, when the energies are most prolific. Such experiences, he stated, are illusionary or beyond the borders of ordinary reality. In other words, do not expect to go into a cave and sit on a golden throne. The entrance to the cave will only be found by those whom the spirits allow to enter. One would be very fortunate indeed.

Unfortunately, there was no time to explore this area on our current trip, but I told Mr. C that I would like to return and explore this area with him but only after first asking the permission of the spirits to enter. When I said the latter, he gave a big smile. I was speaking the right words and he was happy to hear them. Even before these conversations with Mr. C, I already knew that I would return. That is why I wanted to speak to the pretty girl, an opportunity that would present itself later that evening.

As we made our way to the citadel of the White Faces, Mr. C made a rather off-handed comment. Stating it casually and in a matter of fact way, he said that he had once encountered Radu Cinamar in this area. This was also a surprise. Questioning him further, he said that Radu was making a trip to White Faces — perhaps it was his own special pilgrimage of a sort — and that he saw him get out of a car. Mr. C recognized him immediately. It was a spiritual thing. Although he asked him if he was Radu, Mr. C received no confirmation. Even so, it was obvious to Mr. C, but he did concede that there is maybe a ten percent chance that he might be wrong. I then told Mr. C certain private things that I know about Radu, none of which are in print. When I did, he gave me a big smile and shook my hand. There was now no doubt in his mind that he had mysteriously encountered the real Radu.

This whole adventure with Mr. C was something of an epiphany for me. Without any expectation of what I was to discover on my second spiritual sojourn to Sarmizegetusa, I was being confronted with the undeniable logic that I would have to return in order to complete the platter that had been so mysteriously and surprisingly placed before me. As a result, I was no longer too interested in what I would see on the rest of this trip as I knew it would pale in comparison to my future visits. I was eager to return but that trip would be subject to a long time interval. While the rest of the hike to White Face was interesting and enjoyable, it could not measure up to this remarkable encounter with Mr. C.

After taking the longer path to White Faces, we took the shorter path on our way back. This meant going straight down the mountain. After a while, I realized that I had been there before. That was on my trip in 2009 with Nicole. Lenutz and her husband had taken us there from Sarmizegetusa. The forest was unmistakably the same. This path is sometimes so steep and precarious that you sometimes have to grab tree branches to keep your balance. Several people struggled and/or fell down. Some overweight people literally had to slide down certain areas. I did not have any problem negotiating my way, but it requires agility. Once we got down the mountain, we arrived at the road which leads to Sarmizegetusa. We turned the other way and walked a couple of kilometers or so in order to meet our bus and return home.

When we got back to the hotel, it was soon time to eat. After dinner, I had the opportunity to sit down with the pretty girl. Her name is Cristina. My attitude was all business, and I was intent on becoming familiar with all the logistical details for what would be my return trip. Before we began talking, however, I was so struck by her beauty, and I am not just referring to her physical beauty, that unpredicted words just flowed out of my mouth.

"You're beautiful!" I said.

Cristina's response was to get up and hug me, and what I had planned to be only a few minutes of conversation turned into something much more than that. She explained to me that she knew who I was and that people come to their hotel as a result of the books I have written. Her mother even came out and asked me to autograph a copy of the Romanian version of my book, *Pyramids of Montauk*. I was very touched by all of this. As we became familiar and indulged in an informal conversation, I was rather in awe of Cristina, and I am not referring to her beauty. She is one of the most "together" and gracious persons that I have ever met. Cristina has studied law and is currently working on her Masters. At that time, she had a job at a law firm in Orăştie and helps out with the family business when she can. She also explained that she had helped with the interior design of the new rooms. Besides that, she made a point of telling me that she was willing to personally drive me to whatever destinations I wanted to go to on my next journey there. Cristina talked to me a lot about various things. She has a definite aptitude for the esoteric aspects of life, but she has been too busy with law school to read Radu's books or much of anything else outside her specific studies.

Besides being touched by this, a very strong emotion came over me. In some strange way, I was home. Once again, I was being made to feel very familiar in a very strange and far away land, and one that is known quite specifically for its mysterious spiritual aspects. I indeed felt that Romania was opening up its heart to me. This emotion told me quite plainly that I had now arrived at the high point of my sacred journey. I could not help but tell Cristina that sitting there and talking to her was the climax. It was not going to get any better. Glad to share my experience, she hugged me again. It was a brief moment in time but one that I will always remember. From my experience with the time travel adventures of Montauk, I would call it a marker in time and an important one.

As emotionally riveting at this delightful meeting with this new found friend was, it was not until I got home and analyzed my dreams that I realized that Cristina represented the Chrissie in my dream of August 12th. Some aspect of my mind-body complex was obviously tapping into the future. The only connection it could make was with the name of Chrissie from my past. The Firehouse in Sacramento was a perfect parallel to their restaurant in the sacred or sacramental land of Transylvania. Both areas are also in the gold country. The fact that the Chrissie in my dream went next door to the Firehouse further reiterates the truth of the situation. The hotel and Cristina's home is in Costeşti, a small town which is, in a sense, next door to Sarmizegetusa.

I have had plenty of interesting dreams in my life, some of a precognitive nature, but this one was extra special because of the circumstances as well as the intensity of it. It is clear that my dreaming faculties were working overtime and doing a far better job than usual, but they were also connecting my past to my future. You cannot ask for much more on a sacred journey. It is interesting to speculate on how or why my dreams could so decisively predict or connect to the future. While I am certainly not the first person to experience such a thing, it becomes rather obvious that the R.E.M. function of the mind-brain complex does indeed serve the function of a somewhat low-grade time machine. By low grade, I am referring to the fact that it is restricted by certain limitations. That does not mean, however, that there are inherent limitations. These would only be limited by the predisposition of the observer and/or limitations imposed by another source located inside or outside of the mind-brain complex.

Based upon what Mr. C told me about his sacred experiences in the Valley of the Golden Thrones, it is obvious to me that there is something about this area of Transylvania that literally speaks to the mind-body-spirit complex in a way that validates what Cezar and Radu have already offered us earlier in this book. Specifically, they stated that the resident gold in the area serves as a superconductor with regard to consciousness. If a majority of what Radu has written in this book is false, and I do not mean to suggest that it is, he has most certainly offered me a jewel of truth with regard to this one piece of information.

What is most important to me regarding all of this, however, is that these experiences have enabled me to somehow remain "in touch" with the spiritual current of this area ever since I have left. I think of the area a lot with a feeling that is somewhat similar to but different than nostalgia. It is rather like being aware of an energy and the forces associated with it. Was I in touch with the Solomanari or Hultan? Were the two beggars I met at Peles Castle actually disguised members of this ancient priesthood that were testing me? I cannot answer these questions affirmatively or in the negative. It is clear, however, that my adventures, as well as those of Cezar Brad and Radu, are conforming to a very ancient spiritual archetype that has been woven into the fabric of the Romanian culture at its deepest roots.

Later that evening, as several of us sat around a table, someone suggested that I begin doing workshops at this location. I looked at this person as if they were nuts. Others then joined in so as to give this idea enthusiasm. Although I am definitely drawn to the area, it just seemed preposterous. Forced to take it seriously, I then said, "OK. If you organize it, I will come."

The person behind this idea is Vanda Osman, sometimes known as Oz. She has been a professional tour operator since 1982. Sometimes, but not always, she organizes Jonette Crowley's spiritual tours. On this trip, she was a fellow traveller. Going to sleep on this idea, I realized that it made sense. I would therefore have to go back to Cristina the following day and get more information.

That evening, a sacred camp fire was made at the back part of the property. It was a very enjoyable experience, and we were treated to local legends and stories about Zalmoxis, Vlad Dracula, and a shape-shifting white wolf. It is important to mention something here about Vlad Dracula. Completely vilified as a monster or vampire, the local story teller told us why he is so important as a hero to Romanians. For students of common history, it is well known that Vlad was thrust into a situation where his subjects, virtually all Christians, were being enslaved by the Ottomon Empire. His response was to ruthlessly and viciously drive the invading Turks out of Romania, most often impaling entire armies. This created a lot of fear in his enemies. What is not so well known, at least in the West, is that Vlad Dracula's father, Vlad Dracul, was also a great hero to the people but for another reason.

In Chapter 5, Radu and Cezar emphasize the exaltation of the peasant in Romanian culture. Without the peasant, you literally have no subsistence and therefore no culture at all. The Romanian/Dacian people have recognized this since time immemorial. It was typical, however, for the nobles, or boylans as they were called, to individuate from the peasants and to take advantage of them and treat them with contempt. Vlad Dracul was a hero to the peasant because they would take their injustices to him, and he would respond. Usually, he would go to the boylan and ask them to correct the injustice. If they would correct the injustice, that would be the end of it. In the event that the boylan would not correct the situation or just give lip service, more drastic action would be taken, sometimes resulting in impaling. The whole point of the ruthless action was to correct the injustice. This is how Vlad Dracul became an icon to the peasants. His son, Vlad Dracula, followed him in this tradition but became embroiled in bigger issues of national importance. While this is only one aspect of the historical family of Dracula, it is crucial to grasp if you want to have any understanding of the deeper roots of Romanian culture. Hollywood, as well as others, have created a mythos around Dracula as a vampire which grossly distorts the actual dynamics of the culture. The more media you see about vampirism and the more you contemplate the subject, the more you are pulled into that mind-set. If the real Dracula and his father were alive today, they would likely want to impale most of our politicians and the media for taking advantage of the population.

After going to sleep that night, we all woke up again early the next morning to take the journey to what was supposed to be the climax of our trip: Sarmizegetusa Regia itself. As I expected, this was to be anticlimactic compared to what I had just experienced the day before. I cannot, however, speak for everyone else, but there were others who made the same observation. As the bus could not make the final leg of the trip, we had to walk over four kilometers uphill. While it was a long but not particularly grueling hike, I was a little tired of all the hiking I had been doing for the past week. While there were some good moments on our trip to Sarmizegetusa, I will not bother to recount them as they pale in comparison to what you have already read. Vanda Osman took a lot of pictures of the area, and these revealed many orbs in the area of the ruins themselves. For me, however, the best part of that day was at the very end of our long walk back to the bus. There was a creek, and many of us chose to immerse our bare feet in the cold water. To me, it felt absolutely great.

After dinner, I made arrangements to speak to Cristina again. As there had been requests to return to this area, I wanted more information with regard to groups of people. I learned that it can be challenging to take a large group to Sarmizegetusa Regia. There are no buses in the area. As Cosmin had to reserve the bus we were using as early as January, it is obviously an operation that has to be planned well ahead of time. In the event that one wants to take a group without a bus, she said that there is a man with a tractor and a cart. In other words, everyone has to pile into the cart. He can take many people for a reasonable fee, but the tractor moves slowly and the entire journey there could take up to two hours.

I am informing you about the logistics in order to emphasize how challenging it can be to reach this area. Despite the wireless internet and other modern accoutrements of the hotel, one cannot escape the fact that there is a strong element of wilderness in this area. There is also no train to the area. If one wants to fly into the area, one could fly to the city of Cluj, but one is at least an hour and a half away by car. One can take the train from Cluj to Orăştie, but then one still has a drive of about forty-five minutes. One can take a taxi the rest of the way and this can cost between thirty and forty dollars. You have to be careful though. Romanian taxi drivers have a reputation for overcharging as well as changing the fee once you have already made an agreement. All of this can be a challenge to travellers who do not speak Romanian. It is even more challenging to take a group of people.

Cristina also told me that funds had been approved some time ago to actually pave the final road to Sarmizegetusa. That would make things considerably easier for everyone and would also enable a bus to make the trip. For some unexplainable reason, however, the job never gets done. After hearing about this, and combined with other information I have told you as well as some I have not, it is my distinct impression that these challenges have everything to do with the resident spirits that influence this area. One of my friends from Atlantykron, whom I regard highly, has told me that there is fierce spiritual protection around Sarmizegetusa. That is quite obvious if you believe even a little of what Radu has written in this book. She stated to me that the chase for Romanian gold will turn on itself and, further, that the forces behind Sarmizegetusa are more powerful than the Grand Architect of the Universe. This last thought, which came from the deepest part of her psychic nature, was very disturbing to her, but it persisted for at least six months. After all, what could be more important than the Grand Architect of the Universe? I was able to reassure her in a most positive way when I told her that, to me, the only force that could be so powerful would be the Tao itself. From the perspective of my own personal journey, the introduction of the Tao into these circumstances is not only convenient, it fits into the overall pattern of my life. The Tao is always present for all things depend upon it, but it is also subtle and defies definition. As the Tao is tied to infinity, it is fitting that the vortex to another world is reported to be nearby.

Such is it that my adventures have taken me to the gateway to the infinite. While I could say the same about my past excursions and discoveries at Montauk, this is a bit different. The Montauk investigation has led me, two decades later, to the threshold of the secret and sacred heart of Transylvania. All of this is a result of my pursuit of the archetypal forces behind the phenomena that I encountered as a result of studying the Montauk Project. Most people, many of my fans included, get caught up in this debris and remain there. What you read in books and hear from the words of others can only be an outer truth, if it is even truth at all. The only deep or inner truth you will find is inside of yourself. Meeting it or seeing it reflected in the outside world or through the experience of another is nice because it can intensify and further catalyze the internal process. I am very happy that Romania has been such a convenient vehicle for my own spiritual evolution. As part of my work also includes the facilitation of spiritual and personal development for others, I am including an advertisement in the back of this book for those who might like to make their own spiritual journey to Transylvania. One is for the Cotiso Hotel in Costeşti, Transylvania. The other is for Vanda Osman's Joy Travel. Vanda is currently planning a return visit to Sarmizegetusa with myself as a guide. Please note that I do not have a propriety interest in any of these enterprises. My participation in any such tours will be as hired help.

What you have read thus far is only about my spiritual journey. There were some forty plus others who had profound experiences. I am sure they would have many of their own incredible experiences to share. There is some information which has been shared on Jonette Crowley's website, and you can obtain some other views there if you wish at *www.jonettecrowley.com*.

After obtaining all of the necessary logistical information that I could get from Cristina, we enjoyed more stories around the camp fire that evening. Early the next morning, I got to say goodbye to Cristina and her family. It felt more like a hello. As a parting gift, Cristina gave me a full bottle of natural Transylvanian honey. As for Mr. C, he told me that he would learn English by next year so he could talk to me in my native language. We then made our way to the bus for what would be an eight or nine hour trip back to Bucharest.

After arriving in Bucharest about five o'clock, everyone got cleaned up for a traditional Romanian "goodbye dinner" that we would enjoy later than evening. This was everyone's chance to say goodbye to the people we had journeyed with all week. It was both sad and happy as well as a time to revisit our experiences and friendships before returning to the regular world. The meal we had that night was not only one of the best I have ever had in Romania, it was one of the best meals I ever had period. When everyone was finished, it was late in the evening, and Jonette had everyone gather in an empty large room in the restaurant. At the end, she wanted to thank me because, as she said, the entire journey would not have taken place were it not for me. She is referring to the fact of my publishing and contributing to the books *Transylvanian Sunrise* and *Transylvanian Moonrise*. The latter book is one of the few in the West to acknowledge and reveal the importance of Sarmizegetusa as a sacred area, particularly in a context that is both popular, topical and relevant. I took this opportunity to address the group, and it was really the only time I addressed the entire group other than when I gave summations of Radu's books while we were on the bus. I pointed out how this entire adventure really began when I took my first sacred journey to Sarmizegetusa with Nicole Vasilcovschi and Cristina Balan three years earlier. It was just three of us, and it was quite an adventure getting there by switching trains and running down railways throughout the middle of the night. We had no agenda or expectations for that journey. Now, three years later, the spiritual energy had expanded and risen to a higher spiral by reason of my return with forty plus people. I also stated that none of this would have been possible had I not been invited and financed to take my first trip to Romania in 2008 by Dr. David Anderson, a time travel scientist. While I cannot explain all the ins and outs of such extraordinary circumstances, this is the context in which all of us had visited Sarmizegetusa on this trip. I then said that I would be returning and hoped to meet everyone on a higher spiral.

Even though that was our final goodbye, there was much more in store for me on this trip. Jonette was giving seminars over the next two days, a Saturday and a Sunday, and she wanted me to participate in the Sunday seminar. Most of the attendees were not from the tour. For Saturday, she said I could take the day off or attend the seminar. In need of relaxation, I chose to take the day off, spending time with my new friends from Australia and also my Romanian publisher, Sorin Hurmuz. I found out from Sorin that Radu has been silent. For all of the time he has been Radu's publisher, there has never been such a long period of silence and this concerns him. I last heard from Radu, as of this writing, in late December of 2011. Sorin heard from him in January 2012, but that has been it. I also took the opportunity to ask Sorin about Elinor, the mysterious alchemist in *Transylvanian Moonrise* who is supposed to meet me at some point. I asked Sorin about Elinor because, according to the book, he actually spoke to him on the phone. There has been no in person meeting between the two. In fact, Sorin was surprised to hear that Elinor is supposed to meet with me. Specifically, I asked Sorin what Elinor was like on the phone. He said that he was very well spoken and polite but that there was nothing extraordinary about it. All of their conversations were very matter of fact.

I found this rather interesting because the nature of Sorin's interaction with Elinor does reveal that there was an outside source that made contact with Radu and sent him on additional adventures as described in *Moonrise*. What actually happened we can either speculate about or accept from Radu's accounts, but Sorin's statement is corroborative of Radu's experiences, if only in the most abstract sense. I know Sorin well enough to know that he is not part of any knowing conspiracy to create "Radu Cinamar." He was contacted by Radu and the books were forwarded to him to publish. I also know Radu well enough and know enough about him to determine that he is an individual and not a conglomerate of people who use that name to get across their point. Other friends have confirmed that Radu does work in the intelligence sector. It is clear, however, and freely admitted by Radu, that his work is subject to censorship. This is why there have been no new revelations from his quarter for the past few years.

At the end of *Mystery of Egypt*, the third book in the Transylvania Series, I stated that I had received a letter from Radu informing me that Elinor would be meeting me in the next ten months. This did not happen. It is now a full year since I received his letter. I am not disappointed, however, and there is a good reason. Although I am definitely interested in meeting this person, I have intuitively felt that, in some way, it is not time yet. The universe has its own time clock, and I have my own time clock. My intuition has told me that this meeting was premature. I have also been informed that things have come up in Elinor's life that have required him to rearrange his priorities. Keep in mind that security is a very relevant issue in his life at all times.

Sometime during that Saturday morning in Bucharest, while I was waking up from a dream or thinking about it, a sudden thought occurred to me with regard to Elinor. I thought back to my conversations with Madame V. If her husband was an important person in Romanian politics, and if she has her own career and is very well known, it stands to reason that she probably lives in a rather exclusive area of Bucharest. It occurred to me that she might indeed be a neighbor of Elinor or at least live in the same development. I thought this might especially be the case by reason of the fact that she felt a very strong connection to this man when I mentioned him to her. That was all psychic however. I further realized that, due to the nature of Elinor's house and the specialized contracting it would have required, she could probably, by just asking a few questions of key people, determine exactly where Elinor's house might be. Perhaps I was getting too close for comfort. Synchronicity was working overtime on this trip already, and I was stirring up far more that anyone anticipated, even myself. In any event, I learned that Madame V would be at the seminar on Sunday, and I was eager to talk to her again.

When I arrived at the school where the seminar was taking place, Madame V was amongst the first to arrive. When I suggested it was highly probable that she lives in the same neighborhood and area, she readily agreed. I was not, however, trying to smoke out Elinor. These considerations just spontaneously occurred, and I could not help but wonder if I was getting too close. Another seminar attendee, a lady I had met the previous year at the Sphinx, said that she had an opportunity to meet David Anderson through one of her friends, but she was too busy to take advantage of that. The fact that David was in Bucharest in the last year was certainly news to me, and it would have been unexpected news from probably all of his friends at Atlantykron, too. Why was I hearing this? It is no secret that David either has or once had a Time Travel Research Center in Romania, but it was said to be dedicated exclusively to theoretical matters. These days, conversations can take place over Skype; unless, of course, it is so highly confidential that it has to be kept off of Skype. In any case, this woman would have met David in a purely social context with friends of friends. Bucharest is a big city with about three million people. I found it odd that there would be this much cross current with regard to synchronicity. It would not stop here either, but I was beginning to feel as if my presence and extraordinary experiences with synchronicity on this trip might be making certain people uncomfortable.

After lunch, I taught Taoist Chi Gong, speaking very little, if anything, about the various books I have written. To me, this is the most beneficial feature I have to offer. It enables people to heal themselves of all sorts of conditions, even life-threatening maladies. Jonette then summated the seminars of the last two days, also alluding to the trip some of us had just taken. It was then that I had a stunning realization and announced it to the group. I said that it had just occurred to me that I probably have more friends in Romania than I do in the United States. It is not that I do not have a lot of friends in America, but most of them have faded away with time and there is virtually no meaningful interaction. This is the way life flows. Not only do I have an abundance of new friends in Romania, they are "meaningful" friends, and I say that with regard to the fact that they either will play a role in my future or will have the opportunity to do so. There is a lot of live fertile energy for me in Romania. One of the professors who attends Atlantykron has even been hinting for years that I will be moving to Romania. The idea is tempting, but practical business considerations do not indicate that this is anything more but a remote possibility. I would need to learn to speak the language fluently as well.

After the seminar, the executive committee of our tour was invited to visit the house of a couple who had been on the journey to Sarmizegetusa with us. This was basically Jonette, her husband, Cosmin and myself. Later that evening, this couple would take us to their restaurant for what would be the final "goodbye" dinner. I mention the trip to this couple's house because there were aspects to this visit that I consider to be very significant. First, their house was in a neighborhood that was very reminiscent of what I read about Elinor's villa in Bucharest. Like all houses in the area, there were security gates around the entire property. Built in recent times, it was an utterly beautiful house with more nooks, crannies and passageways than you might imagine — a great house to play hide-and-seek in if you were a kid. Once again, I felt as if I was one step closer to Elinor.

The second important item of this visit occurred when most everyone was out in the yard. I was sitting by myself at a patio with a glass table. I was simply resting my legs and eating from the fruit platter that had made available for us. Cosmin came over and filled a champagne glass and placed it on the glass table. As we sat there, the glass slowly began to slide along the table, but it did so very slowly. We both noticed it and could not help but wonder whether it was sliding by reason of liquid on the table or if there was a spiritual current causing it. In my past, by the way, I was once with a highly psychic girl who claimed to be part of the Montauk Project. As we talked, a Diet Coke can began to slide across the table. In that case, there was no liquid on the table whatsoever. It was pure telekinesis, and she hated it when that happened. Later on in our conversation, when we brought up the telekinesis, the can started moving again, just not as strongly. So, this strange sliding of the champagne glass was not a new experience for me. Eventually, we had everyone looking at the glass and wondering whether or not it was moving of its own accord. None of the other glasses on the table moved like that. It became the phenomena of the afternoon. I mention this because, as I realized much later, it was hauntingly similar to the August 12th dream I had wherein the urinal was sliding before it cracked in two. Keep in mind that this particular glass was filled with alcohol, also known as "spirits."

As the sliding of this glass is related to my dream, I will revisit some key aspects here. In my dream, my house was being invaded upon by squatters while I was in the midst of helping the power behind the president. This power had transmogrified into a diminutive goddess dressed up as "Sky Books" through the clothes of my daughter, Sky. I should add here that the fulfillment of tetragrammaton as a magical formula is in the fourth letter of that formula which is *HE* and represents the daughter. It literally refers to the manifestation of the godhead in physical form. Sky Books is not only an advocate for the Goddess, it is the fulfillment of my own magical journey and represents just that. The sliding urinal refers to the virtual impossibility of detoxifying those elements which contradict my mission. When all of the other toilets and plumbing were destroyed, it only reinforces this prospect. That there were squatters in my house speaks for itself. As sliding represents loss of control and also a force acting from the outside, I relate this to the American presence at the sacred sites in Romania, particularly in regard to their resentment and befuddlement over the fact that these remarkable occurrences and revelations were happening in Romania, a country which they consider to be far inferior to America. The main issue for the Americans seems to be that they do not have control of either the territory, phenomena, or circumstances surrounding Sarmizegetusa. As my journey is a spiritual quest and without any desire to own or possess, it is diametrically opposed to the negative forces which would seek to control or access the gold or the spiritual territory that goes with it. As you will learn in a bit, there is a reason this happened to Cosmin's glass and not someone else's.

Our host for the day then took us to his restaurant in Bucharest where we were fed another remarkable meal. When I came into the dining area, I saw Ms. V and she was with her husband, the politician. I will call him Mr. P. Having been told about me by his wife, he asked to sit across from me so we could talk. This was a very pleasant surprise, and I did my best to summarize my personal history in Romania. This started off with the strange story of how I was originally brought to Romania by a time travel scientist. A very intelligent and open-minded person, he was interested and willing to help David as he once worked at the highest level of the Energy Department. In the past, David explained to me that there was considerable political resistance to getting his time reactor technology into Romania. Perhaps this is a sign that times will change. I also explained a bit about the story of Radu Cinamar and Department Zero, but he was quick to point out that this was impossible as he signed off on the budgets during that period, and there was no money marked for activities such as those described by Radu. It was then necessary to explain that the budget was funded through a private company. This is explained in the book and had to do with a company in Uruguay. He was also puzzled that he had never heard about this story. After all, he was a writer himself and is very active in a literary club. Jonette explained to him that Radu's books are known across the world.

Thus it was that I found my spiritual journey either spiraling to or intertwining with the communication network of high echelon Romanian politics. I already know people in the Romanian government from Atlantykron, but this man is at the top level. I was happy to introduce some of these mysteries to him. While he is obviously adept at politics, my meeting and friendship with Mr. P does not necessarily portend a future relaxation of restriction with regard to David's technology and dissemination of information from Department Zero. It does, however, create an awareness at a high political level that was not there before. This gives him, as well as any other politicians he cares to share these views with, an additional lens by which to review and understand the dynamics underlying Romanian politics.

What is of particular interest to me, once again, is how this experience related to my dreams. These ware all about presidential authority and power. While Mr. P is not the president of Romania, he would certainly have a large contingent of Romanians supporting him if he chose to run. I found out that he is very well respected. When my Romanian publisher picked me up to take me to the airport, his eyes bulged when I mentioned whom I had met the night before. He was very impressed and surprised. I have given Mr. P the name of some of my other friends in the Romanian government, and it is my hope that they can interact.

I have already stated that I felt that I was coming too close for comfort with regard to certain issues during my adventures in Romania. Meeting a major politician certainly reinforced that. Even so, there was no discounting the observation that my spiritual journey was taking me into some very interesting and unique spheres. As I have already said, I was stirring up a lot of energy. With regard to political power, I realized that all of this energy I have stirred up could and should be transmuted into a new venture. Accordingly, I have proposed an idea that all of the major government officials in Romania have a gathering at Sarmizegetusa. There is a very important reason for this. It would not only expose them to the super-consciousness of the area, it will have a profound spiritual effect on the well being of Romania. It should be a popular idea because Romanians are rather proud of their ancient heritage.

Romanians are in a very unique position with regard to their own ancient heritage, at least when you compare them to the United States. Other than its memorials, the U.S. does not really have any sacred ground, at least in the sense that the Dacians and their descendants do. The U.S. is not even 250 years old. All the ancient sacred ground in North America belongs to the Native Americans. This is not something the United States government can honor in a genuine manner without making drastic changes with regard to the way they conduct their relations with Natives. Truly recognizing the sacred ground in North America would necessitate recognizing the Montauk Pharoahs and all that that would imply. (See my books *Pyramids of Montauk* and *The Montauk Book of the Living* for further information on this topic). In my view, the United States and their covert operations are completely at risk to the degree they do not honor the heritage of the ancients.

I have already written to Cosmin about this, and he is totally on board. He is also in a very unique position to facilitate such an endeavour as he majored in Public Administration. Cosmin is already very conversant in politics and is an excellent organizer. It is not an endeavor I expect to participate in personally. I am only sharing what I consider to be an excellent idea.

217

Since returning from Romania, the various themes presented in my dreams have continued to present themselves in my life. It has become more intense, quite complex and even uncomfortable at times. These new aspects will not be detailed here as some of them get too close for comfort with real situations and people. As I said, I have stirred up energy on a level that I had not imagined. For the most part, however, my journeys to Sarmizegetusa, past and future, have left me filled with wonder and anticipation of good things to come.

Plans are now being made for my return to Sarmizegetusa, and this will occur, by coincidence, with the "Montauk biorhythm" of August 2013. It was in August of 2003, which was on the twenty-year biorhythm of the Philadelphia Experiment (1943) and Montauk Project (1983), that the Bucegi chamber was breached. In Montauk lore, the year 2013 was considered to be a major biorhythm and a crucial time reference. Even though it was the ten-year biorhythm and not the twenty, 2013 was viewed to be of considerable importance and seemingly more important than that of 2003. These were never my ideas but were fed to me by Preston Nichols from extensive readings at Space-Time Labs in the '90s. If the history of the biorhythm is any indication of a repetitive pattern that will manifest again in the future, we can expect the unexpected as well as great serendipity.

I should also point out that it was never my plan to return to Sarmizegetusa in August of 2013. It is happening via the principles of synchronicity and destiny. By the time most of you will read these words, however, August 2013 will have already passed. Those of you who read it with the initial release of this book, however, can anticipate and perhaps even sense what might happen. While one never knows what to expect with heuristic projections such as this, it is relevant to point out that the discovery near Sarmizegetusa is considered to be a far more sensitive issue than the utterly remarkable chamber beneath the Sphinx. The implications are so powerful, if not staggering, that there is no doubt in my mind that there will be a fifth book. What it includes and whether or not Radu participates, however, are open-ended at this point. It is also a rather awesome prospect to realize that if it were not for the sacred parchment itself and the energy that rides along with it, none of these events would have unfolded the way they have thus far or the way they will unfold in the future. Each and every one of us is in a position of choice.

Thus it is that the progenitors of the *Transylvanian Series* have placed a virtual surfboard in my hands. Accordingly, I have also placed one in your hands. By surfboard, I am of course referring to the parchment. One learns to ride a wave by studying the ocean and seeing how it breaks. You then make your move, judiciously and with as much skill as you have. With regard to myself, I know that it is an adventure ride that will continue for a long time. How long? Into infinity.

EPILOGUE

I do not think it is possible to over exaggerate the importance of this book having come into existence as a result of the secret parchment. It is therefore fitting that I not only reemphasize this point but also share my views on its relevancy as well as how to best utilize it.

My first suggestion would be to heed well the words of Shin Li, Repa Sundhi's assistant, who stated, "...if we remain closed, mean, and suspicious, then beauty, kindness and love cannot penetrate this shell we have created, and then we must conclude that these do not exist. "

People can become inappropriately arrogant when they read a book of the nature you have just completed. It is, after all, outside the boundaries of pedestrian thinking. The purpose at hand should not be to critique Radu but rather to utilize what has been offered so as to inculcate beauty, love, and kindness into your own life. These things are not in the realm of science or making critical observations. They have everything to do with the human factor and the inner personality. It has also been my experience that many people are too ready and quick to point out perceived foibles in Radu's presentation. More often than not, I have also observed that there criticisms are inaccurate. Shin Li's statement is very potent and useful.

We can expect that there will be all sorts of different opinions from the many people who read the manuscript. It has been my experience that most people tend to veer either towards too much cynicism or too much gullibility. There are always shades of gray with regard to any truth you read or story that you hear. The most important point is that you find the information to be useful to your own predicament.

I will now take the opportunity to address the secret parchment itself.

The text itself specifies that the five techniques are actually five efficient ways for spiritual evolution and that they should be made known to anyone interested in deciphering them. The whole point is really spiritual evolution. Radu also states that the secret parchment is a spiritual treasure revealed in a very synthetic and hidden manner. In Chapter 3, he stated that a detailed book of commentary on the five stanzas would not be enough for an exhaustive presentation of this subject. Ultimately, he gradually reached the conclusion that the best way to understand the meaning of these stanzas is through the process of thinking about and meditating on their specific aspects. This is why he chose to present the main ideas briefly and in a way which would "act as a trampoline of inspiration for the reader's analysis" and "guide our steps towards a wider and more mature vision of our lives."

Accordingly, it is my suggestion that you reread Chapter 3 in its entirety. Pay attention to pertinent points that resonate with you and take notes. After that, make a crib sheet of the five precepts or initiation techniques. I will give you my own crib sheet, but you can and should make your own, utilizing what I have offered if you wish. In my own words, the five precepts can be summarized as follows:

> 1) Compassion — There is a divine source of compassion in this universe, and we need to recognize it and link to it.
> 2) All we are is a result of what we have thought — what you think is what you get. This is also representative of the principle of quantum affinity or the Law of Affinity.
> 3) Synchronicity — There are no coincidences. When events or experiences coincide outside the ordinary bounds of probability, this is a meaningful coincidence and there is an intention behind it.
> 4) Vibration — Everything is connected by vibration.
> 5) Will — Align yourself with your own Higher Will and the Divine Source of Creation.

While the general idea of these precepts might not be new to you, there is an energy that came with the release of the parchment. These techniques ride along the crest of that wave. Utilizing them in the prescribed order reinforces this.

Once you have your own crib sheet, review it and commit it to memory. Review these precepts at least daily and see how they can and do flow into your already existing life. This is a consciousness and energy that you want to cultivate and refine on a continuing basis. As soon as you obtain resonance with these ideas, reread Chapter 3 again and continue to refine and cultivate the process. Do not stop.

It is also my suggestion that you reread the entire book again as well as the entire Transylvania Series but only if you are so inclined. Keep in mind, this is your process, not someone else's.

When I first read these techniques, I made my own crib sheet and started contemplating them immediately. This encouraged me to make sure my translator got the entire book translated before my trip to Romania. Additionally, I went out of my way to forward the first rough drafts of the translation to Jonette Crowley in order that she could read it so as to enhance our spiritual journey to Sarmizegetusa. As you have just read, the results were phenomenal. No, it was no coincidence that her name was Crowley. I could not have been more happy with the way things worked out, and Jonette has my eternal gratitude, not only for making it happen but for going out of her way to spend time with me and meet my brothers and sisters at Atlantyk-ron. She was very well received, and they gave her and her husband a standing invitation to return any time they wished.

How you choose to employ these techniques, and whether or not you do, is entirely up to you. If done with an honest attempt, you will have experiences in synchronicity. Ideally, this will help you to discover or reinforce your life path and destiny. Some of you might also find that it leads to you having a desire to visit Transylvania. Towards that end, I have given you a few connections with the ads listed on some of the following pages.

If you follow the path of synchronicity, and these precepts will guide you quite nicely, the path of adventure will never end. It is the path of infinity. Be conscious of it.

Peter Moon
Long Island, New York
December 19, 2012

Acknowledgements

Monica Grigorescu
For translating this book and being a good friend

Cosmin C. Bebu-Vijianu
Jonette Crowley
For making the adventure happen

Cristina Balan
Nicole Vasilcovschi
For accompanying me on sacred journey #1

All members of Jonette Crowley's
Transylvanian Tour 2012
For accompanying me on sacred journey #2

Sorin Hurmuz
For making Radu Cinamar's works accessible

The World Genesis Foundation
All participants and faculty of Atlantykron
For making my adventures possible

Dr. David Lewis Anderson
For introducing me to Romania

Cristina
Alex
Maria
Nicolae
Vasili
Vanda
For adventures in the future

The Montauk Pulse

If you would like to receive updates on the continued adventures of Radu Cinamar and Peter Moon, you should subscribe to the *Montauk Pulse* newsletter which will also feature updates on Dr. David Anderson and other key developments, including the Montauk Project itself. The *Montauk Pulse* has remained in print and has been issued quarterly since 1993. The Pulse directly contributes to the efforts of the authors in writing more books and chronicling the effort to understand time and all of its components. Past support has been crucial to what has developed thus far. To subscribe, send $20.00 to Sky Books, PO Box 769, Westbury, NY 11590. If order is from outside the U.S., please add $12.00 for shipping. You can also subscribe via PayPal to skybooks@yahoo.com or visiting *www.skybooksusa.com.*

Transylvania Tours

If you are considering a sacred journey to Transylvania, look to Joy Travel, founded and run by Vanda Osman, where each journey is designed to enhance your personal transformation and is created to foster multidimensional experiences for the mind, body and spirit.

JOY TRAVEL — 1-800-569-5010
website: *http://www.joytravelonline.com*
email us: *vanda-joy@sbcglobal.net*
CST Registration #2021781-40 648
Corte Loren, San Marcos, California 92069

Cotiso Hotel in Transylvania

If you are traveling to Sarmizegetusa, Peter Moon recommends the Pensiunea "COTISO" which features modern accommodations including wireless internet. They serve excellent food and their hospitality is very friendly.

Pensiunea Cotiso
Located in Costeşti, Hunedoara in the Orăştie Mountains
website: *http://www.pensiuneacotiso.net*
email: *pensiuneacotiso@yahoo.com*
phone: 0722 919 886, 0753 511 527, 0254 246 676

If you are an English speaker, ask for Cristina or Alex

SkyBooks   ORDER FORM

We wait for ALL checks to clear before shipping. This includes Priority Mail orders. If you want to speed delivery time, please send a U.S. Money Order or use MasterCard or Visa. Those orders will be shipped right away. Complete this order form and send with payment or credit card information to:
Sky Books, Box 769, Westbury, New York 11590-0104

Name	
Address	
City	
State / Country	_Zip_
Daytime Phone (In case we have a question) ( )	

☐ _This is my first order_ ☐ _I have ordered before_ ☐ _This is a new address_

Method of Payment: ☐ _Visa_ ☐ _MasterCard_ ☐ _Money Order_ ☐ _Check_

_#_   —   —   —

Expiration Date   _Signature_

TITLE	QTY	PRICE
The Montauk Pulse (1 year - no shipping US orders)...$20.00		
Transylvanian Sunrise (book 1)......................................$22.00		
Transylvanian Moonrise (book 2)..................................$22.00		
Mystery of Egypt — The First Tunnel (book 3)............$22.00		
Secret Parchment (book 4)...$22.00		
The Montauk Project: Experiments in Time..................$15.95		
Note: There is no additonal shipping for the Montauk Pulse if you are in the United States. _Subtotal_		
For delivery in NY add 8.625% tax		
U.S. Shipping: $5.00 for 1st book plus $1.00 for 2nd, etc.		
Foreign shipping: $20 for 3 books		
Total		

Thank you for your order. We appreciate your business.